Reconstructing Catholicism

For a New Generation

❈

Robert A. Ludwig

Wipf & Stock
PUBLISHERS
Eugene, Oregon

Wipf and Stock Publishers
199 West 8th Avenue, Suite 3
Eugene, Oregon 97401

Reconstructing Catholicism
By Ludwig, Robert A.
Copyright©1996 by Ludwig, Robert A.
ISBN: 1-57910-338-3
Publication date 4/4/2000
Previously published by The Crossroad Publishing Co., 1996

For Petra, Patrick, and Mark
and for their peers,
a new generation of hope

Contents

Part Three
CATHOLICISM IN A RECONSTRUCTED UNIVERSE
Challenges and Possibilities from the New Cosmology

Acknowledgments

I am indebted to many in the development of this manuscript. First of all, I'm grateful to DePaul University, particularly my supervisor, James R. Doyle, and my colleagues in University Ministry, for giving me the time from my normal duties and responsibilities to write these pages. Their support in the development of our ministry at DePaul and their willingness to pick up the slack while I was writing have been of prominent value to me. I am grateful, too, to my wife, Kathleen, for her loving encouragement throughout the writing of this book. Her willingness to edit and critique the manuscript and her support for its major ideas have been invaluable. My children, too, have been patient and supportive during the writing process. Without their willingness to set me free to do this work, I simply could not have accomplished the task.

I would also like to thank the several people who generously read portions of the manuscript as it was developing. I am grateful for the suggestions they have made, both supportive and critical, as well as their editorial advice: Thomas F. O'Meara, O.P., Stephanie Quinn, and Catherine Shea. McKim Malville, astronomer at the University of Colorado, was particularly helpful in suggestions related to chapter 8. The reader has benefited greatly from the comments and suggestions provided me during the writing of this book.

Finally, I am also appreciative of the inspiration that I have received from my colleagues on the board of directors of *Call to Action,* a lay-run church-reform group headquartered in Chicago with a national membership exceeding ten thousand. Their continuing efforts to move church reform toward reaching out to young people and the constructive task of nurturing the many positive elements of Catholic renewal have been invaluable. Together, we see the emergence of a new and vital Catholicism expressing itself in countless individuals and communities who have moved beyond juridical consciousness to the experience of love and justice in the ongoing struggles to believe: in ourselves, in God, in the Jesus movement,

in the possibilities for God's reign in our lives and our society — in
a Catholicism that is inviting and searching, building on the core
of a centuries-old wisdom yet continuously renewing and reform-
ing itself in correlation with society, culture, and individuals' hunger
for God.

— Introduction —

From Deconstruction to Reconstruction: A Personal Journey

In 1989 I left my tenured faculty position as director of a very large graduate program at Loyola University in New Orleans to become director of ministry — essentially a campus pastor — at DePaul University in Chicago. For the previous seven years I had been involved in educating adults in their thirties, forties, and fifties, mostly lay people, in pastoral studies and religious education. These people came to our graduate programs with two basic goals: (1) to re-appropriate their understanding of Catholicism in the light of their considerable experience and the cultural shifts that had occurred since their initial socialization into Catholicism; and (2) to equip themselves with the knowledge and skills to become leaders in their faith communities. Evaluative studies have shown that the program succeeded in helping students achieve both of these goals, with the result that most of these adults found their studies to be personally liberating, freeing them from the psychospiritual shackles of an authoritarian Catholicism and enabling them to take the tradition into their own creative hands and relate it in meaningful ways to the contexts in which they live and work.

To a large extent, they were able to move away from *juridical consciousness* toward a free and adult relationship with the tradition, discovering powerful connections between their Catholic faith and their own struggles for human meaning and productive living. When I use the term "juridical consciousness," I'm referring to that mindset that interprets Catholicism as a God-brokering function, legalistically defined in doctrine and rules and carried out by clerics who have been officially empowered to speak God's will and perform divine rites. Juridical consciousness turns metaphorical truth into literal *answers*, and its adherents are robbed of the terrible joy of experiencing life

1

with all of its risks and adventure. One often hears the adjective "official" modifying the terms "teaching," "ritual," or "ministry." There is a long history of mixing Christian faith with the images of governance and law courts, and because Catholicism and the state were so unified after the Emperor Constantine's conversion in the fourth century, there is a Catholic bent toward a juridical understanding of our relationship with God as Christians. Juridical consciousness is a dependency that inhibits one from taking ownership of the tradition, from facilitating one's own spiritual journey, from experiencing the depths of life and mystery, and from becoming an active agent in the community of faith.

Because many of our students were able to move beyond this juridical consciousness, their involvement in graduate studies in midlife provided them an opportunity to *cross over* from a childish religious stance to an easy familiarity with themselves and the various aspects of Catholicism. They were able to find a more mature interaction with the scriptures, doctrines, liturgy, the theological and ethical heritage, through the discovery of metaphor. Their academic work became a personal journey toward what Paul Ricoeur calls "a second naiveté," a new affirmation of the symbols, stories, and rituals that make up the Catholic legacy. Such affirmation grows out of robust correlations of the tradition to their lived experience as the Catholic legacy is connected to the personal, cultural, and institutional contexts in which they live and work.

I left this exciting and fulfilling work to take on a challenge that I thought then would be even more exciting and fulfilling — the effort to help a new generation (some of them, children of these adult students) connect in meaningful ways with Catholicism. It was a risky choice. Was there a viable future for our tradition with young people? I pondered that classic question of religious education, Will our children have faith? turning the title around and asking: Will our faith have children? Would a generation that looked blank at the words "Vatican Two" find a credible Catholicism that could serve as a resource for living as the midlife graduate students had done? Could I find a ministry staff that would create a vital dialogue with young adults who considered the 1960s to be "the olden days?"

This challenge was all the more intriguing since my own children, who were then moving into adolescence, were part of this new generation. Would Petra, Patrick, and Mark ever experience the depths of Catholic faith that I had been privileged to know? Would their lives be blessed with the profound spiritual meaning that I had found in and through Catholicism? These questions pushed me beyond the postconciliar urge to reform through critique toward the more constructive task of helping them and their peers discover a positive and life-giving Catholic faith. I reasoned that this new generation was the future of Catholicism — that if there were to be a viable future for our faith tradition, it was with them and with their success in finding a credible and life-giving Catholic experience. My wife, Kathy, and I have found parenting the greatest challenge of our lives. Trying to help our children into productive adulthood without the support of the authoritarian institutions and structures that our parents' generation relied upon is a daily summons to our patience and creativity. It continually makes us reflect critically on the integrity of our own beliefs and values. To focus my professional life on ministry to young adults was also a chance to focus my life as a father on helping my children sort out their beliefs and values.

Overview of Today's Situation

The Catholicism that today's young people have grown up with is *Catholicism after the Second Vatican Council* (1962–65). The Council initiated enthusiasm for reform and renewal within the church, but that enthusiasm soon led to debate (something with which Catholics weren't particularly comfortable, having been uncommonly homogeneous in both doctrine and practice). After the papal decision against artificial contraception in 1968, the debate became increasingly acrimonious, and a yawning gap began to appear between the church's central administration and a large majority of Catholics, including pastoral leaders and theologians. Since the election of John Paul II in 1978, that gap has grown and hardened, turning into a power struggle about a whole series of issues and concerns, such as mandatory celibacy for priests, the exclusion of women from the ordained ministry, doctrinal uniformity and academic freedom, the morality of homosexual acts, divorce and remarriage, abortion. The result of this prolonged and increasingly angry power struggle has been a growing religious cynicism, grounded in a sense that the church that speaks justice to the world refuses to practice justice within the church itself. Today's young adults have grown up in an increasingly polarized and often cynical church, where they've heard mostly criticism about Catholicism and little of what is positive and constructive. Catholic identity is difficult to figure out in such a conflicted situation, and what is attractive and inviting about this church is not very visible to them. This book is theology, understood as a dialogue between the contemporary situation and the beliefs and meanings enshrined in a broad and diverse Catholic tradition. It represents one believer's perspective but seeks to address the search for theological truth and human meaning in a difficult and transitional period.

Our young people today have grown up in a social context that is best described as "deconstructed." The breakup of family structure, business and political scandals (Watergate, junk bonds, the savings and loan scam, the Iran-Contra affair, the widespread public cynicism of the Reagan-Bush era), the materialistic ambiance of ubiquitous TV commercials and suburban shopping malls, the mounting national debt, educational decline, the rapid growth of theft and violent crime — all of these are symptomatic of the deconstructed world, which is the only world today's young people have ever known. The institutions and systems and structures of public life seem broken or fraudulent or dysfunctional. Not worthy of our trust or confidence, at any rate.

The simultaneity of a deconstructed world, with little encouragement for hope in a transformed tomorrow, and a Catholicism itself in disarray, divided and cynical, has led many to a ravenous spiritual hunger. Young adults long for a constructive worldview. Sometimes this is a felt need, which can be consciously identified and articulated, but mostly it is a hidden need, experienced simply as depression, numbness, a feeling that, as one of my students put it recently, "Life sucks — life really sucks!"

The question this book seeks to address is simply this: How are we to respond to this spiritual hunger? How are people of my generation who care about these young people to respond? How are these young people themselves to respond? The difficulty of writing this book is, in part, that I want to speak to both of these groups — young adults seeking spiritual meaning in a deconstructed world, and midlife adults who find themselves wondering about a meaningful future in a world in which hopeful criticism has turned into cynical deconstruction.

Deconstruction in Contemporary Philosophy

Much has been written in philosophical circles in recent years about the movement from modernity to postmodernity. Many thinkers are questioning the assumptions and presuppositions that flow from the Enlightenment (seventeenth and eighteenth centuries), with its emphasis on rationalism and empiricism and its skepticism about spirituality and religion. Contemporary philosophers want to deconstruct the modern paradigm, largely because of its negative effects on society. Charlene Spretnak describes it this way:

> The assumptions of that worldview have led to widespread ecocide, nuclear arms, the globalization of unqualified-growth economies, and the plunder of Third and Fourth World (indigenous) peoples' cultures and homelands. The psychological costs have been heavy as well: loss of meaning beyond consumerism, loss of community and connectedness with other people, and loss of a secure sense of embeddedness in the rest of the natural world.[1]

Spretnak sees "the postmodern moment" as a great opportunity "because there is finally widespread agreement that many of the assumptions of modernity are false."[2] In Catholicism, this thrust has been focused on the development of postmodern theologies, ecclesial criticism, and church reform. One could interpret the whole sweep of self-criticism leading to the Second Vatican Council and its reforms, not to mention the avalanche of internal critique among Catholics that the Council ushered in, as an exercise in deconstruction. The practical fallout of the Council (which we'll consider more carefully in chapter 2) for many believers has, in fact, been deconstructive: the loss of a pattern of meanings and values that held life together and gave it purpose and direction.

But the other side of deconstruction is *reconstruction*, the effort to put meaning back together through the discovery of new patterns of coherence. Spretnak seems to agree when she writes, "The first phase of post-modern relief efforts, which may be a long one, should focus on two areas: restoring meaning and empowering people at the community level."[3] My hope is that these pages will advance both a restoration of meaning and the empowerment of people — by helping them see Catholicism in contemporary experiential terms and by developing experiential connections to the center of the tradition. In writing this book, I'm presupposing the critical, deconstructive movement of the past decades. I want, however, to focus on reconstruction, attempting to describe Catholicism in a manner that offers people, particularly the young, a coherent theological paradigm of ultimate meaning and practical living. It is my attempt to delineate a Catholicism that is both true to the deepest truths of the tradition and pertinent to today's transformed cultural context. Its focus is the core, the basics, the center of the Catholic tradition, and the integration of this faith into our patterns of living. I hope the book will help facilitate an ongoing process — because that's what the task of reconstructing is: meaning-making and integrating the tradition's wisdom through ongoing reflection on both our experience and the legacy of faith we inherit from others.

Constructive Catholicism

This book grows out of my experience in the years since 1989, both as a father interacting with adolescent children and as a campus minister interacting with "twenty-something" adults. Writing the book itself is a making sense of my experience, an effort to reflect and develop some coherent learnings from these years of discovering firsthand the problems and promise of a new generation. I offer this manuscript as a constructive description of a relevant Catholicism to these young people. I hope it can serve them as a resource in addressing their own spiritual hungers, leading them toward rich experiences of prayer and faith community and the work of service and justice. I want the book, particularly the middle section, to help them grasp *the Catholic potential* — a vital network of people in faith communities focused on Jesus and the reign of God, which is experienced in ongoing personal conversion, sacramental community, and the challenge of making our world more just and peaceful, more secure and celebrative, more loving and creative.

I also offer this book to my peers. In many ways our own critique has run its course. If young people can't find spiritual meaning in religious cynicism, neither can we. We need to find our way back to that which is positive and constructive and life-giving, leaving juridical consciousness behind. The *theological* task of deconstructing juridical consciousness is nearly complete, yet ecclesial dysfunction grows, leading to greater institutional chaos and impending financial collapse. The reform agenda in contemporary Catholicism is intent on structural change: full equality for women and minorities, selection of leaders by the people, more democratic decision-making, small faith communities with greater involvement and participation by all who claim membership, recognition of diversity and pluralism as legitimate, greater commitment to the poor, to social justice, and to ecology, a clear focus on evangelism, spirituality, and community, a returning to origins (Jesus and the dynamic communities of the New Testament) for direction, and a greater openness and willingness to collaborate with persons of other denominations or faiths. Such reforms remain controversial, though less so than media reportage suggests. Indeed, I sense a growing consensus, particularly among pastoral leaders, that only through the adoption of such reforms will the church find a robust future. The commitment to change is such that it proceeds, with or without the support of the hierarchy, creating tensions and conflicts, but also breaking new ground for Catholicism. I hope this book can be a resource for the furthering of this reform agenda. It envisions a Catholicism that is defined, not by the Vatican bureaucracy, but by a broad spectrum of Catholic people who share a spiritual vision for our time, grounded in the central aspects of our long and life-giving tradition. Though some will find it provocative and challenging, I'm hopeful that many others will find it informative and inspiring, providing some sense of direction in a difficult and transitional time.

The *pastoral* task in the present context becomes one of helping people break the chains that bind them (psychospiritual and sociopolitical), but also, and increasingly, there is a need to build bridges — bridges to the heart of the tradition, to the hungers of our souls, to one another, to the work of justice, to the emerging sense of embeddedness in nature and the universe. Now "church reform" means moving away from a preoccupation with Rome and hierarchy and immersing ourselves in the many emergent Catholic reconstructions (house churches, small faith communities, community service programs, peace and justice networks, psychospiritual growth groups, prayer retreats, ecological associations). The task is less and less an obsession with criticism and more and more a giving ourselves to reconstruction — for our own sakes and for the sake of our children. People who seek a new Catholicism must come forward to create it and live it.

The Need for Reconstruction

These pages are, thus, about the future of our faith tradition. Reconstruction is not an effort to return to some romantic past. Rather, it is reconfiguring and reappropriating key elements of the tradition for today and tomorrow. While it draws on the many insights of this passing century, its focus is on the question, Where do we go from here? As we move into the next century and a new millennium, what kind of Catholicism can serve us and our children with relevance and profundity? What kind of Catholicism can inspire and challenge us with credibility and power? The answers to such questions are *our* responsibility, and we dare not leave them to any *official* others.

Richard Rohr provides rationale and support for all this when he suggests that beneath the veneer of today's business-as-usual at a hectic pace, Western civilization is, in fact, in the midst of a major *crisis of meaning*. Referring to what Joseph Chilton Pearce calls "the cracking of the cosmic egg," he writes, "The symbolic universes, inside of which we lived safely, have largely fallen apart, leaving only the private psyche on its lonely journey toward meaning." What we have left, he suggests, is *mere episodic meaning*: "There is no larger mythic story that explains our lives, and each day we must create some personal moment to make ourselves feel significant or even alive. Each of us has only my little story disconnected from any group story and surely disconnected from any Great Story. That is a lonely and tragic way to live." I think Rohr is keying in on something very important today when he insists that "one cannot live on criticism; one surely cannot build anything communal when you start with negation." His concern, as mine, is the next generation: "I am especially impassioned about the next generation. They seem to have nothing. We have left them less than crumbs, only our criticism and cynicism about things. There is an enormous spiritual vacuum...people are dying for lack of vision, for lack of transcendent meaning to name their soul and their struggles." Rohr's point is clear: "It is time for reconstruction. We need to know what we *do* believe, why we are proud of our only past, what is good about even the broken things, and how we can begin a new language of responsibility."[4]

Plan of the Book

This book's contribution is a pulling together of many insights that have been developed by the dedicated work of scholars and pastoral leaders over the past several decades, but with a distinct focus: positive reconstruction. My hope is that it will provide a reader-friendly compendium of the basics — the central themes of the tradition presented in experiential categories. It seeks, first, a clear statement of the need for reconstruction (Part One) by describing the spiritual hungers of a new generation (chapter 1), the frustrating of Catholicism's instinct to reform and renew itself (chapter 2) by failure to implement needed structural changes after the Second Vatican Council, and finally, the exciting work of religious scholars in our time to retrieve the experiential basis of religion generally (chapter 3). The young are increasingly alienated from the institutional church even as they become more and more open to the experiences that lie at the core of our tradition. Reconstructing Catholicism for a new generation means shifting our focus from juridical consciousness to a deeper, more spiritual Catholic experience. It is experience that young people seek, and this book seeks to present Catholicism in experiential terms.

The heart of the book is the middle section (Part Two), which attempts to describe the Catholic experience in a clear, straightforward manner. The method utilized here is evangelism, not propagandizing in the sense of fundamentalist proselytism, but seeking to present the tradition attractively to thoughtful adults engaged in spiritual searching. We start with Jesus (chapter 4) because he is always the center of Christian faith, the inaugural source that must be returned to again and again as the major criterion for Catholic faith. If Catholicism is anything, it is a following of Jesus. Chapter 5 describes the experience of grace as the core of Catholic spirituality, focusing on conversion as a spiritual path. We are called to move from sin and alienation toward grace and reconciliation, from denial of who we essentially are to embracing our human vocation as "the grammar of divine discourse" (Rahner). Chapter 6 explores the experience of sacramental community. The Catholic orientation finds the sacred imminent and present in the material world of shared experience. Sacrament invites us to playful meaning-making through symbol and metaphor in the interactive relationships of sharing faith with others, reaching out to them and opening ourselves for mutual support and critique. Community is the birthing place of faith and the nurturing context where it is refined and developed. Finally in this middle section of the book, in chapter 7 we review the Catholic concern for liberation, justice, and peace as the heart of our mission to the world. The last hundred years of Catholic social teaching has been called "our best kept secret." This is a great tragedy considering the deterioration of confidence in our public life, the gross social and economic inequalities we tolerate, and the resulting loss of hope and cynicism toward society and politics.

A final section (Part Three) is about the larger context for reconstructing Catholicism — making connections to our shifting understanding of the universe and the role that human beings play in the larger purpose of creation. The ecological crisis, the new physics, and the image of Earth from NASA photos have combined to revolutionize our understanding of the cosmos and humanity's self-understanding within an evolving universe. Chapter 8 describes the emergent understanding of the universe — science's new story of creation. Catholicism has a long and rich tradition of grounding spirituality in the cosmos, God's creative act, and the twentieth century brings us a radically new sense of the universe and how it is still coming to be. Chapter 9 discusses how recognizing ourselves within nature occasions a new sense of human purpose. The human vocation is to recognize our embeddedness in the delicate web of life and our unique responsibility, as the reflexive consciousness of the universe, for its future. Chapter 10 describes a green and cosmic Catholicism by picking up the major themes of Part Two and discussing them now in the light of a reconstructed universe and the image of the human it evokes. Catholicism as a holistic spirituality understands human purpose within the dynamic unfolding of divine energy in nature and in cosmos — in space and in time — and seeks to heal human freedom. Such a spirituality is the ground for a new renaissance in human meaning, calling us to the difficult task of liberating nature. Finally in an Epilogue we return to the current situation of young adults and discuss the emergence of a reconstructed Catholicism as a coherent spiritual path.

Part One

A TIME FOR RECONSTRUCTING

❧

Background in Culture, Church, and Religion

While millions of people around the world continue to identify with Catholicism and to find there a spiritual vitality, far too many have no access to this rich religious tradition. Clearly, there are other millions happily connected to widely diverse faith traditions, where they find patterns of ultimate truth and practices leading them toward contact with the sacred, self-esteem, community, and service to others. But many others today are spiritually starving, without any coherent paradigm for meaning and value in human life. They feel no meaningful connection to a genuine faith community. They experience their lives mostly as a treadmill existence of compulsion, competition, violence, and survival. They may report a shallow sense of well-being, but truth be told, they feel unrelated, alienated, empty, without moral purpose or commitment to the future — drifting through life. Douglas Coupland's novel *Life after God* refers to two groups of people "to feel the saddest for":

> Sometimes I think the people to feel the saddest for are people who are unable to connect with the profound — people such as my boring brother-in-law, a hearty type so concerned with normality and fitting in that he eliminates any possibility of uniqueness for himself and his own personality. I wonder if some day, when he is older, he will wake up and the deeper part of him will realize that he has never allowed himself to truly exist, and he will cry with regret and shame and grief.
>
> And then sometimes I think the people to feel the saddest for are people who once knew what profoundness was, but who lost or became numb to the sensation of wonder — people who closed the doors that lead us into the secret world — or who had the doors closed for them by time and neglect and decisions made in times of weakness.[1]

Some of those unable to connect with "the profound" are baptized Catholics who have never experienced any compelling connection to their religious heritage. They've heard words like "grace" and "salvation," but these abstractions mean nothing in their lived existence. They've attended Mass, perhaps quite regularly, but it was perceived by them as the priest's activity, of which they had no genuine understanding or to which they felt no connection. They were passive observers, bored and anxious for the service to be over so they could get on with the rest of their day. They've heard the Gospel sto-

ries, but often these scriptures seemed like fairy tales, again without
any meaningful connections to their own experience and the issues
they struggle with in their lives. These Catholics have no authentic
experiential connection to the tradition.

Others have felt the Catholic door slammed in their face. They're
gay or lesbian, divorced, feminist; priests, sisters, or brothers who
have left the ministry and religious life to marry or simply out of dis-
illusionment with the structures; people who expected organizational
reform and can no longer tolerate authoritarian decision-making.
They experience Catholicism as a rigid ideology, unwilling to integrate the consensus insights of contemporary scholars on issues of
sexuality and population control. They perceive the church as sexist, racist, homophobic, unwilling to be welcoming and inclusive;
controlling and secretive in its employment practices and decision-
making; unwilling to be accountable to its members, particularly
in financial matters, but also in its general policies and procedures
unrelated to the fundamentals of Catholic belief. They see a dysfunctional church, a church no longer focused on spirituality, community,
evangelism, and social justice, but preoccupied with internal control,
trying to shore itself up amid institutional chaos.[2] These Catholics
have left the church — some to find spiritual meaning and community elsewhere, but others with no place to go and now experiencing
simply a loss and an emptiness.

Many others have no spiritual identity, no connection to any religious tradition. They may have grown up as nonparticipants on
the fringes of Catholicism or one of the Protestant churches, or perhaps were never exposed to any religion. Some of these unchurched
persons might be attracted to a reconstructed Catholicism, but they
are not drawn to today's institutional church; they've felt no compelling invitation to address their spiritual hungers, their struggles for
meaning and value, their hopes and aspirations for community and a
transformed society.

Lack of access (true access) and the need for reconstruction go together: providing access must be active, not passive. Central to the
rationale for reconstruction is the vigorous extension of accessibility to those who, whether they are explicitly aware of it or not,
hunger for God. Behind every face is a beating heart, a personal
story, a questing spirit. Putting the hunger for God and one's personal story together is the contemporary work of evangelization. One
of the most eloquent spokesperson for this direction in pastoral ministry is Father Patrick Brennan, a priest of the archdiocese of Chicago

and a prolific author. Brennan suggests four movements that make up contemporary Catholic evangelization:

- Evangelization begins with *listening to people* — hearing their stories, their needs, their woundedness. "Once people have their woundedness and their needs listened to, they discover a deeper need: the need for meaning."

- Evangelization moves on to *a process of conversion and reconversion,* which involves persons in "the cry for more" and "the cry for help." "The cry for more is the cry for God. People in the 12–Step programs don't experience God as an option. The Higher Power is a need, a need to get through each day. That is the conversion Christ calls us to. The cry for help: I need people, I need family, community, relationships. I can't go it alone."

- The cycle of evangelization cries out for *a liturgy and an assembly that provide the culture for conversion and reconversion* and for a clear proclamation of the message. Brennan suggests that current church structures are, by and large, providing neither.

- Finally, there comes the moment of *connectedness or communion.* "Genuine community, not what Scott Peck calls pseudo-community. Something more intense. Genuine life sharing."[3]

Providing accessibility to the richness of our tradition means doing the work of evangelization, but this is not someone else's responsibility. It belongs to all who claim Catholicism as their spiritual home. This book is part of that work.

In this first part, I want to make the case for reconstruction by describing the spiritual hungers of today's young people, the decline of institutional Catholicism, and the work of scholars to help us retrieve the experiential base of religious tradition. All of this is important background for our examination of the basics of Catholicism developed in Part Two.

— Chapter 1 —

A New Generation's
Spiritual Hungers

It is no wonder that we share a suspicion of what words mean and a wariness of relationships. We have been mourning the loss of this world and our lives from the day we were born. Our primary experience is grief, not grace.... We want connection and communication, not distinction and competition. My intuition is that the gift and vocation we bring is one of reconciliation and healing.
　　　　　　　—Jarrett Kerbel (age 27), *Sojourners*, November 1994

I have grown weary of the stereotypes and false representation of my generation—a generation that (believe it or not) gives me great hope. Let me introduce you to some of my twentysomething friends: Analisa teaches on a Navajo reservation. Kathy teaches learning disabled children...and Michael is studying for his doctorate in American history and gay studies. Amy, a fulltime volunteer for Bread for the City and Zaccheus Free Clinic in Washington, DC, loved it so much she extended her one-year term for another year of (yes) *service*. Andrea is in medical school and Mike is a stellar graphic artist. Angela has a golden voice and a passion for AIDS education; Karen was so inspired by Mother Teresa that she traveled to India to meet and work with her.
　　　　　　　　　—Melissa Shirk, *Sojourners*, November 1994

Many commentators today are observing that people born between 1961 and 1980 make up a distinctly unique generation of Americans. They are variously referred to as "Generation X," or "the twenty-somethings" or "the thirteenth generation" (because they are, in fact, the thirteenth generation of Americans after the Revolution). Sometimes naming this generation in these ways is a labeling. This labeling is perceived by young people themselves as stereotyping — a way of lumping them together for a pejorative dismissal. The effort here to describe the generational character that has emerged because of a common set of social and cultural circumstances and shared experiences is not meant as a labeling. Rather, it is an attempt to generalize about a collective uniqueness — what makes their experience of being human special and distinct. As this book is published, these eighty million young people are somewhere between fifteen and thirty-four years old, the largest and most diverse generation (ethnically, culturally, economically, and in family structure) in American history. They have been profoundly affected in their early years by the breakup and reconfiguration of the American family, by the pervasive public cynicism of the Reagan-Bush era, by Americans' growing preoccupation with the economy and a materialist-consumerist identity, by a cultural fixation on erotica and intoxicants, and by adult criticism of the institutional church and confusion about morality, ethics, and religion.

The Generation "After"

They have been described by one writer as feeling like "the generation after" — after 1960, after the Kennedy-King assassinations and Vietnam, after the protests and the sexual revolution, after the heady idealism and the crash — and, worst of all, after the Boomers. "Having watched our immediate elders transform from hippies to Yuppies to New Agers to landowners, we get the feeling we are living in the wake of the postwar baby boom and bearing the economic and cultural burden of a society run on financial credit and social debit."[1]

Another, more graphic depiction of a generational feeling comes from Howe and Strauss in their book *13th Gen:*

> Imagine arriving at a beach at the end of a long summer of wild goings-on. The beach crowd is exhausted, the sand shopworn, hot, and full of debris — no place for walking barefoot. You step on a bottle, and some cop yells at you for littering. The sun is directly overhead and leaves no patch of shade that hasn't already been taken. You feel the glare beating down on a barren landscape devoid of secrets or innocence. You look around at the disapproving faces and can't help but sense that, somehow, the entire universe is gearing up to punish you.[2]

The May/June 1992 issue of *Psychology Today* points out that, because their birth rate was half that of the early years of the baby-boomers, they experience "diminishing demographic clout," feeling irrelevant in a world where their elder boomers command the power, the money, and the media. In addition, "They feel cheated. They see their legacy as a polluted Earth, a racially fractured society, and overwhelming social problems. Many are worried that America's best years are over."³ Worse still, they have to pay the bill for boomers' excess and lack of social responsibility. As the federal deficit spirals out of control and debt piles up, they are more and more aware that the boomers' excessive credit will become their heritage, robbing them of opportunity and a chance to create their own kind of society.

Impact of Cultural Shifts

Clearly, these young people are reaping the harvest of an age of deconstruction, during which time previous patterns of coherence and meaning came unraveled. Those of us who lived through the 1960s sensed that the changes taking place within and without us were profound and permanent, yet we had little idea of what legacy this would leave our children. Nonetheless, the turbulence of the 1960s has combined with the malaise of the 1970s and the cynicism of the 1980s to produce an immense generational impact, described here in terms of the frontiers they've faced:

> When they were born, they were the first babies people took pills not to have. When the 1967 Summer of Love marked the start of America's divorce epidemic, they were the wee kindergartners armed with latchkeys for reentering empty homes after school. In 1974, they were the bell-bottomed seventh-graders who got their first real-life civics lesson watching Nixon resign on TV....In 1979, they were the graduating seniors of Carter-era malaise who registered record low SAT scores and record high crime and drug-abuse rates....[They are] the only generation born after the Civil War to come of age unlikely to match their parents' economic fortunes; and the only one born this century to grow up personifying (to others) not the advance, but the decline of their society's greatness.⁴

Douglas Coupland is a reluctant spokesperson for his generation.⁵ His writings portray today's young people sympathetically, yet as a generation raised on social issues, media events, and TV advertising. In writing *Life after God*, "he found himself drawn to the concept that his was the first generation raised without religion." The book is a series of encounters between a young man named Scout and various characters who have "numbed themselves — via drugs, stupid jobs, empty sex — and are searching, awkwardly, for meaning."⁶ An old friend tells him, "I'm trying to escape from ironic hell: Cynicism into faith; randomness into clarity; worry into devotion. But it's hard because I try to be sincere about life, and then I turn on the TV and see a game show host."⁷ And at one point, Scout himself concludes,

"I think there was a trade-off somewhere along the line. I think the price we paid for our golden life was an inability to fully believe in love; instead, we gained an irony that scorched everything it touched. And I wonder if this irony is the price we paid for the loss of God. But then I must remind myself we are living creatures — we have religious impulses — we *must* — and yet into what cracks do these impulses flow in a world without religion?"[8]

One alarming development expressive of this scorching irony is the epidemic of suicide, which is now the second leading cause of death among American adolescents. Since 1950, the suicide rate for this age group has tripled. Over 2,000 young people kill themselves each year, with 42,496 Americans between fifteen and twenty-five successfully suiciding during the 1970s. Nancy O'Malley's booklet, *Suicide on Campus,* begins by stating that "the epidemic has grown so large and so swiftly that by now it's almost certain your life has been touched by suicide. Either a friend, a friend of a friend, a young person you know, or a member of your family has turned the will to live back upon itself."[9] In the fall quarter at DePaul in 1993, we had six students attempt suicide. Unfortunately, two were successful. The loss of personal meaning, however, shows itself in countless lesser ways: drug and alcohol abuse, reckless sexual activity, eating disorders, clinical depression, apathy, and alienation.

Changes in Family Life

The millions who make up Generation X have grown up in radically different family contexts, resulting in changed values and attitudes. America's divorce rate doubled between 1965 and 1975. A child born in 1968 faced three times more risk of parental breakup than his or her counterpart in 1948. On a summer day not too many years ago I was urging my daughter to turn off the TV and do something. Her reply ("But there's nothing to do") met my suggestion that she visit her friend Christine. "She's with her father this weekend." "Well, go visit Sarah." "She's at her mother's." "Petra, how many of your friends' parents are divorced?" After a brief moment of reflection: "Practically all of them!" Howe and Strauss comment on the impact felt by this profound shift in family structure:

> According to one major survey of the 1970s-era marital disruptions, only one-fifth of the children of divorce professed being happier afterward — versus four-fifths of the divorced parents. Half the kids of divorce recall having felt unwelcome in their new pieced-together fam-

ilies. At best, divorce brought kids complicated new relationships with moms, dads, and unfamiliar adults — and new time-consuming hassles shuttling back and forth between parents trying to schedule in a little "quality time" under awkward circumstances. At worst, divorce meant violent quarrels, split loyalties, estrangement from one parent (usually the father), maybe even a move away from one's house and friends. And, for most 13er kids, divorce has brutal economic side effects: moms gone all day, less money, homes sold.[10]

A 1988 survey found that barely over 50 percent of American youths age fifteen–seventeen were living with both their birth-mother and their birth-father. Another 15 percent were living with their formerly married birth-mother and no father; 13.5 percent were living with their birth-mother and a stepfather; just under 5 percent lived with a never-married birth-mother and no father; 3.2 percent lived with their birth-father and no mother; the remaining 10 percent lived with adoptive mothers and fathers, relatives including grandparents, and other such arrangements. "Over the span of this one generation, the proportion of children living with less than two parents increased by half, and the proportion of working mothers of preschool children doubled."[11]

Changing gender roles, away from male-dominance and toward greater mutuality, is another important factor affecting this generation's experience of family. Since 1960, the number of working mothers with children under age six has increased threefold and, according to the U.S. Bureau of Labor Statistics, is now more than 60 percent of all such mothers. Working mothers with children between six and seventeen years of age have almost doubled, with more than three-quarters of such women now in the work force. Working mothers meant day care for toddlers and less supervision for older children. It also meant shifting gender role-expectations among spouses in the home, with males being called upon to do more housework and meal preparation and expected to take more responsibility for supervision of children. These changing expectations have resulted in some behavior shifts, as well, but much less than most women now want or need, creating conflict and tension in two-parent families. Parent-child relationships went through changes, too, becoming less authoritarian and judgmental and more egalitarian. Howe and Strauss point out that "the dominant cultural image of the 1970s-era parents became that of a *pal* who is overly permissive, always understanding; they never get very angry. There are no boundaries or limits set."[12]

The results of the shifting family context are still unknown, but studies seem to support the view that "these changes in family processes have made the early life course of children both less stable and less economically secure."[13] This is particularly the case among African Americans, where the number of single-parent families is proportionally much greater than in other parts of American society, and where the precarious economic situation is exacerbated by worsening employment prospects and the decline in inflation-adjusted income transfers to poor families during the 1980s.[14] In considering the impact of the changing family on Generation X, one thing seems clear: these young people have been able to rely less on parents and their authoritarian guidance and have had to accept greater responsibility — frequently by default — for decisions affecting their own everyday lives. Greater freedom, for sure, but also greater burden, less clarity, more room to make poor decisions, less access to the voices of experience.

Undoubtedly the changing family and its consequent result in greater autonomy and independence of children are tied to other aspects of the new social environment. For example, street gangs appeal to many young people because they provide a sense of belonging, discipline, group expectations, and demands. There are greater security risks and a growing incidence of violent crime, making neighborhoods dangerous, even for routine activities. There is an earlier norm age for sexual activity and an increase in promiscuity and STDs (including the AIDS epidemic). Studies show a higher incidence of addictive behaviors, including the resurgence of marijuana use even at the high school level, widespread alcohol abuse, eating disorders, and a new wave of cigarette smoking. All of these factors affect young people's self-esteem and their relationships with peers and family. They affect their attitudes toward society and the future, their performance at work and in school. All of this fuels a deep, though frequently hidden, spiritual longing. But where to turn for spiritual nurturance?

Drugs and Alternative Consciousness

The use of drugs provides young people with access to another level of consciousness. Many try to escape the pressures and tensions of everyday life and the added anxieties involved in developmental transitions to adolescence and young adulthood by getting high. The momentary experience of numinous mystery in a spiritual dimension is transcendence from the pragmatic utilitarian experience of ordinary conscious awareness. The glimpsing of a more profound level raises deep questions about reality and meaning and makes the return to ordinary consciousness troublesome. The absence of the numinous and the profound in contemporary culture, even religious cultures, creates a disdain for pragmatic existence and a cynicism about everyday life. Drugs introduce flashes of the numinous, but without any coherent pattern of entering into and relating to it; drugs produce a sense of ambiguity and profound questions, but without any "answers." Religion is fundamentally about relating to the numinous and living within the framework of ultimate mystery with storied patterns of meaning (myth), but most young people have no such experience of religion. The psychological effects of drug usage, even moderate and intermittent usage, are a distancing from everyday and pragmatic meaning, increased anxiety and cynicism, and a hunger for relationship to the numinous. This is an important feature of existence for today's young people, quite apart from any addictive experience.

Ubiquitous Advertising and *Homo Economicus*

Still another feature of contemporary American culture affecting today's young people is the enormous growth of advertising and societal preoccupation with the economy. Since they've grown up with television, they have been assaulted from early age with media sales pitches — from McDonald's "food, friends, and fun" to Calvin Klein's erotic cologne and underwear, the beer companies' beach parties, and Levi's description of their 501s as "the last great mystery." They have been *sold* spiritual values (freedom, belonging, community, intimacy, and love; self-esteem, the acceptance and affection of others, beauty, truth, and fulfillment) through hamburgers and haircuts, beauty aids and clothing, soft drinks and credit cards, and, perhaps most of all, basketball shoes. Buying and consuming are the way to happiness. This is the message that has been drummed into their psyches, beginning with ads that accompany Saturday morning cartoons and continuing with MTV spots, the sides of buses, slick magazine layouts, and even what you see on the silver screen before the feature film begins. Advertising, manipulative invasions of our consciousness and our subconsciousness, besieging us minute by minute, day after day, through creative design and hype — this has been the constant environment in which today's young people have grown up.

Simultaneously, most of Generation X have been clued into the untrustworthiness of these messages. Parental responses to desires fired by ads have usually included warnings: "they're just after your money," "the real toy doesn't work like they make it look," "this is a con job — they just want you to buy their stupid product." However, it's frequently the parents' credibility that suffers. Mom and Dad (or, Mom or Dad) are seen as the ones who don't really know, or worse, who really don't want their children's happiness. Early on in life, parents and advertisers are at war — a conflict that expands dramatically in adolescence, with a peer group that is saturated with ad-dominated consciousness, isolating parents still further.

Sharon Daloz Parks suggests that our cynicism about advertising and our awareness of its manipulations does not mean that we remain unaffected. The images of advertising and their accompanying values and yearnings are being orchestrated by people "who have reflected on the nature of the human imagination so as to place it in the servitude of market logic. . . . Such understanding [of the imagination] makes attempts to craft and engineer the public soul possible. Our patterns of desire, our 'choices' are increasingly the creation of someone else's understanding of our imagination."[15]

Meanwhile, society as a whole is focused on *Homo economicus,* the human as defined by production and consumption. The good person is the person who is producing and consuming, and human value is interpreted economically. Thanksgiving weekend is now "shop 'til you drop weekend," and "How good a Christmas was it?" refers to the amount of spending shoppers did. A papal visit is measured by its impact on the local economy. Whatever creates jobs is viewed positively, even if the jobs are environmentally destructive or socially pathologic. Weekly, or even daily, we hear the economic news: interest rates, housing starts, wholesale upturns, manufacture downturns, balance of payments off, bond market up, the weak dollar, the bear market, unemployment figures, this month's economic indicators. Politicians rise and fall, depending on the public's perception of the economy and how well it is being stimulated and managed. Everybody works, everybody shops, everybody consumes, everybody works longer and harder and more efficiently, so everybody can buy more and more. Corporations cut costs, downscale, reengineer, relocate subsidiaries, redefine their market share. Life itself is delimited by the ubiquitous economy, demanding this, necessitating that, requiring more of this but less of that, providing opportunities for the opportunistic and tragedies for those who don't read the *Wall Street Journal*. To grow up in a world of *Homo economicus* is to experience a radically diminished human spirit.

Decline in Religious Literacy and Socialization

A precipitous decline in religious literacy and socialization is yet another factor shaping Generation X. Today's young people, according to Gallup findings, know little about the religious tradition in which they have been raised and feel little sense of ownership of or belonging to an organized religion. A survey report, with commentary and analysis by George Gallup, Jr., and Robert Bezilla, published in 1992 states that significant numbers of today's young Americans "are turned off by churches and organized religion."[16] They report that "a glaring lack of knowledge of the Ten Commandments and basic religious tenets is found among youth today. Many do not know the meaning of Easter." Compelling statistics cited:

- Only 12 percent of teens interviewed feel that religion has a great deal of influence on their generation; an additional 30 percent say it has some influence, and another 28 percent feel it has very little influence.

- Friends, home, school, music, and television are rated ahead of religion (and books) as factors which teens believe are having the greatest influence on their generation.

- Only one teen in every four expresses a high degree of confidence in organized religion.

- Only 41 percent of teens report attending religion classes, and a mere 36 percent are active in a youth group at church.

This data is clearly supported in my own experience teaching Religious Studies classes at DePaul these past five years. One student who considered herself a good Catholic didn't understand the terms "Old" and "New Testament." Two out of forty-five raised their hands when asked if they had "*ever heard of* the U.S. bishops' pastoral letters on peace and the economy." Only a small minority of incoming DePaul students report an active commitment to an organized religion that they have studied and know something about. And clearly, the only Catholicism many young people know about is in the context of their elders' growing cynicism toward church and their own media-enlarged experience of unyielding patriarchy, pedophilia scandals, sexual phobias, and institutional chaos. One young woman recently told me of what it was like for her growing up Catholic in a family headed by her divorced mother. The mother insisted that all the children go to Mass every Sunday. Despite the angry complaints she and her sisters registered as adolescents, off they went to church on Sunday morning. Then, in the car on the way home, at breakfast, and off-and-on through the rest of the week, they would hear their mother complain bitterly about the priest's arrogance, his offensive homily — about sexism and patriarchy in the church and the demeaning of women. But when Sunday morning next rolled around, there was Mom getting everybody up and off to Mass again. The young woman was socialized into a critical, angry, bitterly cynical Catholicism, which she and her sisters wanted no part of. Was the mother herself aware of and possessive of a deeper, more life-giving faith? If so, she never shared its meaning and values with her daughters.

This orientation shows up again and again in my survey of first-year college students taking our Introduction to Religion course. When asked what the major contemporary *religious* issues are, students consistently bring up the credibility of the church, pedophilia in the priesthood, reproductive rights, the ordination of women, priestly celibacy, and the church's teachings regarding human sexuality — hardly the basics of our tradition! When I push them and ask what the major *spiritual* concerns facing their generation are, I get a very different set of responses: the need to belong and feel loved; concern for interfaith understanding and the self-righteous exclusivity of the Religious Right; self-esteem, mutual respect and civility, human rights; increasing violence and abuse; ecological concerns; the problems of addiction; and the loss of meaning and hope for the future.

Spiritual Hungers

The irony is that today's young people exhibit simultaneously a distrustful distancing from institutional religion and a new openness to spirituality and profound human values. Marketing experts appeal to these values in advertising their products to Generation X. Transcendence, belonging, self-esteem, community, trust, love, even mystical consciousness are used to sell hamburgers, beer, jeans, cologne, and underwear. Would that our religious communities were as interested in the young's spiritual hungers as are business and enterprise. The same Gallup report referred to above points to "six basic needs of young people":

1. The need to believe that life is meaningful and has a purpose;

2. The need for a sense of community and deeper relationships;

3. The need to be appreciated and loved;

4. The need to be listened to — to be heard;

5. The need to feel that one is growing in faith;

6. The need for practical help in developing a mature faith.[17]

These spiritual hungers await appropriate responses, but such responses, clearly, must address young people where they are and must offer them something credible and authentic — a vision of life that is compelling and challenging and a practice that denotes a path that is inviting, adventurous, and demanding. There is a begging for such spiritual wisdom. No one is more straightforward in declaring this need than Coupland's hero, at the very end of his long journey in *Life after God:*

> Now — here is my secret:
>   I tell it to you with an openness of heart that I doubt I shall ever achieve again, so I pray that you are in a quiet room as you hear these words. My secret is that I need God — that I am sick and can no longer make it alone. I need God to help me give, because I no longer seem capable of giving; to help me be kind, as I no longer seem capable of kindness; to help me love, as I seem beyond being able to love.[18]

A New Openness

There are indications of an openness to pursue such a spiritual quest among many young people today — evidenced in their interest in meditation and mysticism, vegetarianism, and community service. The interest is decidedly experiential, not doctrinal or juridical. They want direct experience of God and community, hands-on service to those in need. They want to do rather than merely hear about. Rushkoff hints at this openness when he insists that Generation X is itself "a life philosophy designed to help us cope with the increasingly disorientingly rapid deflation of our society, both financially and culturally." This philosophy is based, he says,

> on a commitment to reject the traditional values and linear reasoning of the dominant culture and instead embrace the postmodern swirl, . . . a conscious effort to avoid engaging in anything that requires descent into the rat race or consumerist angst, a neo-Buddhism where

attachments of any kind break the awareness so valuable to surfers of a consumer culture.[19]

Such a philosophy of life (though one could argue whether what Rushkoff describes is, in fact, such) already speaks to an openness to the wisdom of the great spiritual traditions, including Christianity. The Jesus movement was born in just such a deflationary world among a peasant culture that wanted no part of Rome's imperial pretensions. But, again, rejection and detachment are only prerequisites to the constructive task, which has something to do, I think, with developing this "neo-Buddhist awareness." Interest in spiritual doers and in doing spiritual practices are expressions beyond simply rejecting a deconstructed culture.

Rushkoff himself agrees that liberation from yesterday's constraints brings with it the sense of being cast adrift:

> It must be nice to have something external to believe in. Something that doesn't move. Something absolute. Having no such permanent icon (no God, no Country, no Superhero) we choose instead — by default, actually — to experience life as play, and trust that the closer we come to our own true intentions, the closer we will come to our own *best* intentions.[20]

This absence of something to believe in and the movement toward play and the pursuit of one's true intentions is an excellent perspective from which to view the task of reconstructing Catholicism. The missing piece in Rushkoff's description of a generational choice is the wisdom of experience present in the great spiritual traditions that can serve as a precious resource in making meaning and developing authentic responsibility. The association of Christianity, particularly Catholicism, with negative constraints for so many people today, while readily understandable, is unfortunate, since in its origins and at its best throughout history it has been experienced as a liberation. Liberation and believing go together; trusting one's own true intentions (the deepest desires of the human spirit) and surrender to God go together; pursuing our *best* intentions (love and service, compassion and justice) and discovering the experiential truth present in the wisdom traditions go together. But this is already a reconstructing approach — something beyond what most young people today have perceived in their interaction with religion in general and with Catholicism in particular. The thesis of this book is that reconstructing Catholicism by focusing, not on juridical consciousness, but the Catholic experience, can address their hungers, appeal to their aspirations, and help heal their wounds, offering them a way to live with meaning and hope in the future.

While recognizing the severe challenges facing those who seek to help young people in developing their spiritual lives, one could see the opportunities as exciting. The challenges clearly include the reluctance of so many of the young to commit themselves to anything and their continual need to ask *why?* (to question *everything*), their skepticism toward authority and rejection of hierarchy, and their cynicism about religion. Nonetheless, there are important positive orientations that motivate today's young people. Gallup and Bezilla point to three: "From what we know about young people in America at this time, they appear to be motivated by three basic drives: (1) a search for meaning in life and their purpose in the universe; (2) a search for meaningful and sensitive relationships with others; and (3) a desire to serve others."[21] My own experience finds great promise in this new generation's freshness and candor — in their practical idealism and willingness to give generously of themselves, in their efforts to overcome prejudice and discrimination, in their spectacular honesty about themselves (the brokenness and emptiness they feel inside) and our world, in their distancing themselves from our consumerist-materialist addictions, and in their openness — a searching, almost begging, openness.

— Chapter 2 —

Vatican II and
the Graying of Catholicism

Unfortunately, today's Church is crippled by its failure to address fundamental justice issues within its own institutional structures and so becomes a stumbling block to its own members as well as to the broader society. Therefore we appeal to the institutional Church to undertake reform and renewal of its structures and to all the people of God to give witness to the Spirit who lives within us and seek ways to serve the vision of God in our human society. We see many young adults and children of Catholic families who are reluctant to affiliate with a Church they view as authoritarian and hypocritical. We call for a fundamental change so that young people will see and hear God living in and through the Church as a participatory community of believers who practice what they preach.
—Call to Action's *Call for Reform* (1990)

As cultural decadence and a desire to serve others opens a new generation to a spiritual quest for the profound dimensions of being human, for ultimate meaning and transpersonal values, institutional Catholicism is fraught with conflict and threatened by organizational collapse and financial ruin, yet the vision of a renewed and reformed church continues to assert itself in countless ways. Vatican efforts to restore a preconciliar Catholicism have, for the past fifteen years, polarized Catholics in a prolonged and angry conflict, focusing the church on peripheral concerns: traditional ordination requirements, doctrinal uniformity, organizational standards, and an unyielding approach to sexual ethics. The Vatican asserts that the church doesn't have the authority to ordain women, since Christ chose only men as his disciples. The new Catholic catechism is purposely written using noninclusive language. Annual international synods of bishops, originally intended to continue the work of transforming the church that the Council had begun, have been carefully controlled and managed by the pope and the Vatican offices so as to resist change and to reassert centralized jurisdiction. Theologians, such as Hans

Küng, Charles Curran, and Leonardo Boff, who advocate change are discredited and sanctioned. A growing number of issues (e.g., the morality of abortion and homosexual acts, the ordination of women) are declared *undiscussable*. Only men who submit to such centralized control are appointed as bishops, regardless of their gifts and abilities. All of these attempts to resist change and restore Vatican dominion are met with louder calls for reform, and the movement for change broadens and becomes increasingly bold. The result is a widening gap, a deeper power struggle, a too often mean-spirited conflict.

The Perception of Young People

While restorationists and reformers carry on an acrimonious debate about who is gender-fit to proclaim the Gospel and preside at the Eucharist, too many young people assume that issues such as this are at the center of Catholicism. Surely, they conjecture, the very heart of Catholicism must be its restrictive teachings on human sexuality and the authoritative bureaucracy that promulgates it. Papal pronouncements about the immorality of artificial contraception are mostly ignored among a generation battling AIDS and concerned about the global population explosion, but where such statements are thoughtfully considered, the frequent response is that the source of such assertions is neither alert to the epidemic of teenage pregnancies nor HIV-aware. The young perceive the church as unjust and immoral in its treatment of women and gays and preoccupied with maintaining its own power rather than serving the spiritual and moral needs of the world. Too often, in this protracted contention within the church, juridical consciousness commands center stage, whether one is rebelling against Catholic patriarchy and authoritarian dictates or seeking a restoration of the "real" (1950s) Catholicism. Meanwhile, clergy sexual abuse looms as the governing image for Generation X's cynical sense of ecclesial hypocrisy and organizational discipline gone amuck.

While there are many examples of local churches that are spiritually alive and dynamically focused on evangelism, community, and social justice, unfortunately these are the exceptions, frequently hidden from the public eye — or perceived as the heretical fringe. Chapter 6 of this book looks at a growing network of such faith communities, some of them parishes or campus ministry centers, others without any formal institutional ties or canonical status. Meanwhile, the dominant perception of Catholicism among young people today is an institution in decline and growing old, its members controlled by an addictive guilt and deep patterns of codependency and without much genuine interest in either "the profound" or service to those in need. The enthusiasm and excitement of a changing church, retrieving its ancient dynamism and reclaiming its mission to the world — the vision of church that gripped me in my late teens and early twenties — has largely been eclipsed by an image of a desperate power struggle pitting the Vatican against the common sense of the clergy and the people alike, a struggle in which what is truly essential is being lost and forgotten.

Vatican II: A Vision Betrayed

Angelo Roncalli, who became Pope John XXIII in 1958, shared this sense that Catholicism needed to renew itself by forging a vital connection between its core beliefs and the needs of our contemporary world. On January 25, 1959, just three months after his election to the papacy, a vigorous yet elderly Pope John surprised the church and the world by announcing his intention of convening an Ecumenical Council. In succeeding months he frequently spoke of his hopes for the Council. It would address the longing for unity among Christians and the critical issue of world peace. It would bring about an *aggiornamento* (the Italian word for "updating") of the church, revitalizing it and bringing it into closer relationship with the actual contemporary world. In May 1960, the pope again advanced his purposes, making it clear that the Council was not going to be under the control of the Roman Curia: "The government of the Church is one thing," he said in nominating the preparatory commissions to draw up the Council's agenda, "and the Council is another."[1] The commissions, which were made up of bishops from all over the world, including some well-known liberal names, met at the Vatican in November 1960. Here the pope told them that their task was not so much to concern themselves with points of doctrine or discipline, but "to show in its true light and restore to its true value the quality of human and Christian life."[2] He again used the term *aggiornamento*, the word he seemed to favor most in giving his lead to the Council. It meant not merely a bringing up-to-date of the church's message, but an attempt to find the way to reawaken an awareness of the spiritual reality of life. "We must recover our courage," said John. What was needed most was for the church to take stock of itself, of its own

life and the appearance it presents to the broader world, in order
that it can again announce the deep and universal vocation of all humanity in a world that was sated with the seductions of materialism
and greed.

John XXIII's vision is as relevant today as it was more than three
decades ago. Between then and now, his hopes for the Council itself were largely realized, as the most authoritative teaching body of
the Catholic Church presented a radical call for renewal and reform,
shifting its focus from internal maintenance to pastoral leadership
toward spiritual renewal, building community, the work of peace-
making, and social justice. But the Council itself never addressed
implementation of this vision through specific steps of structural
change and precise patterns of ecclesial reform that would give the
pastoral dimension priority over the juridical and provide agency to
pursue *aggiornamento* with freedom. The pope's aspirations and the
Council documents had all the right instincts, but left the vision gen-
eralized and within the hands of a hierarchical structure made up
exclusively of celibate men, whose power was now imperiled. Conservative power blocks, threatened by loss of ecclesial control and a
startling shift away from the juridical and the canonical, never gave
up and have been able gradually over these intervening decades to
put the old face back together again. The first step was convincing
John's liberal-minded successor, Paul VI, not to follow the counsel of
his own international panel of experts who made up the papal birth
control commission. In 1968, this pope, who had championed the
Council's vision, issued his encyclical letter *Humanae vitae,* reaffirming the prior teaching against any form of artificial contraception,
despite an overwhelming majority in his own hand-picked commission to change it in the light of contemporary insights regarding
human sexuality and the need to control human population.[3]

A decade later, the Council's vision found a formidable opponent
in the election of the charismatic Karol Wojtyla as John Paul II.
His conservative leadership has put Vatican II in a deep freeze,
resisting change at every turn, appointing party-line clerics as bishops, and creating a credibility gulf between the Vatican and the
church's hierarchy, on the one hand, and most pastoral leaders, theologians, religious educators, and dedicated Catholic believers, on the
other. Had Vatican II's direction and vision found implementation,
the work of reconstructing Catholicism would already be in place,
addressing today's spiritual hungers and leading the way toward psychological and social liberation, inspiring Catholics and others to

integrate the faith of Jesus and do the work of love and justice. Alas and alas, such is not the case. Nevertheless, the Council ignited a firestorm with its radical call for *aggiornamento*, ecumenism, and retrieval of the church's mission to the world, and that vision continues to be the basis for reconstructing Catholicism.

Vatican II's Call for a Paradigm Shift

Vatican II said almost nothing about human sexual behavior, and what it did say balanced the earlier focus on reproduction with a new emphasis on the expression of mutual love.[4] The Council documents emphasized, not the authority of the pope and the role of the priesthood, but the authority of the bishop and local church and the role of the laity. The goal of the Council, again, was to move the church away from peripheral concerns, stressing the spiritual hungers of all humanity and the need to retrieve the vital center of our tradition in addressing them. Jesuit theologian T. Howland Sanks describes the teachings of Vatican II under seven major emphases:

- *A shift from a closed and defensive posture to one of openness and willingness to listen and learn:* Most obvious in the document "The Church in the Modern World," where the Council urges the "duty of scrutinizing the signs of the times...to hear, distinguish and interpret the many voices of our age," the emphasis is on dialogue with and participation in the "world."

- *Ecumenism, reconciliation with believers of other denominations:* Most explicit in the *Decree on Ecumenism,* but found throughout the conciliar documents, a focus on the bond of unity that Christians share and a deep desire to overcome that which separates by recognizing that "men on both sides were to blame" for the historical separations between Christians and by accepting "with respect and affection as brothers" those whom it had previously regarded as heretics and schismatics.

- *The need for continual reform and renewal within the church itself:* Admitting that there have been "deficiencies in conduct, in church discipline, or even in the formulation of doctrine," the Council legitimizes changes and development by recognizing "how great a distance lies between the message she offers and the human failing of those to whom the gospel is entrusted."

- *A shift from the "classical mind" to a historical consciousness:* The movement away from a preoccupation with immutable essences and unchanging truths to a recognition of the historical location and context of scripture, discipline, and doctrine is incorporated in the documents in its distinction between "the substance of the ancient doctrine" and "the way in which it is presented."

- *Pluralism, diversity, and differences of discipline, liturgy, and governance within the church and the churches:* Saying that "the heritage handed down by the apostles was received in different forms and ways, so that from the very beginnings of the Church it has had a varied development in various places, thanks to a similar variety of natural gifts and conditions of life," there is a relativizing of European modes and a legitimization of pluralism.

- *Collegiality, which recognizes a corporate responsibility for the church and its mission,* with the need for those in authority to listen to and carefully consider the views of those whom they lead: While not denying the hierarchical nature of the church, the Council redresses the imbalance left by the incomplete treatment of this subject occasioned by the forced suspension of Vatican I by pointing to the collegial nature of priesthood, episcopacy, and among individual churches and the universal church.

- *Ministry as service grounded in baptism:* Leadership in the Christian community is not to be thought of in terms of domination or merely the exercise of jurisdiction within a circumscribed institution, but rather as "a true service . . . *diakonia* or ministry" directed to all nations and to every creature and involving the laity as well as those who hold office in the Church."[5]

The work of the Council was fueled by Pope John's final exhortation, an encyclical letter addressed "to all men of good will." Published in April of 1963, just two months before he died of stomach cancer and before the second session of the Council convened, *Pacem in Terris (Peace on Earth)* is a resolute call for peace in the world — for all persons, but especially for national leaders, to give themselves unsparingly to the establishment of true and lasting peace. Biographer E. E. Y. Hales claims that the pope "succeeded in lifting himself right out of his political and even out of his clerical environment onto the lofty plane of Father-in-God of all men, irrespective of their creed, their colour, their continent, irrespective even of their acceptance of his own fatherhood."[6] In this document the pope issues a definitive affirmation of religious liberty as a fundamental right of all people, a clarion call for the realization of women's rights, an unmitigated condemnation of the arms race and of the use of nuclear weapons. Against national chauvinism and racism, the pope declares the equality of all and the unity of all. Every person possesses a dignity that others must respect and that he or she must assert. Laws that deny or fail to recognize this dignity have no juridical value. The world's goods were meant for all, and the equitable sharing of wealth is a duty and imperative. There can be no economic or cultural imperialism, but each culture and nation deserves its own respect and esteem. Above all, we must remember that we are clothed with a spiritual nature and have a spiritual destiny — more than consumers and producers in search of material gains, we are capable of love and find our fulfillment only in exercising this capacity to the fullest. We belong to God and to one another; this is our deepest identity and our noblest vocation.[7]

The seven emphases of the Council's teachings described above demonstrate how influential the dying pope was in leading the Council. Taken collectively, the teachings of Vatican II amount to *a massive paradigm shift* in Catholicism, leaving its medieval European forms behind and moving the tradition into a global and contemporary context. The church that had for centuries hoped for a restoration of a Catholic culture throughout the West was now setting a quite different course, reconciling itself to a world of global pluralism and diversity and seeking its place of spiritual leadership not in retreat but through engagement. A sculpture memorializing John XXIII hangs in St. Peter's Basilica at the Vatican; in it the artist has portrayed a benevolent Pope John compassionately reaching out to a hungry and poor humanity. Lined up behind the smiling pontiff are the bishops of the church with their pointed miters on their heads and their crosier staffs in hand. They wear quizzical looks, as if to say, "Where are you leading us?" John knew where Catholicism needed to go: toward the people in loving service, with a message of justice and peace in a world torn apart by greed and violence. It could no longer preoccupy itself with its own internal institutional concerns but was called to seek a profound dialogue with human beings everywhere about our common spiritual vocation as children of God and brothers and sisters of one another. Relinquishing its religious triumphalism, its centuries-old withdrawal from "the world," and its politics of privilege, the church was being led, reluctantly, toward a retrieval of its humble origins in Jesus of Nazareth with a pastoral mission of liberation and healing. But without an agenda to implement this direction, which, in effect, amounts to a pastoral revolution, Catholicism awaits a reconstruction from below — from the laity, particularly from the young. Meanwhile, the stand-off between restorationists and revisionists has left young people with little or no access to or ownership of Catholicism —

and the church, left and right, liberal or conservative, looks grayer and grayer.

Double-Speak and Institutional Chaos

A few years ago a business research method called "positioning thinking" was applied to the Catholic Church. The request to apply this method of critiquing institutional communication problems, which has been utilized broadly in major corporations, came, not from the Vatican or a committee of bishops, but from a group of lay people who were concerned about the disarray and chaos that had followed in the wake of the reforms of Vatican II. Prior to the Council, "the institutional Church had a clearly perceived position in the minds of the faithful. To most, the Church was the teacher of the law. Much emphasis was placed on rules, rewards, and punishment."[8] After Vatican II, as the church moved away from this posture of law and order, rules and regulations were downplayed, and flexibility took the place of rigidity. Yet "what was painfully lacking was a clear presentation of what the new church was about. The faithful quietly asked, 'If you are not the teacher of the law, what are you?'" Unfortunately, there was no clear distillation of what had transpired, no program in simple language to explain the new directions. There was "no attempt to reposition the church in the minds of the laity. Even in the minds of the clergy, for that matter. And with no answers, confusion walked in and many people walked out."[9]

The lack of a pastoral plan to implement Vatican II's vision and the subsequent power struggle to keep juridical consciousness on the front burner have created a major identity crisis among Catholics themselves and a sense of bewilderment for those who observe from the outside. When clergy, bishops, and laity in the "positioning thinking" process were asked, "What is the role of the Catholic Church in today's world?" never was the same answer received twice. While the Council had called the church back to its origins and to the fundamentals of spirituality, evangelism, community, and social justice, the communication patterns — from the Vatican's declarations down to the Sunday homily and weekly bulletin of the local parish — continued to betray this teaching, proclaiming instead more rules and regulations, usually focused on sexual matters, almost always affirming hierarchical control, frequently demeaning women or a host of other subpopulations of believers, affirming patterns of codependency rather than those of liberation and healing. The institutional results have been predictably disastrous: "For the first time, regular Mass attendance dropped below 50 percent of the Catholic population.... There are 20 percent fewer priests, nuns, and brothers today than there were 10 years ago. Vocations have dropped by 60 percent."[10] More and more dioceses and even the Vatican itself experience serious financial difficulties. Reconstructing Catholicism means taking John XXIII's lead and the Council's vision seriously: it means focusing on the basics of the tradition and integrating them with our lived experience.

A Uniquely American Catholicism

Catholics in the United States, as a group, welcomed the Council's teachings, seeing in them a signal to proceed with the process of inculturating Catholicism in a uniquely American way. Vatican II occurred at a critical moment in U.S. Catholic history, providing authoritative legitimacy to a shifting consciousness already emerging in America — a consciousness that in some ways has its roots as far back as the American Revolution. Historian Jay Dolan maintains that the real revolution, which took place "in the minds and hearts of the American people" and emphasized equality and a spirit of independence, affected the small group of American Catholics profoundly. He argues that already in 1790 a distinctive vision of Catholicism was taking shape in the United States under the leadership of our first American bishop, John Carroll. That vision called for "a national, American church which would be independent of all foreign jurisdiction and would endorse pluralism and toleration in religion; a church in which religion was grounded in intelligibility and where a vernacular liturgy was normative; and finally a church in which the spirit of democracy permeated the government of local communities."[11] This early revisioning was eclipsed by the massive influx of European immigrants that began in 1820. They brought with them European clergy. These clergy had been influenced by the destructive impact that the French Revolution had on the church with the state's confiscation of church lands and the execution of bishops, priests, and religious. They were also influenced by the subsequent pressure that Rome brought to bear for a conservative centralization in the aftermath of the Revolution. Nonetheless, by the end of the nineteenth century, a uniquely American Catholicism again appeared with the so-called Americanists.

Influenced by creative thinkers like Orestes Brownson and Isaac

Hecker, a new generation in the 1880s and 1890s, led by Bishop John
Ireland of Minnesota, began to search for ways to adapt the church
to the new age in which it found itself:

> The basic ideas of this movement involved the adaptation of the
> Church to modern culture; the idea of God as one who acts in history
> and is revealed through it; the vision of the Reign of God as moving
> toward realization in history; the need for an active, energetic laity;
> a more tolerant view of Protestants; the superiority of this American
> version of Catholicism to that of the Old World.[12]

Pope Leo XIII issued a condemnation of Americanism in an 1899 letter, *Testem Benevolentiae*, in which the experiment in adaptation was
seen as heresy "for espousing the activist individualism, self-confident
mystique and optimistic idealism of American civilization."[13] Dennis McCann, a Religious Studies colleague at DePaul, suggests that
what Rome was most concerned about was "an emerging style of
religious praxis nurtured by the experience of Catholic people in
America" — "a certain liberty" in the church that reflected the revolutionary American principle of "self-governing association" and its
extension to all institutional sectors of society.[14]

The condemnation of Americanism, together with the condemnation of modernism (including, of course, Pius IX's famous *Syllabus
of Errors*) less than a decade later, signaled an end to this spirit of
independence and the beginning of the twentieth-century Romaniza-
tion of the U.S. church. With new European immigrants continuing
to come to America, Catholicism increasingly reflected the church
that had shunned the Enlightenment and the culture of modernity
that it spawned, conservatively clinging to the ancient regime's authoritarianism and a medieval worldview. Still, within decades the
vast numbers of immigrant Catholics had become more and more
assimilated into American culture, reigniting the deep dissonance between America's openness, pluralism, and love of liberty, and their
Catholic subculture. As the children and grandchildren of immigrants
participated in higher education, particularly with the G.I. Bill at
the end of World War II, the assimilation process produced a generation of acculturated Catholics, perhaps epitomized by John F.
Kennedy — worldly, modern, participating fully in the center of
American culture, and increasingly distanced from the conservatism
and authoritarianism of institutional Catholicism. Kennedy's ascen-
dancy to the presidency symbolized this assimilation process, and
it coincided with the opening of the Second Vatican Council. The
Council reforms were broadly perceived in America as the church's

permission to pursue this assimilation without guilt — to embrace modernity. Given the long history of wanting to blend American openness, pluralism, and democracy with Catholic faith and practice, there was a rush to see the Council as an authoritative signal to move resolutely in that direction.

Historian David O'Brien has suggested four key historical factors that shaped the American Catholic subculture, which has largely collapsed in recent decades:

- *Immigration:* Catholics were regarded by other Americans as "outsiders" and responded not by setting aside their ancestral traditions, but by reaffirming their Catholicism, using the church to strengthen family ties and provide meaning and identity in the bewildering world of American industrial cities, where most of them settled.

- *Blue-Collar Workers:* Earlier American Catholics were mostly blue-collar workers, providing the backbone of political machines and trade unions and expressing social attitudes derived from viewing American society from the bottom up.

- *Explosive Growth:* The U.S. Catholic population grew from three million (mid-nineteenth century), to 17 million (1914), to 40 million (1962). This steady, rapid growth meant that church leaders had little time or energy to devote to problems outside the Catholic community itself.

- *Minority Status:* Throughout these two centuries of expansion, Catholics thought of themselves as a minority in a basically Protestant culture, depending upon their own resources and sticking together in defense against non-Catholic hostility, emphasizing loyalty and solidarity.[15]

O'Brien sees the changes in the American church since 1962 as an "unraveling of the historic American Catholic subculture" and the beginnings of a new era for Catholicism here. Besides greater Catholic participation in higher education and more economic strength (today's Catholics are per capita the most affluent religious denomination in America), he cites the upheavals in American society in the 1960s, the erosion of rural communities and ethnic neighborhoods, and the shift of economic and political power away from industrial sections of the country, as factors bringing about the "disintegration" of the Catholic subculture. But perhaps the key factor in bringing about this collapse was the coincidence of all these developments at the very hour of Vatican II: "The council's declaration on religious liberty lessened a tension long felt by American Catholics. Historic papal resistance to church-state separation conflicted with American fidelity to the First Amendment. Vatican II insisted on the duty of each person to follow his or her conscience. But while this lessened tension in one respect, it set up another. With the individual conscience emphasized, church members were more likely to clash with church authority."[16]

Selective Catholicism

The emphasis on individual conscience translated religious liberty into what sociologist Andrew Greeley describes as "selective Catholicism."[17] He argues that since the Council there is a dramatic emergence in America of a do-it-yourself Catholicism in which believers pick and choose what they will believe and what teachings they will follow. Greeley argues that perhaps four-fifths of the regular Sunday church attenders, while remaining loyal to the Church, ignore official Catholic teaching in those areas where they judge papal and episcopal leadership to be incompetent, especially those issues related to sex, above all birth control.[18] A study conducted by University of Notre Dame researchers Joseph Gremillion and Jim Castelli confirms what Greeley is saying, providing survey evidence that "core Catholics" are no less likely than unchurched or nonpracticing Catholics to make up their own minds: "If they agree with the church on an issue, it is because the church position makes sense to them and they actively decide to agree. If a church teaching does not make sense to them, they will refuse to agree, no matter how often or how clearly or how authoritatively the church has spoken on it."[19]

Greeley describes this new phenomenon as "the communal Catholic" — loyal to the Catholic collectivity and sympathetic toward its heritage, but refusing to take seriously the teaching authority of the leadership of the institutional church.[20] This new selective style of affiliation with Catholicism brings with it "a desire for new religious forms...which provide personalized experiences of community" and greater involvement in service and social justice efforts.[21] How this development will extend into the next generation, which eschews hypocrisy and insists on self-honesty, is becoming increasingly clear: they have almost no definition delimiting Catholicism nor any exclusive allegiance to it. They see the smorgasbord table of beliefs and practices even more broadly, now including a panoply of world religions, rites and practices of indigenous peoples, and various New Age spiritual developments. Ravenous spiritual hunger in a decadent culture and the American tradition of openness, individualism, and free thinking make "selective Catholicism" a virtual imperative for young people today.

An effective pastoral response to this cannot simply be a louder drumming of the church's teaching authority, including sometimes threats and manipulative efforts to control. The themes echoing recently from the hierarchy's public utterances seem to assume still a juridical consciousness: the divine authority of pope and bishops, the unique ministry of the priesthood and its tie to *official* ritual prayer and sacrament, the chosenness of the male gender, the definitive truth of a procreative sexual ethic, the exclusive priority of Catholicism as *the* path of salvation. Perhaps they are simply not cognizant of the degree to which a broader and broader population of present and potential believers now assume the religious liberty proclaimed at Vatican II and translated into the American idiom of individual responsibility and freedom of thought and expression.

This book suggests another direction and assumes that people need to be informed and persuaded. More than anything, they need an experiential understanding of the core of the Catholic tradition and psychospiritual bridges to the struggle for meaning today. Independent thinking and personal judgment are critically important, and they require that Catholics make genuine connections between their own experience and the key aspects of the tradition. This is what reconstructing Catholicism is all about. We need to emphasize Jesus as healer and liberator, the dynamics of sin and grace as grounded in our humanness and in our choices, a sense of divine immanence in the material and social worlds, the necessity of community as both support group and spiritual laboratory, and the mission of all the baptized to both personal and social dimensions in the path of liberation. The force of history in Catholicism since Vatican II, particularly in the light of recurring trends in America, seems to be urging the need for reconstruction from below.

The Graying of Catholicism

Nothing speaks louder to this matter than the fact that in the years since the appearance of Vatican II's revolutionary designs for a renewed and reformed Catholicism, the church in the U.S. and its organizations have gotten older. Today one sees the graying of Catholicism — not just in groups like the Serra Club and the Knights of Columbus, but at summer institutes on religious education and pastoral ministry and even in reform-minded organizations like Call to

Action. A growing percentage of young people who were baptized
Catholics as infants have experienced no meaningful socialization
into the church or its traditions — gone are the days of twelve
to sixteen years of exclusively Catholic education. They have little
ownership and tend not to participate, particularly as leaders, in the
organizations and activities of groups directly tied to church. As religious communities build larger infirmaries and prepare to close down
and as the numbers of clergy dwindle, young people frequently look
elsewhere for inspiration, spiritual community, and opportunities for
service. There is a great thirst for the wine that Vatican II ordered,
but the old wineskins of yesterday's church are inadequate. There is
an urgent need to get on with reconstructing Catholicism.

Profile of Tomorrow's Church

The vision of what it means to be church — the church that reformers seek and work for — takes shape in comments made by Rosemary
Ruether at the 1994 Call to Action conference ("We Are the Church:
What If We Meant What We Said?").[22] Ruether describes today as
a *kairos* (critical moment) in human history in which much of the
planet finds itself caught between the great hopes that emerged from
the surprising end of the Cold War and the horrors of poverty, violence, profligate materialism, and environmental devastation. Such
a *kairos* calls the church to a transcendent sense of itself, radically
free from the system of lies and oppression that tends to dominate globally. The church is called to return to its authentic, deeper
self, becoming the community that lives in and through grace. She
describes five qualities of the needed church:

1. *Multicultural:* The church needs to be authentically catholic,
not hegemonically European, white, and male, but truly inclusive of
every continent, race, ethnicity, and class, both genders, and great
cultural diversity. Rather than a haven from cultural and class diversity, to be catholic is to be at the crossroads of all cultures
and races.

2. *Committed to the Poor and Oppressed:* The church is called
to solidarity with the most marginalized and destitute in the existing
systems of power, reversing its current preferential option for the rich
with a preferential option for the poor. In order to do this, the church
must live by repentance — in deep mourning and contrite struggle to
heal the suffering and liberate the victims of social, economic, and
political oppression.

3. *Liberated from Sexism:* The church is called to embody equality and mutuality of women and men and to extend its welcome to a diversity of sexual orientations. Today, more than ever, the church must deepen its awareness that it is called to be "a new humanity" that transcends cultural divisions — where there is neither Greek nor Jew, free nor slave, male nor female, but a community of equals.

4. *Democratic:* The church needs to move beyond the organizational patterns that it adopted from fourth-century Roman imperial systems to an egalitarian and participatory church polity. The present hierarchical, patriarchal, monarchical, fascist structure, which is interpreted by the Vatican as a divine intention, is nonessential, nonnormative, and an embarrassing contradiction to the radical egalitarianism of Jesus' own community. Today the church needs to assume democratic patterns, allowing for broad participation in forming church policy and shaping church decisions.[23]

5. *Acknowledging Its Fallibility:* The church must recognize that it can err, that it has erred, that it lives by faith and not absolute certainties. The church must recognize its institutional need to repent, accepting its humanness, liberating it to live by a radical and ultimate trust in God and to form perspectival truths that are constructed of the best insight and wisdom we can muster.

Reconstructing from Below

There is little indication that the central bureaucracy of the church will shift its current approach to any of the above anytime soon. Indeed, it seems intent on enshrining the opposite of what Ruether and other reform-minded Catholics are calling for. In the meantime, however, Catholicism is being reconstructed from the bottom up. Increasingly, Catholics are being liberated from the patterns of passivity and dependence with which they were socialized, transcending the relationships of domination and submission, and becoming free and responsible adult Christians. Developing a confidence in our own mature autonomous responsibility is crucial to shaping a church in which today's young adults will find a spiritual home. Most young people are prematurely autonomous, having learned to fend for themselves quite early in life. They will not be drawn to a church that practices dependency and submission to authoritarianism.

Becoming knowledgeable about the Catholic tradition, about scripture, church history, and theology, is another crucial ingredient in reconstructing Catholicism. Happily, the numbers of well-informed lay Catholics — people who are aware of how the church became what it is and are able to bring vision to their understanding of tradition — are growing steadily. Knowledge is power. The more Catholics are able to sort out what symbols in our tradition are really meaningful and what truth claims need to be seen simply as assertions of power, the more free they become. The chapters in Part Two of this book are meant to provide the reader, young or old, with a deeper understanding of what is essential in Catholicism. Access to such an understanding of Catholicism means coming at this tradition experientially.

— Chapter 3 —

Retrieving the Experiential Base of Religion

> Faith is for me a mix of intellect straining to understand God, my senses, and what Van Morrison calls "the inarticulate speech of the heart." Music, the water and mountains of my Puget Sound home, the garden grown from seeds, and my kitchen full of bread, roasted garlic, wine, and friends daily show me God. Faith is the invisible spring in my core that feeds the river of my daily life.
> —Debbie McLaughlin (age 29), *Sojourners*, November 1994

If the institutional church and its hierarchy are no longer recognized as the definitive sources of authority in spiritual matters, where can one turn for truth about the profound? The answer is simultaneously simple and complex: *experience is the new authority*. Learning to attend to one's own experience and to search out the experiential basis of tradition creates a communal dialogue that becomes compellingly authoritative. We are opened to experience spirit movement in our own lives and that of others. We begin to listen to and to discern the divine initiative that acts in our own lives and in history, inviting us to surrender and risk, to vitality, authenticity, and compassion. Perhaps this sense of openness to spirit and divine initiative is the most accurate description of *faith*.

The modern inhibition to this openness, pervasively observed in Western culture in recent centuries, is unique in human history. Scholars can find no parallel anywhere at any time. We seem uniquely closed to spirit, disconnected from the larger reality that is all-pervasive mystery disclosing itself to us in multiple ways. This closedness and disconnectedness have cut us off from our own deepest meaning. Modernity brought with it faith in reason and science and shed the wisdom traditions, making religion an inward, private matter of the individual. Religion, which is meant to facilitate spiritual experience by opening us to the profound, frequently became in the modern West a mechanism to suppress such openness. Modern

45

religion put God in a juridical box, serving as a method of constraint that protected us from wonder and mystery by providing "answers." Its focus was not experience and life, but words and concepts leading to the world beyond. As rational scientific certainty powered the engines of progress in an effort to harness nature and dominate indigenous peoples and democratic capitalism released the power of self-interest in unbridled competition, religion was relegated to helping one observe social convention and maintain self-control in order to attain salvation after death, in heaven.

The popular novel *The Celestine Prophecy* summarizes the shift that occurred during the Enlightenment and its results today in Dobson's explanation of the Second Insight:

> Four centuries ago we shook off our feeling of being lost by taking matters into our own hands, by focusing on conquering the Earth and using its resources to better our situation.... Our focus gradually became a preoccupation. We totally lost ourselves in creating a secular security, an economic security, to replace the spiritual one we had lost. The question of why we were alive...was slowly pushed aside and repressed altogether.[1]

Charlene Spretnak describes a trivializing of religion and a distancing from the sacred as this preoccupation with progress and practicality flourished:

> Because modern Western culture has enthroned science (or, rather, an arrogant notion of that mode of inquiry) and the *scientific* skepticism toward anything that cannot be quantified, religion has been pushed to the cultural periphery in Eurocentric societies, except for occasional exploitation by politicians. The sense of the sacred — our human perception of the larger reality, ultimate mystery, or creativity in the universe — has become so diminished.... Clearly, modern society is out of touch with the insights of the great wisdom traditions, those rich cultural repositories of thousands of years of human development of relationship with the sacred.[2]

Experience and Authority Today

Sociologist of religion Peter Berger suggests that experience is today the ground of all religious reflection and affirmation. One must attend to one's own experience of human existence, but also to the experience of others, by listening and using "a weighing and assessing frame of mind — not necessarily cool and dispassionate, but unwilling to impose closure on the quest for religious truth by invoking any authority whatever — not the authority of this or that

traditional *Deus dixit,* but also not the authority of modern thought
or consciousness." In other words, one must be open. Included in
this listening to the experience of others is an effort to seek out the
experience present in religious traditions, which are understood as
"bodies of evidence concerning religious experience and the insights
deriving from experience."[3]

Thus, a two-way dialogue is generated. We search the tradition
in an effort to retrieve the experiential base of story, ritual, ethical
code, dogma, ecclesial practice — all of which arose, originally, from
the experience of spiritual communities and embodied their best insights into meaning and truth. And we search our own experience
(family of origin, formative events, developmental and circumstan-
tial crises, significant relationships, peak moments, illness, death and
loss, creative impulses, the challenges of work and parenting, dreams
and nightmares, emotional patterns, sexual feelings, our hopes and
our sufferings, our wonderings and our questions) for depth and
meaning and ultimate significance. Attending to our own experience
helps us to understand the experience embodied in tradition, and our
understanding of that experience helps us to understand our lived
experience.

Our insights become increasingly authoritative as we sift and sort,
practice self-disclosure with a spiritual director, with friends, in community, receiving their feedback and listening to their experiences.
We never arrive at absolute certainty, but we can find the certainty
of faith, ultimately making decisions grounded in our own freedom,
but also in trusting relationships and a breadth of experience. My
guess is that Moses and Jesus experienced the authoritative word of
God through some similar kind of process. They felt the movement
of spirit and divine initiative by reference to what was happening in
their own lives and by reference to the experience of others as related
to them in and through their religious traditions.

Revelation is too often thought of as words and concepts, but
these are, in fact, the interpretive expression of a prior experience, an
experience received in, and interpreted by, faith — first experience,
then interpretive expression:

> God's activity with man cannot be conceived of as a series of iso-
> lated events each accompanied by a word of interpretation. If it is
> man's whole self that is in question, there must be an organic process
> in which the words issue out of life and point back to what is non-
> verbal in life.... Words bring meaning to light by interpreting what

has been given in experience; there is not full intelligibility until such interpretive words are spoken.[4]

Experience and Myth

Scholars of religion have emphasized experience as the foundation and the driving energy of the great world religions and of the religious expressions of indigenous peoples. What begins as powerfully transforming religious experience becomes story and teaching carried on in communities influenced by charismatic leaders whose purpose it is to share the original set of experiences with others. The originating experiences are individual and communal and directly tied to a people's situation in life. Yet they are experiences of transcendence, which go beyond the mundane and the ordinary and push the limits of language. Experience of the sacred cannot be contained in ordinary descriptive prose; rather it seeks more imaginative expression that is meant to provoke and evoke similar experiences in those who hear the stories or receive the teaching. The purpose of sacred story is not merely the narrating of past experience (even in the rich language of poetry), but the initiation of the hearer(s) into the experience of the sacred as well. It seeks to arouse wonder and awe before ultimate mystery and mystical union. Sacred story is almost always acted out in ritual and engaging practice, drawing others into the story and thus into these experiences. In this way, experience becomes myth and ritual, narrative and practice, and the founders' experience is embodied communally by a broader spectrum of social bonding. Too frequently today, however, people have inherited the stories and the rituals, the disciplines and communal regulations, but with little or no connection to the core experience itself. Religion is for many a set of repetitive words and concepts, external observances, but without the shattering and life-transforming experience of the sacred.

Mircea Eliade spent his life studying myth and ritual across cultures and from various historical epochs, searching out the experiences that lie at their center. "Myths describe the various and sometimes dramatic breakthroughs of the sacred (or the "supernatural" into the World. It is this sudden breakthrough of the sacred that really *establishes* the World and makes it what it is today."[5] According to Eliade, religious myths narrate a sacred history, which is a "true history" because it always deals with *realities*. Mythic events lie outside of ordinary time, either in a primordial "time before time" or in an eschatological "time after time." Yet these creative events serve as a model for events within time, and the experiences that myths narrate are made accessible through ritual.

Ritual dramatizes this sacred history, bringing mythic events momentarily into time and making them contemporaneous with the communities of practice through dramatic enactment. Believers or practitioners are invited into that sacred time and experience it as their own, as they ritually identify with the mythic characters. Far from the modern understanding of myth as an untrue story, he sees myth as "an ultimately true story" about that which is most real — about origins and destiny, yes, but therein also about the depths of meaning in the present. The creative power at "the beginning" is made present, healing, reconciling, and giving vitality now, providing believers with an empowering experience of the sacred. The ritual experience regenerates existential/historical time by putting us in touch with the creative energy and unthreatened power of being that is present in the original event. Present experience is revitalized and made creative in and through our access to sacred time in myth and ritual. For the believer, then, there is an absolute reality, the sacred, which transcends this world but manifests itself in this world, thereby sanctifying it and making it real. Ordinary experience is thus sanctified through participation in sacred experience.[6]

Experiencing the Numinosum

C. G. Jung's empirical study of religion led him to describe the core of religion as "a careful and scrupulous observation of...the *numinosum*," which is a word Rudolf Otto used for Eliade's "the sacred." The *numinosum* is "a dynamic existence or effect, not caused by an arbitrary act of will. On the contrary, it seizes and controls the human subject, which is always rather its victim than its creator." He sees this experience of *numinosum* as "an involuntary condition of the subject...causing a peculiar alteration of consciousness." For Jung, religion is not primarily about creeds or dogmas, but this experience of the *numinosum* and "the loyalty, trust, and confidence toward a definitely experienced numinous effect and the subsequent alteration of consciousness."[7] Jung's critique of religious institutions was that the foundational experiences have become "congealed in a rigid, often elaborate structure," with the result that modern men and women mostly turn inward — to the psyche — to be seized by the *numinosum.*

The psychological experience of the *numinosum* (revealed in dreams and in depth reflection on experience, particularly through psychoanalysis) bears striking parallels to the experience yielded in religious myths. Myths, he says, are the human expression of our search for truth—ultimate truth, responses to our most fundamental questions about identity and meaning. And they inform our experience—by bringing images from the unconscious into our conscious awareness. Jung sees the same symbols and themes emerging again and again across the mythological landscape and in psychoanalysis, leading him to conclude that they arise from a "collective unconscious." Our experience of mystery, our quest for identity (who am I, really?), the haunting reality of our mortality, the quest for love, and a sense of belonging—these are universal experiences in human life, and they give expression to myths. The human tendency to interpret our profound experience in certain patterned ways results in what Jung call "archetypes." Myths are, thus, markedly the same even when their cultural contexts vary widely. They are about fundamental human experiences (psychospiritual longings?) that find similar symbolic patterned responses in our imaginations, because we tap into a common spiritual source. They provide hope and encouragement as we journey through the labyrinths of life's adventures. The mythic story is also, and profoundly so, *my story*, making its truth immediate and compelling in my own experience. My search for authentic identity (my "true self") and direction in life is also the search for God. Myths are God's words to us, arising from the collective unconscious, asking us to risk, to trust, to hope, to love, seizing us and inviting our surrender.

The Power of Myth

Joseph Campbell is perhaps the name most popularly associated today with myth, particularly for young people. His own writings and many public lectures prior to his death in 1987 generated a broad following among those who resonate with his sense that myth opens us to life's adventures and to the rich fullness of the human experience.[8] Then in 1988, his conversations with broadcast journalist Bill Moyers, taped in the last months of his lifetime, became a PBS video series, *The Power of Myth*. The original airing of this six-part series drew 2.5 million viewers each week. The response to this video series was so enthusiastic that the tape transcripts were edited into a best-selling book, *The Power of Myth,* and tens of thousands of the video-cassette series have made these conversations between Campbell and Moyers available to millions in libraries, schools, churches, and video rental stores.

Myths are about the challenges that every person must face in the varying experiences of human living. They provide us with clues to living and interpreting our experiences — nonrational answers to our shared human condition and the world of mystery that envelopes us. Campbell's words in the opening segment of the video series proclaim the power of myth for the spiritually starving in today's diminished culture:

> We have not even to risk the adventure alone, for the heroes of all time have gone before us.
> The labyrinth is thoroughly known. We have only to follow the thread of the hero path.
> And where we had thought to find our abomination, we shall find God.
> And where we had thought to slay another, we shall slay ourselves.
> And where thought to travel outward, we shall come to the center of our own existence.
> And where we had thought to die alone, we shall be with all the world.

Myths are about the transformation of consciousness through trials and revelations, about liberation from desire, fear, and social convention and the discovery of vitality. They call men and women to a deeper awareness of the act of living itself, guiding us through trials and traumas from birth to death.

> People say that what we're all seeking is a meaning for life. I don't think that's what we're really seeking. What we're all seeking is *an experience of being alive,* so that we actually feel the rapture of being alive.... We're so engaged in doing things to achieve purposes of outer value that we forget that the inner value, the rapture that is associated with being alive, is what it's all about.[9]

Myth opens us to this inner value by providing us with a field of references, metaphors that crack open eternity:

> Eternity isn't some later time. Eternity isn't a long time. Eternity has nothing to do with time. Eternity is that dimension of here and now which thinking and time cuts out.... The experience of eternity right here and now is the function of life.[10]

Campbell sees the real danger facing persons as overreliance on the intellect, which he suggests is "a secondary organ." The intellect must serve "the humanity of the body":

It is a part of the Cartesian mode to think of consciousness as being
something peculiar to the head, that the head is the organ originating
consciousness. It isn't. The head is an organ that inflects consciousness
in a certain direction, or to a certain set of purposes. But there is a
consciousness here in the body.[11]

Persons need to listen to the spiritual and heart demands (what he
calls "following your bliss"), bringing the world to life by reaching
for life ourselves. "The real danger is in you, holding you in — your
ego, doing what the environment tells you to do. Slay the dragon by
following your bliss." When we follow our bliss, we live life with a
sense of its mystery and of our own mystery — a way opened to us
in and through myth: "Myth helps you to put your mind in touch
with this experience of being alive. It tells you what the experience
is."[12] Myths are "metaphorical of spiritual potentiality in the human
being,"[13] showing the way to realizing wonder and mystery and the
experience of awe before this mystery.

Campbell and Catholicism

Campbell himself was brought up as a Roman Catholic, which, on
the positive side, taught him to take myth seriously, to let it operate
on his life and to live in terms of the mythic motifs.

> I was brought up in terms of the seasonal relationships to the cycle
> of Christ's coming into the world, teaching in the world, dying, resur-
> recting, and returning to heaven. The ceremonies all through the year
> keep you in mind of the eternal core of all that changes in time. Sin is
> simply getting out of touch with that harmony.[14]

Anyone who has not known Catholicism in such experiences "has
no realization of the ambience of religion within which you live.
It's powerful; it's potent; it's life supporting. And it's beautiful. The
Catholic religion is a poetic religion. Every month has its poetic and
spiritual value. Boy, that got into me. I'm sure that my interest in
mythology comes out of that."[15]

But Campbell also experienced a negative side of Catholicism
"in the Church's tendency to take symbols and rituals literally and
thereby cause them to become *locks on the door* to the experience
beyond."[16] When the metaphorical sense is eclipsed by *concretiza-
tions,* religion becomes ideology. Rather than evoking an experience
of the sacred, Catholicism often functions as a defense against such

experience, facilitating a "no" to the adventure of life. This shutting out of transcendence was even more the case in Catholicism's emphasis on the Fall: "With that fall in the garden, nature was regarded as corrupt. There's a myth that corrupts the whole world for us, and every spontaneous act is regarded as sinful — because nature is corrupt and has to be corrected and must not be yielded to."[17] Campbell experienced the church as preoccupied with this sense of natural corruptness — and of using it as an instrument of intimidation to justify its own God-brokering function: "The Church tells you...you are in sin, and we've got the medicine for you right here. And when you've got an invisible cure for an invisible disease, you've got something you can sell."[18]

His critique of the church was so ardent and his enthusiasm for Hinduism and Buddhism so potent, that he spent most of his adult life at a distance from his Catholic roots, sometimes even expressing hostility toward Western traditions generally. But at the end of his life, he reconciled Catholicism and his love of mythic truth in a profound experience of a brass crucifix that hung on the wall of his room in St. Francis Hospital in Honolulu. It was a fitting completion to his spiritual journey. "Instead of the usual suffering Christ with head bowed and body bloodied, the figure on the cross in Campbell's room was fully clothed, with head erect, eyes open and arms outstretched in what seemed an almost joyful embrace of the divine."[19] Campbell saw in this figure one who had awakened to the depths of life's adventures and to the great Mystery that is its source, one who had surrendered to the sacred and been transformed. "For him this was the mystical image of Christ that reflected the state of *at-one-ment* with the Father...he experienced emotionally what he had understood before only intellectually."[20] His intellectual understanding of this great Christian symbol as life-giving had emerged years before. In *The Hero's Journey* he summed up its meaning this way:

> If you think of the crucifixion as a calamity that is the result of your sins and Adam's sins and all that — that Jesus had to come down, give himself up on the cross for death and look sad there — that is one reading. But you can read it another way: as the zeal of eternity for incarnation in time, which involves the breaking up of the one into the many and the acceptance of the sufferings of the will.... That's a total transformation of the idea.[21]

Catholicism as Myth

What's most important about Campbell's experience is not just the transformation of an idea, but the shift to understanding his native Catholicism mythically. Is Catholicism a myth? Can one relate the insights of Eliade, Jung, Campbell, and other scholars of myth to Christianity and Catholicism? I would say clearly yes — and, indeed, effective pastoral practice demands it. Bernard Cooke has written about the need for Christians to focus on the Jesus story as our "master myth": "the basic story into which all the other stories fit or at least are meant to fit; this is the story that explains what human life as a whole is all about."[22] If Catholics are to find Christ as their mythic center, however, it is equally important that they develop what Cooke calls "a hermeneutic of experience": "a set of principles and insights and critical judgments that equips us to interpret our experience."[23] Catholic liturgy and sacraments provide participants with precisely this, according to Cooke.

Alan Watts's book *Myth and Ritual in Christianity* was one of the first efforts in the contemporary situation to present Christianity constructively as myth. He defined myth as "a complex of stories — some no doubt fact, and some fantasy — which, for various reasons, human beings regard as demonstrations of the inner meaning of the universe and of human life." In contrast to understanding the Christian life primarily as a set of concepts to be believed or even as a pattern of moral behavior ("being good"), seeing Christianity as myth means a focus on the concrete — "consisting of vivid, sensually intelligible narratives, images, rites, ceremonies, and symbols."[24] Christianity is utterly diminished when it is seen mostly as words and ideas. Watts's mythic approach seeks to move our understanding of this rich tradition in a different direction: "Far from retreating into a subjective and private world of its own, its entire concern is to transcend subjectivity, so that man may 'wake up' to the world which is concrete and actual, as distinct from that which is purely abstract and conceptual."[25]

For Watts, Catholic Christianity is

> one of the most incomparably beautiful myths that has ever flowered from the mind of man, or from the unconscious processes which shape it and what are in some sense more than man....So understood, the marvelous symbols of Christianity might still — one is tempted to say, might begin to — have a message for Western man, that anxious and restless eccentric who has "no time" because he has reduced his present to an abstract dividing line between past and fu-

ture, and who confuses his very self with a past which is no more and a future which is not yet.[26]

More recently, in *The Catholic Myth* Andrew Greeley argues for a distinctly Catholic imagination, which he sees as more *sacramental* — more likely to imagine God as present in the world and the world as revelatory instead of bleak. Basing his argument on his sociological research, he suggests that in Catholicism "Image and experience and story come before formal religious doctrine and are likely to have more raw power than purely propositional teaching can possibly possess."[27] People are drawn to Catholicism and remain Catholics largely "because they like being Catholics — that is, because they are loyal to the poetry of Catholicism." By poetry, he means "everything beyond the prose and propositional articulation" of the Catholic heritage. "The poetry is broader, deeper, and richer than the prose heritage, but not opposed to it. Rather, it envelopes and embraces the prose tradition." This model of poetry enveloping prose has, indeed, been the case for most of Christian history, during which time "most people had very little prose religion and very much poetic religion."[28]

An Experiential Dialogue

Cooke and Watts and Greeley are on to something. They seem to recognize that, while ideas are important and critical reason a fundamental human faculty, people's spiritual orientation in life is not primarily ideas and critical discourse. It is experience — their concrete lived experience and the interiority it shapes — that lies at the center of our spiritual passions and commitments. The heart of any spiritual tradition is the experience of God. Our encounter with mystery, the sacred, the *numinosum* shapes our identity and our relationships, our thinking and our behavior. Within Catholicism, I suggest, there are four key aspects to the experience of God: the Jesus experience, the experience of grace, the experience of sacramental community, and the experience of personal and social liberation. In the next part of this book we will examine these four aspects in succeeding chapters.

The dissonance that Joseph Campbell experienced with Catholicism is not wholly atypical. The rich spiritual tradition that he experienced as a boy fired his imagination as he pursued mythic truth and gave him a deep sense of supernatural *realities*. But he could not be satisfied with the institutional church's interpretations, its constraints and negativism. He was drawn into an active spiritual quest and assumed the freedom to search far and wide. What Catholicism had intimated in his childhood was verified in his life-long enchantment with sacred stories from countless sources: truth is metaphorical and universal. Neither a literalist nor an exclusivist stance will do. Human experience drives us toward God, who opens us from within to hear the stories of God's presence and activity everywhere in life. Reconstructing Catholicism today means taking the spirit of metaphorical truth and broad inclusivity as fundamental to the Catholic urge, and it means a free and freeing dialogue between our own experience and the experience embodied in the tradition. Many young people today are eager for such a dialogue and hungry for the spirituality it may yield. What many lack, however, is information about the key elements of the Christian tradition itself, explained in experiential terms. They await an experience of a revitalized Catholicism focused on essentials.

Part Two

THE CATHOLIC EXPERIENCE

❋

Essential Building Blocks for Reconstructing Catholicism

C ATHOLICISM IS ESSENTIALLY *an experience.* It is the human experience informed and understood metaphorically by the experiences of others, stretching back two thousand years and beyond, and by the rich and diverse pattern of stories and symbols, practices and ideas, that interpret and hand on those experiences. It is *the experience of God,* the immense mystery that is both source and continuing context of everything that exists, informed and interpreted through the historical event and symbolic understandings of Jesus of Nazareth. Catholicism is *a network of diverse communities,* relationships that stretch back to the community of Jesus himself and the various faith communities spawned in the spectacular release of spiritual energy provoked by his life and teachings. Catholicism is *a pattern of meaning-making* — a set of beliefs and values that give direction to individuals and communities about the human adventure, in all of its ambiguity, with all of its suffering and pain, joy and fulfillment. Catholicism is *a spiritual tradition in process,* developed through the centuries by those who were drawn, first to Jesus, then to the communities that he inspired, finding resources in ancient Judaism and the pagan religions of ancient Greece and Rome, as well as the rural nature religions that stretched across premedieval Europe. Catholicism is *a people* that spans the globe, fully 20 percent of the world's population, the vast majority increasingly found in the poor and underdeveloped countries of the southern hemisphere, a highly diverse and pluralistic people whose experience of Catholicism is also highly diverse and pluralistic.

Catholicism *was a political empire* that brought church and state together to rule most of Europe and then to colonize much of the rest of the world. It *was a cultural synthesis* that integrated reason and the arts, commerce, government, education, and family life with religion in medieval Europe. It *became a religious denomination,* losing its political power in the rise of the modern nation-states and much of its religious and moral influence in the Protestant Reformation and the onslaught of intellectual criticism accompanying modernity's turn to rationalism and empiricism. In many ways, the twentieth century is an important turning point for Catholicism — institutionally per-

haps tragic, but providing also a great opportunity for the recovery
of its spiritual identity in the retrieval of its origins and its unique
blending of mythic power and practical wisdom. *Its new context is
global pluralism, democracy, and individual self-determinism.* Catholicism can no longer control people, but it can inspire them. It can
no longer claim political privilege, not even spiritual exclusivity, but
it can persuade and influence and contribute much to the dialogue of
meanings and values. It can no longer pretend to broker God to the
world, but it can invite people to a rich spiritual experience in which
they discover God in and through the sacramental community, where
the memory and presence of Jesus and the movement of grace lead to
a profound personal and social experience of liberation.

Reconstructing Catholicism means no longer clinging to a juridical
past, grasping instead the real opportunities of the present. It means
reclaiming our spiritual heritage, embodying it in vital and diverse
communities of faith and service, scheming strategies for justice and
the extension of human rights, for the expansion of opportunity and
the peaceful resolution of conflict. The chapters in Part Two describe
a vibrant Catholicism in its new historical context.

— Chapter 4 —

The Jesus Experience

Catholic Christianity stresses that access to the original long ago event of Jesus Christ is mediated through people. It cultivates a romantic vision of hands clasping hands, linking backward through time until they touch the hand of Jesus Christ who holds the hand of God. . . . Each generation of Christians, since the first, has preserved the memory of Jesus and, as best they could, lived within, acted out of, and passed on his Spirit. Tradition is a premeditated act of fragile people not wanting to lose what they love. . . . The messy truth is that Christ comes to us fingerprinted by every generation that ever embraced him.

— John Shea, *An Experience Named Spirit*

"Jesus Christ. Jesus Christ. Yesterday, today, and forever!" These words from the solemn Easter Vigil service proclaim the very heart of the Catholic myth. At the center of the Catholic experience is Jesus of Nazareth. He is founding source, enduring inspiration, and himself the great metaphorical symbol, the *sacrament* of God. He is the source of spiritual wisdom, healer and liberator, the one to whom we look as model of how we are to live before God and the universe, with others in relationships and in society. Jesus shows the pathway in life's journey and calls us to follow him. He teaches us to "be compassionate as God is compassionate" (Luke 6:36), to embody as he does the disposition of God toward self, others, the whole cosmos. He is called "Lord" and "Savior," "the Son of God," "Christ" — all of them ways of describing his role in the spiritual journey of Christians. Throughout the centuries Catholics have named their experience of Jesus variously, seeking to be faithful both to his memory and to the spiritual dynamics present in culture and history.[1]

What is crucial to note, however, is the reality of their experience — something very elusive in the culture of modernity, which looks suspiciously at spiritual experience. Karl Rahner relates a conversation he had with a modern Protestant theologian whose the-

ories Rahner perceived as overly rationalistic. "You're actually only
dealing with Jesus," Rahner injected, "when you throw your arms
around him and realize right down to the bottom of your being that
this is something you can still do today." The theologian's reply is
curious: "Yes, you're right, of course — if you don't mean it too pie-
tistically."[2] At the heart of the Catholic experience is an unyielding
conviction that, yes, this is something you can still do today — and
that such an embrace makes all the difference for life.

Historians' Account of the Jesus Experience

Jesus is encountered and known in history and through faith. The
Gospels contain his words and sketches from his life and dramatically portray the impact he had on the first Christian communities.
They are *portraits* of Jesus that spell out *the Jesus experience* as it
was understood and lived in the early communities of his disciples
and devotees, several decades after Jesus' death. They blend memories of the historical Jesus with interpretive images drawn from
ancient Judaism — particularly in the three "macro-stories" found
in the Jewish scriptures: (1) the story of bondage and liberation (the
Exodus story); (2) the story of exile and return (the story of the Babylonian captivity and Judah's restoration); and (3) the story of sin and
reconciliation through sacrifice (the priestly story).[3] In the light of
these three macro-stories, Jesus is seen as Liberator, Messiah/Christ,
and Redeemer. We will explore this interpretive matrix of literate Judaism and its role in the development of the Gospels' images of Jesus
later in this chapter. For now, however, it is important to recognize
that the character of the Gospels themselves is not in the manner of journalistic accounts providing us factual biographies; rather,
they are the early communities' *faith interpretations* of the spiritual
wisdom that flows from Jesus, related to their own historical and cultural contexts. They contain "not only the memories of the historical
Jesus, but those memories added to and modified by the growing beliefs and changing circumstances of the movement.... They tell us
what these early Christian communities had come to believe about
Jesus by the last third of the first century."[4]

Historical scholars, who seek to describe the facts and circumstances of Jesus' life and teachings without the benefit of faith, draw
upon the Gospels as one source among many in their search to
understand *the historical Jesus*. Their work utilizes cross-cultural anthropology, Greco-Roman history, and literary analysis of a broad

spectrum of texts, many of them outside the Christian scriptures.[5] These scholars tell us that Jesus was born and lived probably his entire life in Galilee among a destitute peasantry and that he was executed by order of the occupying Roman authorities in the manner of crucifixion, undoubtedly because he was perceived as a revolutionist. Earlier he had been a disciple of John the Baptizer, who himself was executed by the Galilean tetrarch Herod Antipas.

Following John's death, Jesus' focus had shifted from an apocalyptic expectation that God would act in *dramatic future action* to save the poor and redress their oppression. Now Jesus spoke of God's reign as *present healing* — a healing accomplished only in a clear giving over of one's allegiance to God. Split allegiance, then as now, meant physical and mental illness. Such was the result of internal conflicts and of the abuse to self-esteem that the intimidating presence of an occupying power (Rome) and its local collaborators could render. Such a healing is, thus, also a social liberation. It implies the withdrawal of fealty to damaging conventional structures and the recognition of God as *Abba* (translated "Papa" or "Daddy"). Jesus brought liberation among the Galilean peasants, who bore the burden of oppression from both imperial Rome and the local and regional collaborators, by urging them to reject the shackles of the conventional wisdom and develop a radical trust in God, whose stance toward us is always compassion. He invoked the liberating traditions of Exodus Judaism and Israel's prophets in a program of "free healing and open eating" (Crossan), proclaiming the way of compassion through faith and hope in a God who seeks justice and reverses the experience of anguish, grief, and sorrow in a radical egalitarianism.

John Dominic Crossan, for example, describes the Jesus event as an "ecstatic vision and social program" that sought to rebuild society upward from its grass roots on principles of religious and economic egalitarianism. He sees Jesus' "deliberate conjunction of magic and meal, miracle and table, free compassion and open commensality," as "a challenge launched not just at Judaism's strictest purity regulations, or even at the Mediterranean's patriarchal combination of honor and shame, patronage and clientage, but at civilization's eternal inclination to draw lines, invoke boundaries, establish hierarchies, and maintain discriminations." Jesus, he says, "did not invite a political revolution but envisaged a social one at the imagination's most dangerous depths."[6]

A Spirit Person

Marcus Borg elaborates on "the imagination's most dangerous depths" by emphasizing Jesus' relationship with spirit. The most crucial characterization of Jesus, he says, is that he was "a spirit person." It is precisely his spiritual experience that is the source for everything else that can be said about him. Borg's description of this term "spirit person" is important:

> Spirit persons are known cross-culturally. They are people who have vivid and frequent subjective experiences of another level or dimension of reality. These experiences involve momentary entry into nonordinary states of consciousness and take a number of different forms. Sometimes there is a vivid sense of momentarily seeing into another layer of reality; these are visionary experiences. Sometimes there is the experience of journeying into that other dimension of reality; this is the classic experience of the shaman. Sometimes there is a strong sense of another reality coming upon one, as in the expression "The Spirit fell upon me." Sometimes the experience is of nature or an object within nature momentarily transfigured by *the sacred* shining through it. Bushes burn without being consumed; the whole earth is seen as filled with the glory of God (where *glory* means "radiant presence"). The world is perceived in such a way that previous perceptions seem nothing more than blindness.[7]

For Borg, an accurate gestalt of the historical Jesus hinges on this sense of him as a deeply spiritual person, whose practice of prayer and fasting indicate a powerful experiential awareness of God — and an intimate relationship with God. All the other pieces of the picture of the historical Jesus — his healings and exorcisms, his wisdom teaching, his social critique, his own gathering of disciples — are grounded in his profound experience of relationship with God, who is radically compassionate. It is possible, perhaps even plausible, to think that Jesus may have been associated with the Jewish mysticism of his day. Such holy men as Honi the Circle-Drawer and Hanina ben Dosa, both of whom joined contemplative prayer and miraculous works, were part of a form of Jewish mysticism contemporaneous with Jesus. Whether there is any connection between Jesus and this movement we do not know, but it is certain that Jesus himself took spiritual experience very seriously and that such experience became the basis for everything else he was about.

Jesus' spirituality led him to know God, whose central quality was *compassion*. Borg points out that in Hebrew (as well as in Aramaic), the word usually translated as *compassion* is the plural of a noun that in its singular form means *womb*. In the Hebrew Bible, *compassion* is both a feeling and a way of being that flows out of that feeling. Sometimes it is very specifically linked to its association with *womb*: a woman feels compassion for the child of her own womb; a man feels compassion for his brother, who comes from the same womb.[8]

So *Abba* is also "womblike," and to know God experientially means, also, "to feel with" God's children — feeling the feelings of others in a visceral way, particularly feeling the sufferings of others. Jesus felt the sufferings of his peasant culture in a profound way, and his ministry was in response to these lowly ones.

A Revolutionary Peasant

Crossan emphasizes that while the Gospels are about "the Jesus experience," Jesus himself is about "the kingdom experience." This is to say that Jesus' focus was on relationship with God and with God's presence breaking into life. Jesus' teachings and his activity are about a subversive God of compassion breaking into the world of conventional wisdom and a society ordered by imperial hierarchies and strict purity regulations. For him, understanding the historical Jesus hinges on understanding his *peasantness*. Jesus was not part of the elite, not even a middle-class. Jesus was a peasant. Crossan points out that the Roman Empire was "characterized by an abysmal gulf separating the upper from the lower classes." On the one side of that great divide were the ruler and governors (who made up 1 percent of the population but owned at least half the land), the priests (who owned perhaps 15 percent of the land), military generals, bureaucrats, and merchants.

> On the other side were, above all, the Peasants — that vast majority of the population about two-thirds of whose annual crop went to support the upper classes. If they were lucky, they lived at subsistence level, barely able to support family, animals, and social obligations and still have enough for next year's seed supply. If they were not lucky, drought, debt, disease, or death forced them off their own land and into sharecropping, tenant farming, or worse. Next came the Artisans, about 5 percent of the population, below the Peasants in social class because they were usually recruited and replenished from its dispossessed members.

Since Jesus is identified as a carpenter (*tektōn*), he belonged to the Artisan class, those who had been pushed into a dangerous space between Peasants and the Expendables (outcasts, beggars, and slaves).[9]

Understanding class is important because it gives us a social context in which to understand much of Jesus' activity, which can only be seen as revolutionary. Whereas the dominant understanding of God and virtue in the Jewish social world of Jesus' time was "Be holy as God is holy," Jesus' message was "Be compassionate as God is compassionate." Borg makes the tension between these two understandings of God and one's imitation of God clear:

> The central conflict in the ministry of Jesus [is] between two different social visions. The dominant social vision was centered in holiness; the alternative social vision of Jesus was centered in compassion.... He directly and repeatedly challenged the dominant sociopolitical paradigm of his social world and advocated instead what might be called a *politics of compassion*.[10]

Borg sees Jesus as both a social prophet and a movement founder — similar to the classical prophets of ancient Israel in his critique of the elites (economic, political, and religious) of his time, and one who began a Jewish renewal movement "that challenged and shattered the social boundaries of his day."[11] He attacked both the arrogant presumptions of the Roman occupiers with their oppressive policies and the Jewish purity system that distracted people's religious energy. Both Rome and Temple combined to create a world of oppressive economic hardships and sharp social boundaries between pure and impure, righteous and sinner, whole and not whole, male and female, rich and poor, Jew and Gentile. In this volatile socioreligious context, Jesus spoke of *basileia* ("rule"), usually translated "kingdom," but inadequately so. His focus is a contrast of rule, power, sovereignty:

> The basic question is this: How does human power exercise its rule and how, in contrast, does divine power exercise its rule? The Kingdom of God is people under divine rule — and that, as ideal, transcends and judges all human rule. The focus of discussion is not on kings but on rulers, not on kingdom but on power, not on place but on process. The Kingdom of God is what the world would be if God were directly and immediately in charge.[12]

Jesus challenged the power and rule of his own time and place by "eating with tax collectors and sinners," by breaking the Sabbath laws, by proclaiming the direct and immediate availability of God unbrokered by religious intermediaries, and by advocating what Crossan calls "a radical egalitarianism." The latter term is a way of describing Jesus' invoking of "the peasant's dream," which is a hope-filled vision wherein both the religious and political elite that oppress them are replaced by a society of equals:

> The radical vision to which I refer...nearly always implies a society of brotherhood in which there will be no rich and poor, in which no distinctions of rank and status will exist...the elimination of religious hierarchy in favor of communities of equal believers. Property is typically to be held in common and shared. All unjust claims to taxes, rents, and tributes are to be nullified.[13]

The leveling of hierarchies and the elimination of brokerage meant Jesus was often in conflict with the authorities, a condition that eventually led to his violent demise.

Jesus' social context led him to contrast the rule of present authorities with the more profound and universal rule of God. Power and riches are pretensions that will fade. Ultimately, only God rules. Human beings are vulnerable. All they have is, finally, gift. To recognize one's real situation is to recognize the reign of God. Purity regulations distract from this and assume a divisive posture, pitting Jew against Jew, even perhaps peasant against peasant, in a competition to win spiritually that which has been taken by the Romans: a sense of self-worth. Jesus, however, proclaimed a God of compassion — a radical politics, indeed.[14]

A Teacher of Wisdom

When we put Jesus as Spirit Person and Jesus as Peasant together, we get a sense of a third image: Jesus as Teacher of Wisdom. Again we turn to Marcus Borg for a description of wisdom teacher as a religious type:

> The subject matter of wisdom is broad. Basically, wisdom concerns how to live. It speaks of the nature of reality and how to live one's life in accord with reality. Central to it is the notion of a way or a path, indeed of two ways or paths: the wise way and the foolish way. Teachers of wisdom speak of these two ways, commending the one and warning of the consequences of following the other. There are two types of wisdom and two types of sages. The most common type of wisdom is conventional wisdom; its teachers are conventional sages. This is the mainstream wisdom of a culture, "what everybody knows," a culture's understandings about what is real and how to live....The second type is a subversive and alternative wisdom. This wisdom questions and undermines conventional wisdom and speaks of another way, another path. Its teachers are subversive sages.[15]

Jesus was a subversive sage. What he taught was spiritually stunning and politically dangerous. The reign of God is the narrow path that overturns conventional wisdom and reverses its polarities. His wisdom challenged both religious sages (Temple and priest, purity laws and Pharisee) and their political counterparts (the conventions of hierarchies and boundaries, patronage and clientage, law and order). One must abandon the reign of conventional wisdom and embrace the reign of God; conventional wisdom breaks up and the reign of God breaks in; a pattern of controlling expectations and intimidating fear must give way to the generous compassion of a God who doesn't play by our rules. The wisdom of Jesus threatens the presumed authority of conventional power structures, but it heals those who have been ravished by that power, exorcising their demons and empowering them with a freedom from fear and a radical confidence in a compassionate God. The rewards and punishments of conventional wisdom cannot compel those who have crossed over to the reign of God and now dine in truly egalitarian resplendence.

Jesus' wisdom teaching takes two forms: one-line aphorisms and extended parables. These startling proverbs and graphic stories are invitational forms of speech in which the hearers are invited to see something they might not otherwise see. "As evocative forms of speech, they tease the imagination into activity, suggest more than they say, and invite a transformation in perception."[16] While the aphoristic one-liners are usually strung together in the Gospels as we now read them, in Jesus' own teaching ministry they were stunning expletives that cleverly cut to the marrow: You cannot serve two masters; Leave the dead to bury the dead; It's not what goes into the body, but what comes out, that defiles. Here Jesus turns complicated religious debates of his time toward the simple wisdom of faith. Rationalizations, minutiae, and procrastinations are the result of our ego-saving mental gymnastics. The point is to surrender. Only a radical faith can heal and give life — and such a faith liberates us from the complicated spiritual prisons constructed by the interplay of social oppression and psychological scheming.

Similarly, Jesus' parables give God room by shattering the deep structure of our accepted world, removing our defenses and making us vulnerable to God. The great parables of Jesus reverse the expectations of his audience: they expect a priest and Levite to stop and provide aid to the wounded Jew, and they don't expect a Samaritan to do so; yet Jesus' story makes plausible a situation in which the priest and the Levite, not wanting to make themselves impure, pass by the wounded Jew, while the Samaritan shows compassion. Jesus' audience expects a father to reward his faithful son and not to reward a son who has squandered his inheritance and herded pigs, but Jesus' story reverses this expectation: the prodigal father rewards his wayward son upon his return, and the faithful son demonstrates a jealous anger. In both of these stories (and many others), Jesus stuns his hearers by undermining the conventional wisdom, suggesting that a God of compassion is simply not playing by our rules. Letting go of one's polarities and hardened perceptions of reality is the key to an opening to the mystery of God, whose ways we cannot predict and whose compassion is always a surprise.[17]

The Historical Jesus

The stories that Jesus told cut to the spiritual marrow. His sayings reinforced the provocative nature of his stories. His healings and exorcisms and table-fellowship with outcasts — these activities *did* what he *said*. The *basileia* of God was proclaimed in word and deed, cutting like a two-edged sword into the rules of his hearers, demanding decision, inviting response, prompting the surrender of faith, but also surfacing fears, inciting anger, polarizing crowds. Jesus was himself a parable. His presence and activity evoked uncertainty about that which had always been certain, ambiguity where clarity had been. Jesus confronted his hearers with *sacred mystery*, with the ultimate mystery that lies at the heart of the human condition and, indeed, at the center of the universe itself. He exhibited a radical confidence in that mystery, which he called *Abba*, and he confronted those who encountered him with an experience of God's immense compassion.

From the many recent historical studies, one gets a compelling image of Jesus as a young man (probably only in his early thirties) possessing of extraordinary personal charisma, remarkable spiritual wisdom, and great moral courage. Clearly, he was focused on God as the source of compassion and critical of the norms and conventions that governed his cultural world. But he did more than speak. He enacted his spiritual insights by reaching out to the sick and the possessed, the downtrodden poor and the outcast, and by engaging in symbolic actions necessitating a response. Jesus provoked his contemporaries, confronting them with their own freedom, demanding their response. To encounter Jesus was to be swept up in decision about the depths of life's meaning and one's own patterns of living.

It was, really, to encounter oneself before God. That explains why the Gospels focus on the Jesus experience: for them, it truly was the experience of God. All that the Christian tradition has held about Jesus revealing God and even being God is captured here experientially: his very person unmasked idols and therein made present God's *basileia*. People were left to see and hear, to be converted and healed; or to shut their eyes and be dull of hearing, to shun the truth of human vulnerability with greater and more desperate ego-illusions (see Matt. 13:34–35). Retrieving this Jesus of history, whose life and teachings unleashed an explosion of spiritual energy that would eventually become the Jesus movement and then the Christian movement, is essential to reconstructing Catholicism today.

The Death of Jesus

What would happen to Jesus was probably as predictable as what had happened already to John. Some form of religiopolitical execution could surely have been expected. What he was saying and doing was as unacceptable in the first as in the twentieth century, there, here, or anywhere....It seems clear that Jesus, confronted, possibly for the first and only time, with the Temple's rich magnificence, symbolically destroyed its perfectly legitimate brokerage function in the name of the unbrokered kingdom of God. Such an act, if performed in the volatile atmosphere of Passover, a feast that celebrated Jewish liberation from inaugural imperial oppression, would have been quite enough to entail crucifixion by religiopolitical agreement. And it is now impossible for us to imagine the offhand brutality, anonymity, and indifference with which a peasant nobody like Jesus would have been disposed of.[18]

Crossan's reconstruction of the circumstances of Jesus' death by crucifixion provides us with a final word of historical description about the man from Nazareth. His bold teaching and provocative activity led his enemies to do away with him. Jesus was swiftly eliminated, his charismatic power ceased and his clever tongue silenced. The Gospels' elaborate "passion narratives" are filled with interpretive references, describing much more than the facts in their efforts to make theological sense of his humiliating end. They are written from another vantage point, the experience of Jesus risen from death, present to them in visions and in a revelation received in faith: this Jesus whom men have crucified, God has raised from death. In a certain sense, even in death Jesus proclaims the rule of God over the conventional powers — for those who believe in him. Martin Hengel tells us that crucifixion was a political and military punishment, utilized by the Romans particularly on the lower classes (slaves, violent criminals, and the unruly elements in rebellious provinces). The chief reason for its use was "its allegedly supreme efficacy as a deterrent." It was public and usually accompanied by other forms of torture — meant to terrorize the populace into imperial compliance. "By the public display of a naked victim at a prominent place — at a crossroads, in the theatre, on high ground, at the place of his crime — crucifixion also represented uttermost humiliation, which had a numinous dimension to it."[19] Jesus' followers refused to buy into its deterrence and were not intimidated by its terror. Grief-stricken, yes. Discouraged, for a time. But finally inspired by the faith of Jesus to experience in this most agonizing and humiliating death still another expression of God's *basileia*. Francis Schüssler Fiorenza says, "Belief in Jesus' resurrection is belief in God's justice that vindicated the life and praxis of Jesus and had the effect of affirming that life and that praxis."[20] And Crossan puts it this way: "What could not have been predicted and might not have been expected was that the end was not the end. Those who had originally experienced divine power through his vision and his example still continued to do so after his death — in fact, even more so, because now it was no longer confined by time or place."[21]

The Resurrection Experience

The Greek word *egēgertai* (translated "was raised to life") or *ēgerthē* (translated "has risen") refers to the common experience of waking from sleep. But in late Jewish apocalyptic expression it was used metaphorically to connote a transition from this age to the future age when God will rule. It denotes the interventive activity of God for those who are dead and in the grave — not as a return to this life in the manner of a resuscitated corpse, but rather a radical transformation of one's personal existence beyond death, a restoration to primordial harmony and perfection.

> In resurrection God's Spirit touches and transforms this body-person so completely that he or she enters into an utterly new existence which can be characterized in terms of the traditional understanding of Adam's and Eve's existence in the Garden of Eden, *viz.* as involving union with God, harmony with oneself, and victory over death.[22]

The followers of Jesus believed that God had intervened on his behalf, raising Jesus and reversing his crucifixion: this Jesus whom worldly powers have rejected, God has affirmed; this crucified Jesus who was condemned by both religious and civil authority, God has endorsed; this abandoned and God-forsaken Jesus, God has chosen and claimed; this broken and beaten Jesus whom oppressive rulers have killed, God has restored and given a new life.

Further, the raising of Jesus is itself a proclamation about the fate of humankind and history, a further elaboration of God's *basileia*. For the followers of Jesus, his resurrection is seen as determinative for everyone else, indeed for all of creation. It opens up the promise of God as a future horizon of life restored to its primordial wholeness. Yet in the Gospel narratives it is clear that this divine act is known only through God's revelation of it, to which the only response is either faith or unfaith. One does not "sort of believe" in the resurrection of Jesus. It is known as revelation and thus treasured as divine truth. It requires the same act of trust and entrustment that believing in God's rule required in Jesus' own ministry. When one believes in Jesus' resurrection, it is a further surrender to God's reign and to a "following of the Lord" that is integral to it. The Easter narratives in the Gospel accounts are stories of revelatory disclosures grasped in faith by disciples. These accounts are also characterized by themes of vocation and mission: to believe in the resurrection is to feel oneself called to follow him, to be one with him in death and resurrection. If we trust that God has raised Jesus from death, then Jesus' own trust has been vindicated. There is an implicit invitation to trust *Abba* as he trusted *Abba*, grounded in a powerful sense that *Abba* is, indeed, trustworthy. This imitation of Jesus' faith-surrender is at the very center of discipleship in the Gospel narratives.

But the Easter appearance stories contain still more. They are stories about *coming to faith*. In these stories, the disciples become witnesses of the resurrection, as nonrecognition becomes recognition ("and their eyes were opened and they recognized him," "she knew him them," "they knew quite well it was the Lord"). Fear and despair are transformed into confidence and joy. Anxiety becomes forgiveness and peace. These *witnesses*, in believing that God has raised Jesus from death, are brought to new life themselves; what they believe about Jesus, they come to believe about themselves as well. They feel themselves affirmed, endorsed, chosen, and claimed by God, and they too are gifted with restoration and newness of life. They too know themselves as reconciled, as having moved from this age into the age of God's rule, as rescued from their bondage, their alienation, their sinfulness by God. The personal transformation experienced by the witnesses of the resurrection is more commonly referred to as "conversion" — involving the disciples in an experience marked by emptiness, liberating freedom, and courageous hope.

Surrender to God: Liberation and Boundless Hope

The death/resurrection experience led the followers of Jesus to see that God acts most dramatically in those places where we are weak and dying, where we have exhausted our resources and have to let go. God is most obviously active in our emptiness and vulnerability, when we have surrendered. We are prone to think just the opposite: that God is acting where we are strong and together and successful. But Jesus' resurrection is saying something very different: that where we let go and let God, there we can most clearly see God's saving action. Empty tomb, empty womb — there is a consistency throughout the tradition that affirms the activity of God where humanity is impotent: where we cannot, God does. The insight this offers us, however, is more: God does even where we think we do. Far from limiting God to those places beyond human capacity (to the miraculous), the sense here is a deeper humility. God is acting always; God rules. Even where we think it is only us, or especially us, it is God's power and God's rule that is the context for all activity. Yet such power and rule is vulnerable to human violence. God's rule is realized and actualized only in the turning of human hearts, in the free surrender that recognizes divine sovereignty.

Ironically, such surrender brings with it an empowering liberation. In the apocalyptic context, resurrection was the promise of the new age of God's rule. The Pharisees taught that God would reward those who had made themselves righteous by fidelity to the Law with resurrection at the end of history. It was part of the myth of Judaism, debated among the people, but widely believed. The revelation that Jesus had been raised, thus, came to them as parable, a reversal of conventional wisdom, an advent of God's rule, as stunning completion to their experience of Jesus. Given the context of late Palestinian Judaism, to believe that God had raised Jesus had at least two implications: (1) that the endtime of God's rule had already begun and (2) that God was not playing by the conventional rules. God's judgment was already upon the earth, already breaking into history. God had revealed history's verdict, and the long-awaited reign of God had arrived. But the criterion for salvation was not fidelity to the Law in all its minutiae. Indeed, the scandal of Jesus risen is precisely this:

that *Jesus* is risen — one who lived in tension with the Law and who died a condemned blasphemer had been raised up by God. The crucified and God-forsaken Nazarene *tektōn* who seemed to revile the Law, the friend of tax collectors and sinners, the teacher whose stories were a scandal — God had raised *this one* from death. It was not fidelity to a narrow understanding of Torah that had vindicated Jesus. Rather, it was his solidarity with spirit and peasant, his own surrender to the God of compassion. Robert Goss writes: "In his *basileia* practice, Jesus asserted God as the saving reality of solidarity and justice for the oppressed. Through the resurrection God affirmed the validity of Jesus' *basileia* message of the end of domination; by raising Jesus, God said *no* to human oppression."[23]

For those who received the revelation of Jesus' resurrection, a truly scandalous truth emerged: resurrection/salvation is gift, pure gift, completely from beyond ourselves. Over against those who demanded compliance to purity regulations, it cannot be earned or won or bought. There is no way of cleverly achieving it. It is gift to those who surrender in faith and accept the rule of God now. This means that moralism is over. It is as though the Law, with all of its rigorous demands, had been repealed. God's salvation is not meted out according to the Law. It is gift freely given to all who will but receive it. Their joy was not only in knowing that Jesus had been rescued and that his life and teaching had been vindicated. Their joy was tied also to *their own* radically new freedom: freedom from the Law, freedom from fear and control, and freedom for the liberating work of compassion and justice.

Such work could proceed energetically because of the boundless hope that Jesus' resurrection brought: if God had raised Jesus from death, then anything can happen. Their belief freed their imaginations from the prisons of their own ego-worlds. God is not limited by the structures we place on reality. God is free. God can do anything. The only way we can understand their experience is to imagine the most outlandish thing possible and then to think of it actually realized — something like the tearing down of the Berlin Wall and an end to communist rule in Eastern Europe. When the impossible happens (Nelson Mandela is president of a South Africa no longer plagued by apartheid), when we actually experience something that we thought was totally out of the question, then our imaginations are freed to think of equally outlandish things as possible. What is possible is no longer limited by our expectations: our cities can be disarmed and peaceful; the planet can be restored to its primordial resplendence; a truly multicultural community can emerge to end racism; a woman of great faith and leadership skill can serve the church as pope. Such was the loosening of imaginative energy in the disciples' hope born of their faith in Jesus' resurrection.

Access to Jesus and His Spirit

The *basileia event* becomes the *Jesus event;* the Spirit that had descended upon Jesus and filled his life with divine energy is given over to his disciples; the God of compassion who visited humankind in Jesus now works through a network of communities, the Jesus movement, healing and liberating others in the name of Jesus, who lives and reigns with God. As the quote from John Shea at the beginning of this chapter indicates, Catholicism stresses that access to Jesus Christ is mediated *through people.* It is one generation of believers

> confiding to the younger generation the sufferings and glories of Jesus Christ, the Son of God and Savior of the World. What is important is not the bare fact that the conversation takes place, but what happens between the people who tell and listen to the story of Jesus Christ. Present day contact with Jesus Christ occurs through *a chain of people* stretching over 1900 years.[24]

People carry the experience of Jesus and of his Spirit in their hearts and in their viscera, and they pass it on to others through the scriptures, in the sacraments, in the community. It is important to recognize that people are central to all three aspects of mediating tradition (Word, Sacrament, Community):

> We tend toward "false objectivisms" which give the impression that Christ arrives independent of his flawed followers. We say we reach Christ through the scriptures. But what is the New Testament but the witnessing words of people who had to speak of what they found through Jesus of Nazareth? We say Christ is present in the sacraments. But what are the sacraments but the creations and recreations of people bent on continuing the salvific experience Jesus inaugurated? We say Christ is present in the Church. But what is the Church but the collectivity of us all...? Scriptures, Sacraments, and Church are ventures of divine-human cooperation...divinely inspired creations of people which have become the privileged locale of contact with God. Christ is present in Word, Sacrament, and Church. But to say that Christ is present we do not have to say that we are not present. The history of Scripture, Sacraments, and Church show that they have been created, participated in, reinterpreted, and reformed by people.[25]

Unfortunately, this focus on the role of people in passing on the experience of Jesus developed into a new sense that *God is brokered through others* — that some *have* Jesus and that they may or may not *give* Jesus to others. The development of a brokerage consciousness in Catholicism refers to earlier comments about juridical consciousness. There is a sense of mediating function that can imply possession of Jesus and his *basileia* experience, even control over it. Such a sense is in total contrast to the Jesus discussed above. Catholicism, in wanting to faithfully preserve and authentically hand on the inaugural experience, has over the centuries developed patterns that appear to conflict flagrantly with that inaugurating experience itself. In reconstructing Catholicism, we need to focus again on the rich and powerful experience that stands at the beginning of our tradition and to seek fidelity to it. Still, in Catholicism there will always be the need to see the role of people as key in bridging the tradition's deepest meanings and values from one generation to the next, and it is within this understanding of the centrality of people that we look briefly now at the experience of Jesus in the early Christian communities.

Jesus in the Gospels

Jesus in the Gospels is more than spirit person, peasant revolutionary, teacher of wisdom, or even crucified and risen Lord. He has become *discloser of the sacred* and *divine event*. As the Jesus movement expanded and grew — from a reform movement within Galilean Judaism, to a new interpretation of Judaism itself with a radically unique vision of its future, to a competitive relationship with Pharisaical Judaism in the world beyond Palestine, to the inclusion of more and more Gentile believers in the great urban centers throughout the Mediterranean world — the Jesus event was continually reinterpreted in extremely creative ways. The experience of those who joined the movement blended Jesus' teachings and the stories about him with the spiritual currents already present in these new cultural contexts. In addition, the risen Jesus continued to "speak" to these followers in revelatory visions and ecstatic prophecies, frequently in relation to issues and concerns that these communities were facing. Jesus stories were used to proselytize new converts, to instruct them in the meanings and values of the faith communities, to defend the integrity of this spiritual path against its critics (both Jewish and Gentile), to deepen and enhance the community prayer life and the development of uniquely Christian rituals, and to address the philosophical and ethical concerns with which such communities had to wrestle. In all of this, new images of Jesus emerged and the portraiture of Jesus changed.

Increasingly, it was important to describe him in terms of the movement's foundation and the unique divine revelation that had occurred in and through him. The Jesus of history became meta-phorized. Now he was spoken of as Son of Man, the Son of David, Christ/Messiah, Son of God, Founder of the New Israel and Giver of a New Law, *Kyrios* (Lord), the One whose birth heralds a new age, the Wisdom of God (*Sophia/Logos*) Incarnated, the Lamb of God, the Great High Priest, and on and on. The Gospel narratives describe him in these terms because this is who the Gospel authors and the communities they represented knew him to be in the light of experience and developments as these unfolded after his life and death. In a sense, the Gospels provide us a picture of the early com-munities' issues and concerns and how they responded to them more than they give us an accurate picture of Jesus in his own life circum-stances. It is important to see that the Jesus tradition is alive, flexible, adapting to new circumstances, and therefore changing, and that the Gospels give us snapshots of this developing tradition at particular points in time. They are testimony that the Jesus event didn't happen once upon a time, but that it happens again and again. Throughout all this, there are elements of continuity with the historical Jesus, but these elements are more closely understood experientially than they are in strictly verbal, much less factual, terms — which is to say that *what happened* in Jesus' own lifetime (the unmasking of idols and the disclosure of God as compassionate mystery in a critique of conven-tional wisdom, healing and triumph over demons in coming to faith and creating alternative communities of equals) *continued to happen* in the lives of his followers. The followers of Jesus discovered a free-dom from fate and a belonging to God, and this was the experience of salvation.

The New Testament interpretations of Jesus are a rich resource for contemporary spirituality because they speak to the perennial dynamics of the human condition and our quest for salvation, de-scribing in narrative form the human predicament and its solution in relationship with God. They do so by describing the Jesus ex-perience in terms of three macro-stories embedded in their Jewish heritage: (1) the story of bondage and liberation in the Exodus event; (2) the story of exile and return from captivity in Babylon; and

(3) the priestly story of sin and reconciliation through sacrifice.[26] New Testament stories and images are magnificent metaphors for understanding the deep story lines and hidden plots operative in our lives. Like Campbell's comments on myths, the Jesus narratives put us in touch with *what's really going on* in the world about us and in the depths of our own souls. The encounters with Jesus in the first centuries after his life and death yielded great spiritual insight — truths that continue to speak to our hungry spirits — and the Gospel narratives offer us those insights about spirit and life in the form of Jesus stories.

Bondage and Liberation

All of us know the pain of bondage. All of us yearn for freedom. We seek liberation from our social and psychological prisons, from the shackles of human tyranny and spiritual enslavement. Some of our enslavements are imposed externally by sociopolitical structures or the repression of others. Others are primarily of our own making, internal constructs that prevent us from being who we want to be and doing what we want to do. When we hear Martin Luther King's "I Have a Dream" speech or listen to Pete Seeger's rendition of "Oh, Freedom," something deep inside us resonates. We hunger for freedom and for the sense of self that comes with it. We long for liberation and for the esteem and dignity that is integral to it.

Freedom is one of the great themes of spirituality East and West, and it is central to the Jewish tradition that informed and inspired Jesus and his New Testament interpreters. "For the people of ancient Israel, the story of the exodus from Egypt was their *primal narrative*. It was the most important story they knew. It was the primary story shaping their identity, their sense of who they were, and their sense of God."[27] From this story came Israel's greatest prophet-hero Moses; its foundation document, the Pentateuch (the first five books of the Bible, also known as the Torah); and one of Judaism's central ritual celebrations, Passover. It is the story of God's compassion for an enslaved people and their deliverance — a story of bondage, liberation, a journey, and a destination. It resonates with our own experience of bondage: "bondage to cultural messages about what we *should* be like and what we *should* pursue — messages about success, attractiveness, gender roles, the good life";[28] bondage to our family of origin script, the role identity we were given as we grew up; bondage to a variety of addictions; bondage to damaging patterns in relationships; bondage to the social structures of racism and sexism; bondage to our desires and fears. The solution to bondage, of course, is liberation, but the story tells us that leaving Egypt and coming out from under the lordship of Pharaoh means *passage through the wilderness,* where we are gripped by fear and anxiety, tempted by idols, but also encountered by God and invited to a radical trust. "The journey lasts a long time — forty years according to the story. Its destination is life in the presence of God. Yet God is not simply the destination, but one who is known on the journey. It is a journeying *toward* God that is also *with* God."[29]

The New Testament presents the story of Jesus precisely in these terms. Jesus is liberator, a new Moses, who leads us out of our bondage and into the presence of God, who shows us the way through the wilderness, facing down the temptations, dealing with our anxieties and fears, surrendering to God. To identify with Jesus is to go into the waters with him and to come out on the other side, to leave behind our old self and to accept a new identity, to suffer the wilderness as the nurturing ground for freedom. Jesus' death and resurrection is metaphor for journey from slavery and oppression to liberation and freedom. He walks with us in the wilderness and heals us, nurturing us even as he teaches us detachment as the liberating path.

Exile and Coming Home

Another macro-story in Judaism is that of exile and return. In 587 B.C.E., Judah was conquered by the Babylonians. The Temple was destroyed and Jerusalem laid to waste. Many of the inhabitants, particularly the learned and those who showed leadership capabilities, were taken into exile to prevent any attempt to rebuild or create pockets of rebellion. Those who were exiled were taken some eight hundred miles from their homeland, which had always been understood spiritually as the center of the universe. The destruction of the Temple caused a severe crisis: the symbolic seat of God had been desecrated by violence. As refugees in an alien land, the Jews suffered marginalization, victimization, and oppression, the loss of all that was familiar and dear. They yearned for return to Zion. Finally, in 539 B.C.E. Cyrus the Great led Persian armies to victory over Babylon, and he issued an edict of liberation, allowing all foreign exiles to return to their homelands. The period of Jewish history that followed, marked by the rebuilding of the Temple and focus on their scriptures and the sacrificial cult, was known as the "Restoration."

"Next to the exodus, this experience of exile and return was the most important historical event shaping the life and religious imagination of the Jewish people. It seared itself into their consciousness and became for them a metaphor for their relationship with God."[30]

The image of exile and return speaks to universal human experience. All of us know estrangement, alienation, the emptiness of being separated from *home*. It is the experience of being *lost*. The story of the wayward son who journeys to a distant country to squander his inheritance on a life of debauchery and the prodigal father, who "while he was still a long way off" sees him, is moved with pity, and runs to greet him with an embrace and a kiss (Luke 15:11–32), is a story that speaks to our depths. Coming home is coming back to ourselves, finding our intimate origins, letting go of folly and pride, returning to the source of love. "Exile is central in the symbolism of the Garden of Eden story in the book of Genesis. The garden — paradise — is the place of God's presence, but we live outside the garden, east of Eden."[31] The New Testament interprets the Jesus event as a return, an overcoming of our lostness, a homecoming. The parables of the Lost Sheep, the Lost Drachma, and the Lost Treasure are all parables of finding, of being found. In and through Jesus, we are found. To follow him is to return to the source of compassion and mercy, forgiveness and love. It is to find God and to be found by God. The story of Jesus is the story of our reconciliation with the sacred.

Sin and Reconciliation

Finally, Judaism treasured the institutions of sacrifice: Temple, priesthood, and cult. This is the story of human sinfulness, of breaking the covenant that binds us to God, of renewing that covenant through sacrifice. The sacrificial cult is about relationship, about human and divine sharing in a sacred meal, about blood mingling as a symbol of shared life. In Jesus' time it was broadly perceived among the peasants as a priestly brokerage, which exacted great economic hardships on the poor. The Jesus event, then, became interpreted as a new covenant and he as the Great High Priest. Jesus is seen as the Lamb of God, whose sacrifice takes away the sins of all the world, establishing a divine-human bond that can never be undone. When the Temple was again destroyed, this time by the Romans, following the revolutionary uprising from 67 to 70 C.E., it was interpreted by Christians as affirmation that the Temple had been replaced. The communities that gathered for the breaking of the bread, renewing

Jesus' table-fellowship and sharing his body and blood, were enacting ritually the everlasting covenant established in and through Jesus. His death restored relationship with God, vanquishing human sinfulness and establishing mercy and forgiveness as God's attitude toward sin. Christians understand themselves, then, as a "priestly people," whose sacrifice is for a reconciliation of the world in justice and peace.

Guilt is integral to the human condition. We break trust in our relationships. We fail in our obligations. We don't live up to our own ideals and expectations. We know ourselves to be sinners. The world is filled with sin: injustice and violence, cheating and dishonesty, gross inequities and the denial of opportunity. Children by the millions starve; human rights are trod upon; nations spend billions on weaponry; the planet verges on ecocide. Sin is personal; sin is social. Human insensitivity, racism and sexism, pride and greed, pollution and murder fill the news reports. Our hearts are hardened with cynicism and self-seeking. Yet feeling guilty, wallowing in guilt, being paralyzed by guilt solves nothing. The resolution given in Jesus is atonement (read "at-one-ment"): we are washed and forgiven, released from guilt, "justified" (read "acquitted"). Preoccupation with righteousness and purity renders us helpless to serve others, but connecting our lives to Jesus' sacrifice sets us free for service, for compassion and the works of justice.

Jesus Today

The Jesus experience is as vital and life-giving today as it was two thousand years ago — and at least as challenging. Many people today hear "Jesus" only on the electronic airwaves from fundamentalist preachers espousing a narrow judgmentalism and right-wing politics. Or perhaps they associate "Jesus" with an otherworldly focus that condemns human nature and sees clinging to him as a way to heaven. But Jesus is much, much more. He embodies humanity's most noble dreams and represents a God whose compassion beckons us beyond the tawdry materialism and manipulative power plays of today's conventional wisdom. We are called, in and through Jesus, to liberation, to reconciliation, to come home — which is what we long for, but also what we fear. To follow him is to take the narrow path, the road less traveled, requiring great courage and a full heart. It means accepting our vulnerability and risking the security of status and success, betting our lives, as he did, on *Abba*. It means surrendering to the rule of God and confronting every lesser rule, including that of our own ego. But it means, also, a rich and life-giving relationship with God and with companions.

At a recent religious education conference in New Orleans, following a presentation on "Religious Education in the 21st Century," a distraught man in the audience stood up, his face flushed and his veins bulging: "I'm sick and tired of hearing 'Jesus, Jesus, Jesus!' When are we going to get back to what our religion is really all about — rules and regulations?" The rediscovery of Jesus at the center of Catholicism moves us in a new and exciting direction. Jesus bids us travel our life journey with him, fasting and praying, facing down the temptation of idols, opening ourselves to God's spirit and making God's compassion our own, becoming healers and exorcists, social revolutionists who seek a place for everyone at the table. He invites us to recognize the trials and opportunities of our own existence as fundamentally tied to a relationship with gracious mystery. We respond not so much with our verbal *yes* or *no*, but with the way we live life. The New Testament provides a compelling image in Matthew 25:31–46:

> Come, you whom my *Abba* has blessed, take for your heritage the *basileia* prepared for you since the foundation of the world. For I was hungry and you gave me food; I was thirsty and you gave me drink; I was a stranger and you made me welcome; naked and you clothed me, sick and you visited me, in prison and you came to see me.

— Chapter 5 —

The Experience of Grace

> Grace is much more than a static possibility of love. It is an out-
> pouring, a boundless burning offering of God's self to us, suffering
> with us, overflowing with tenderness. Grace is God's passion.... The
> love that creates us may be haunting, but it is not enslaving; it is
> eternally present, yet endlessly open. Free will is given to us for a
> purpose: so that we may choose freely, without coercion or manipu-
> lation, to love God in return, and to love one another is a similarly
> perfect way.
>
> — Gerald May, *Addiction and Grace*

The Jesus experience gives expression to something even more fundamental and universal in human existence: *the experience of grace.*
Catholicism holds that human beings actually share divine life, that
God gives Godself to us in loving us. This sense of human participation in divine life is what Catholic spirituality is all about, and it
is probably the least understood aspect of Catholic tradition today.
To understand the experience of grace, we need to ask about God,
about the human person, and about the relationship between God
and persons. We need to ask about the dynamic interaction between
the divine and ourselves, about freedom and the ability to refuse
divine love in sin.

We begin by examining the experience of St. Paul, whose letters to
various Christian communities are probably the earliest New Testament documents. Paul's spiritual experience was a shattering of his
previous religious understandings and a true encounter with sacred
mystery. He understands the Jesus experience in a larger context:
God's relationship with human beings. God was revealing Godself
in Jesus, but further, in that revelation God was also giving human
beings *a new existence.* For Paul, this new existence was a surprising gift, which dramatically demonstrated God's passionate love for
creation and God's desire to share divine life with us.

Paul's Understanding of Grace

Paul uses the term *charis* (grace) to describe the Jesus experience. For him, a Pharisee who experienced conversion to Christianity through an encounter with the risen Jesus,[1] Jesus represented the end of life under the Law and the beginning of the life of *charis*. As a Pharisee, Saul (his name prior to his conversion) believed in resurrection as the reward that would be given to all those who had been faithful to the Law. Judaism imaged the end of time as a great court trial. Humanity had been indicted because of Adam and Eve's sin, and the indictment would go to trial only at the end time, known as the *eschaton*. God had given Israel the Law as a way, a path, and to live the Law's commands, to follow its path, was to set oneself right before God. The trial's verdict would be either justification (acquittal) or condemnation (guilty). The justified would be raised from the dead to live an eschatological existence in everlasting life with God. Obedience to the Law was the way to justification.

This new eschatological existence is life in the numinous. It is the original life — the existence first given to human beings at the dawn of creation. As Robin Scroggs says, "Authentic life consists in a return to an original situation which is made possible by the risk taken of giving up striving for selfhood and by accepting selfhood, rather, as something already present. The quality of this new but original life is one of self-acceptance, love and joy."[2] Its opposite is the life of sin: life characterized by anxiety and distrust, in which we try to prove ourselves worthy and acceptable. These two forms of human existence, eschatological existence and sinful existence, provide a context of tension — a tension familiar to all of us, whether we use this language or not. To be alive is to be drawn and pulled in conflicting directions, aware that we are free and must decide. This tension was exposed in profound ways in the activity of Jesus, and its exposure continued in the proclamation that he had been raised from the dead and given a new eschatological existence.

Paul experienced this tension, and his spiritual conversion grew out of it. The followers of Jesus were claiming that Jesus had risen. For Paul, from the Pharisees' standpoint, such a claim, were it true, had two important implications: (1) the eschatological time was already beginning; and (2) God wasn't playing by the expected rules. Indeed, if Jesus had been raised, the efficacy of the Law and the importance of obeying the Law were called into question. In and through his conversion experience, which may have endured for several months or even several years, Saul became Paul and shifted his allegiance from the Law to Jesus Christ. This profound spiritual experience focused on *grace*. Salvation was not to come later, at the end, but was already here: eschatological existence was a present reality in and through Jesus Christ. Obedience to the Law was not the way to such existence — indeed, such striving could only frustrate the possibility of such consciousness. No, eschatological existence is given freely, is *charis,* through Jesus Christ, to all who open themselves to accept it in faith. Thus, to believe in Jesus risen is to open oneself to eschatological existence now: the verdict has been rendered in God's raising of Jesus, through whom all humanity has been justified. Rather than living life as a preparation for a trial, now one can live on the other side of the trial, rejoicing in the verdict — this is the good news (Gospel) for Paul.

The end of the Law's efficacy and the beginning of *charis* as the way of salvation led him to a rethinking of the whole of Judaism. In his letter to the Philippians he writes:

> As far as the Law can make you perfect, I was faultless. But because of Christ, I have come to consider all these advantages that I had as disadvantages. Not only that, but I believe nothing can happen that will outweigh the supreme advantage of knowing Christ Jesus my Lord....I am no longer trying for perfection by my own efforts, the perfection that comes from the Law, but I want only the perfection that comes from faith in Christ, and is from God and based on faith. (3:6–9)

Paul wasn't claiming that Judaism was an erroneous religion and that Christianity was a true one. His insight is much more profound: "You cannot save yourself, put your trust in God, who has already claimed you in his raising of Jesus from death." Abraham, the father of Judaism, had been saved by his faith; he put his trust in God and followed that trust. Circumcision was the sign of that faith, not the saving event itself. To follow in Abraham's way, he reasoned, was to follow Jesus, whose trust in God was radical and complete. And the Gentiles, who never did think the Jewish Law could save, had to take a new look at what they thought could: their mystery cults, their philosophical wisdom, their prestige, wealth, and power. None of these could provide access to God's approval and acceptance, either — only trust, which comes to us as gift.

For Paul, in light of the new postresurrection situation, sin is not transgressing the Law. Rather, sin is the state of *unfaith*. Sin is not trusting in God, attempting instead to justify oneself. That is why the

Pharisee is a sinner, not only when he fails to fulfill the Law, but precisely when he does fulfill the Law. His obedience to the Law is an act of unfaith, a striving to secure his own existence, an attempt to prepare his defense for the day of judgment. Sin is the anxious attempt to save ourselves. For the Jew of Paul's day it meant obedience to the Law: circumcision and dietary restrictions. Torah could be applied to almost every facet of life. For the Mediterranean Gentile it likely meant the effort to enact wisdom. For us today, it is still different: achieving success, amassing a fortune, looking good, keeping physically fit, being dedicated to civic idealism, doing works of charity, doing religious things — all of them life-projects grounded in a striving self. It is not that any of these things are wrong in themselves; rather, they are wrong when they are ways for us to earn a sense that we are loved or worthy of love, that we are *ultimately valuable*. The only way to know that we are loved, treasured, cherished, affirmed, is through trusting that we are, through entrusting ourselves to God. Learning to trust God's love, simply opening ourselves to God's overflowing compassion — that is what faith is. And when Paul speaks of obedience, he means obedience to Jesus' faith. Jesus trusted his *Abba* all the way, even unto death by crucifixion, but God did not abandon him in death, raising him up and giving him a new eschatological existence. To live that kind of trust — that is obedience for Paul.

And all of this is *charis*. It is not earned by what we do or don't do, but rather is God's free gift to us. It is God's initiative that allows us to let go of our anxieties and to trust. The first *charis* is what God has done in Jesus Christ. The second *charis* is what God does in us, opening us to the Spirit that was in Jesus, allowing us to trust as he did. Such trust is not of our own doing — that would be another kind of self-justifying activity. Such trust is a simple openness, grounded in the acceptance of our vulnerability and our powerlessness, an abandonment, a surrender. Jesus surrendered, even unto death; we surrender, opening ourselves to a new and liberated existence. This experience of surrendering trust is *charis* and allows us to be *charis* for one another, to reflect this radical and unconditional divine love to others. That was Jesus' compassion, reflecting the compassion of *Abba*. Our trusting surrender can allow us to love others, not in order to justify ourselves, but precisely because we know experientially that we are already cherished and loved, and we know that this same compassionate God loves others in precisely this same way.

Similarities to the Buddhist Path

Catholic Christianity has always seen the tension between sin and grace as the context for *all* human existence — and the great challenge of spirituality. Christian spirituality means dying to sin and rising to the new life of grace, letting go of our most fundamental anxieties in a surrender to God and actually living life in the numinous, participating in the life of sacred mystery. But this experience of gifted surrender is not seen as a once and forever event. Rather, conversion is an ongoing journey, and the tension between untrust and trust, sin and grace, is a permanent feature of human life, challenging us again and again to "let go and let God." Buddhism sees a similar tension and poses a similar path: from illusion to reality, from darkened consciousness to enlightenment, from a sleeping existence to waking up. The Buddha is "the one who woke up" (note the parallel to Jesus as the one who was awakened, was raised).

The Buddhist path begins with the insight that human existence is fraught with anxiety and psychospiritual suffering.[3] This is the first of the Four Noble Truths. We are dissatisfied and always experience a sense that things should be different than they are. No matter how good life may be, it can still get better, and in any case, we don't want it to deteriorate and get worse. We experience an unsatisfactoriness and a dis-ease and are anxious about our life, wanting more of this, less of that, trying to hang on to the good we have and not lose it, hoping to avoid disasters — like growing old, sickness, and death. Mortal existence is anxious existence. It is characterized by what the Buddha calls *dukkha*. This sense of dis-ease and dissatisfaction is grounded in *tanha* (craving, desire, thirst). We continually thirst for more. Our desire is insatiable. We crave — material things, psychological and social experiences, spiritual well-being. A little creates a hunger for more, and a lot is not enough. *Dukkha* arises from *tanha* — our existential anxiety is grounded in an unquenchable thirst. This is the second Noble Truth.

The cessation of thirst (*tanhakkhaya*) is simultaneously the cessation of our suffering/anxiety; to extinguish our thirst means the end of our dis-ease and dissatisfaction. Buddhists call this *nibbuta* (cool, in the sense of being cool after a fever, healthy and well again). Cooling our feverish craving — chilling out — is the key to transcending our permanent state of dissatisfaction. But this is easier said than done, since even our desire to cool our thirst is an expression of *dukkha* and *tanha*. We crave to stop our craving! Cooling our ravenous appetite — relief from the heat of our greed — is *nirvana,* the ideal state of being, but getting there is a delicate task, in some ways more passive than active. It is a letting go, a surrender, a giving up, that leads to *nirvana.* This is the third Noble Truth.

The way to the cessation of thirst is the path (*magga*) of the Buddha, the famous Eightfold Path. This is the fourth Noble Truth. This way involves faith and wisdom, morality and meditation, but it is primarily understood as the path of detachment. The path of letting go is the path of waking up: we let go of perceiving life from the vantage of our thirsting ego (reality as seen through the lenses of our fears and desires), and we wake up to reality as it really is. Being present to reality, perceiving it truthfully, opening our minds to what is, the practice of mindfulness — this is the Buddhist path. It is called "the middle path" because the Buddha sought to avoid two extremes: rigorous asceticism on the one hand; and living by hedonistic desire on the other. Buddhist wisdom is that both extremes are expressions of our dissatisfied thirst. The middle path seeks to transcend the thirsting through the balancing of awareness and detachment.

The most important Buddhist practice is *meditation.* In and through the right practice of meditation, one gradually cools one's thirst and ever so gently becomes awake and alert. It is the disciplined practice of paying attention to what's happening — to one's breathing, to one's bodily posture, to the flow of one's consciousness, to what one is feeling. What surfaces in this practice of attentiveness is a recognition of a myriad of fears and desires that arise in our consciousness, making us anxious. Meditation doesn't deny the fears and desires, nor the anxiety. The practitioner simply notes that all this is going on, distracting one's attention from breathing. Buddhist meditation leads one away from distractions, away from the internal noise that arises in the silence, away from the need to fill up the empty space of solitude — not in and through consciously avoiding the distractions, the noise, and the urge to fill up the emptiness (will power); but precisely in becoming aware that all this is going on, gradually becoming experientially aware of our *dukkha* and our *tanha.* In and through the discipline of meditation, attentive mindfulness replaces anxious grasping, and one makes peace with the empty silence. The mind is healed, blindness is replaced by sight, and detached compassion supplants controlled and controlling uneasiness. The path toward enlightenment is a life's journey, requiring persistent practice and great patience — gradually letting go and becoming free.

Catholic Spiritual Practice

The Catholic path involves meditation and prayer, ascetical practices such as fasting and solitude, conscious and active participation in community and the sacramental rites, and doing compassionate service. It leads us toward a deeper and deeper participation of life in Christ, identifying with his letting go in death, receiving the gift of a transformed consciousness and a new existence in resurrection. It is the journey from unfaith to faith, from a preoccupation with one's own desires and fears to a life of compassionate presence. This spiritual path is ritually acted out in baptism, where one goes into the water to die to sin and comes forth from the water to live in Christ. The going into the water is a going into Christ's tomb — a letting go, an experience of powerlessness and emptiness, a surrender, a leap of faith. The coming out of the water is rising with Christ to a new, numinous, eschatological existence. This ritual enactment of the Christ myth is a symbolic acting out of conversion: from sin to grace, from life unto oneself to life in community, from ego identity (Buddhism's "small self") to identity with Christ (Buddhism's "Buddha self"). The physical movement — into the water and forth from the water — is also a reenactment of Israel's liberation from bondage, through the Sea of Reeds and, again, across the River Jordan. It is a liberation *from* the bondage of fear and desire, from a life of untrust, from alienation and exile, from sin and death. It is liberation *for* life in Christ and the *basileia,* for *charis,* for radical compassion (the service of love and justice). The action of baptism symbolizes a life's journey along the path of conversion, a commitment to follow in the way of Jesus, to open ourselves to the Spirit, to withdraw from the conventional wisdom and to adhere to his wisdom, to move beyond structured hierarchies and boundaries in a life of radical egalitarianism, to make his healing mission and his open table our own, to join him in death and resurrection. This is the life of grace, the gift of God through Christ and the Spirit.

The Rapid Spread of the Christian Movement

One of the characteristics of Catholic Christianity is its openness to translation through enculturation. In the first decades after Jesus' death, the movement spread rapidly throughout the Mediterranean area, creating communities mostly in the great urban centers of the empire (at first in Jerusalem, but soon thereafter at Antioch, Alexandria, Rome). Christians developed creative correlations between their faith in Jesus and the key sociopolitical and intellectual currents of the Greco-Roman world, attempting to translate the spiritual wisdom of a Galilean peasant revolutionist into the shifting social demography of imperial cities, where change could be met and even sought out, where the empire was, and where the future began. It was in the cities that foreigners gathered, travelers visited, and people connected, and it was here that Christianity found a ready audience for its Gospel and the experience to which it led. Merchants, artisans, persons enslaved and displaced by war or piracy and now set free, political exiles, the hearty noncitizens who gathered in voluntary associations, oftentimes across ethnic and religious groupings, were spiritually and socially ready to embrace the radical vision of the illegitimate Christian movement and make a home for one another in the compassionate communities of faith. Freedpersons (persons who had obtained manumission from slavery) and single or widowed women were chief among the many groups in imperial cities caught up in "status dissonance" (a term that points to the crisscrossing of status categories that was an emerging feature of city life in the otherwise rigid hierarchy of the Roman world). Conversion appealed to such as these in a manner not unlike the way the *basileia* experience appealed to Galilean peasants. Their communities, usually led by Jews who themselves or whose ancestors had migrated to imperial cities to flee the violence and destruction of uprisings in Palestine, were the first *ecclesiae* — a term that later will be translated as "churches." Such communities became the birthing place for the writings that eventually became the New Testament and the creative context for the development of a uniquely Christian ritual pattern. Here, too, the Christian movement began to converse with a wide variety of spiritual philosophies.

Grace and Morality

During the course of these first few centuries the new Christian movement continued to grow in popularity and influence and became more and more organized. Increasingly, Christian thinkers made peace with the conventional wisdom in many parts of the Roman Empire. Particularly after Christianity became politically legitimate in the Emperor Constantine's Edict of Milan (313), the experience of *charis* was understood and described in dialogue with the key intellectual currents of Greco-Roman culture, and the focus of grace became less and less the experience itself and more and more the lasting effects of grace on persons. Grace became associated with moral power — as cause and effect. The earlier emphasis on the dynamic, personal presence of God in Christ and the experience of relationship and conversion was replaced by a new emphasis on the moral life and our ability to choose good and avoid evil. Grace was more and more seen as the basis for living a morally virtuous life, and increasingly grace was understood as being brokered by the church, particularly in and through its sacramental rituals. This is the beginnings of what we've been referring to as juridical consciousness.

Paul's sense of grace was somewhat distorted, sometimes actually turned completely upside-down. Some Christians, influenced by spiritual movements such as Gnosticism and Manichaeism, developed a practical dualism that looked upon the body and human emotions as needing to be bridled and controlled by reason. Ironically, the life of grace became more and more identified with this process of control, mistrusting human drives and the imagination. Human nature was pejoratively associated with concupiscence (destructive, hedonistic human passions) and our sinful appetites, and grace came to mean overcoming our humanness, transcending the body and the emotions, neutralizing our needs and our drives. Gnosticism taught that there were two gods: an evil god was responsible for material creation, and a good god offered spiritual salvation (redemption) through release from our imprisonment in matter. Christianity condemned this dualistic philosophy, but also fell under its influence. Some believers wanted to become angels, despising their humanity. Virtue meant an asceticism of controlling feelings and drives, overcoming our needs. The moral ideal that was fashioned by such an anthropology was asexual, completely in control of the senses, without any emotional needs. The grace of baptism was seen as a human necessity (a metaphysical imperative), that without which one could only languish in a sea of wretched appetites, captured by concupiscence, destined for eternal punishment. Christian spirituality was more and more focused exclusively on "redemption" from a material creation that was seen mostly as an occasion of sin.

The church became focused on redemption from the Fall, seeing human nature as oriented toward evil — and itself as a broker for the healing medicine of grace, without which there was no salvation. Salvation itself was seen as a heavenly afterlife achieved through virtuous living, and virtuous living could occur only with the help of grace, which was mediated by the church. Human freedom as the universal capacity to choose freely was denied: we could only sin. True freedom (the ability to choose the good) was seen to be given in grace, and grace was given to some and not others, but always only in and through the church, its sacraments, and its moral teaching. With hindsight we can now see that the very things Jesus had militated against — a brokering of God and a focus on virtue, hope for future salvation rather than the experience of salvation now — were beginning to overshadow the *basileia* experience of radical trust in a compassionate God with its implications for social revolution. The Pauline experience of *charis* was looking more and more like his earlier experience of life under the Law.

Grace and Being in the Middle Ages

By the thirteenth century, Christianity had become "Christendom" in a common-law marriage of church and state. The church's brokerage function was well-established and even civil society was ruled by powerful bishops, not the least of whom was the bishop of Rome. The institution of the papacy had evolved and become the center of patronage and clientage in medieval Europe. A cultural renaissance was reversing the spiritualism of Platonic thought, turning Europeans away from otherworldly designs and toward the material world.

Thomas Aquinas (1225–74), wanting to incorporate the new interest in natural science and the humanistic enthusiasm of the Renaissance into a Christian understanding, sought to reconcile the classical worldview (with its emphasis on reason and this-worldly interests) with Christian faith (with its emphasis on revelation and a supernatural destiny). He turned to the newly rediscovered philosophy of Aristotle. Every substance, according to Aristotle, has a purpose, a reason for its existence. Christian revelation announces communion with God as the goal of human existence. Aquinas reasoned that the beatific vision (communion with God in heaven) is our purpose. But a merely human existence cannot achieve such an end, so God gives us grace (which he saw as a new, supernatural existence), in and through which we are elevated and given the capacity to pursue our true purpose. Grace (supernatural existence) is given by God so that we can achieve the end for which God created us in the first place.

Thomas drew upon Aristotle's notion of causation to explain the meaning of grace, which was focused not so much in the will as it was in being. With grace, merely human being becomes supernatural being. We can understand Aristotle's sense of things by considering a piece of clay being worked on by a sculptor. Throughout its successive manipulations, the clay remains the same but the form it takes changes, until at last it advances to the final, aesthetically satisfactory object that is the end of the sculptor's activity. Here we see what Aristotle called the four causes: the final cause (the purpose of the object — to decorate a living room and to hold fresh flowers, for example), the material cause (the clay out of which it is made), the formal cause (the actual form the clay finally takes, a vase), and the efficient cause (the sculptor who fashions the vase). Grace is the new form (formal cause) that we are given by God so that we can attain our true and final purpose.

Thomas's brilliant correlation of the Christian experience of grace with Aristotle's philosophy became accepted as the basic Catholic teaching about grace. However, it was soon challenged — by Martin Luther and other reformers in the Protestant Reformation because of its focus on being rather than relationship. Luther himself rediscovered Pauline teaching about grace and found rich resonance with it in his own experience of conversion. Just as Paul had sought to follow the way of obedience to Law and found the way of trusting surrender through grace in his own powerful spiritual experience, so did Luther. Catholicism, in his experience, had taken on the character of the Law and so emphasized earning salvation through obedience to church authority that it had lost the vital center of personal relationship to God. Grace as formal cause that elevated human being to supernatural being didn't match his experience of himself as always a sinner. As he looked around at church leaders in a world of patronage and clientage and the papacy's brokering activity, he didn't see much supernatural being either. He took his stand on the Pauline teaching (justification by faith through grace) and on his own powerful experience of trusting surrender, eventually leading to a formal breakup of Christendom. Such a sundering probably would have happened anyway, since the grand medieval synthesis was collapsing with the rise of independent nation-states and the emergence of capitalist economic experiments. Yet Luther's spiritual teaching should not be understated. He confronted Catholicism with its historical contradictions and introduced scripture as a greater authority than hierarchy, hinting that spiritual experience itself was more authoritative than the juridical power of ecclesial rule.

The Roman Church condemned the Protestant Reformers and sought to carry out its own institutional corrections in the Council of Trent (1545–63). While it earnestly tried to reverse the corruption, theological ignorance, and lack of discipline among the clergy, it took a strongly defensive posture on doctrinal matters. It reasserted Thomas Aquinas's teachings and the authoritative role of hierarchy over against Protestant teachings. In many ways, Trent established juridical consciousness as the way of Catholicism, insisting on the inadequacy of human nature and the helplessness of humanity in sin and defining the church as the mediator of grace to fallen humanity. Sin and grace were seen as mutually exclusive states of being. One could pass from the state of sin to the state of grace only through the church's sacraments (baptism and penance), and grace was increased through obedience to the church's teachings and doing virtuous acts. It was the church that held the key to salvation — the power to save and the power to condemn.

Grace and Juridical Consciousness Today

Many Catholics today first heard about grace from the perspective of this juridical consciousness version of the original *charis* experience. Grace was presented as an antidote to immorality. Catholics were taught that they were born with original sin, so baptism was required to "wash away" its effects. Grace was seen as something of a supernatural add-on to human nature, which had been hopelessly wounded by Adam's sin and which was now incapable of achieving the true end of life, communion with God. Human nature was tragically flawed and insufficient in and of itself. Grace was, thus, supernatural (above and beyond nature itself) and mediated in and through the church by baptism. The supernatural virtues (faith, hope, and charity) were said to be "infused" into the soul at baptism, providing the capacity to pursue the real reason for our existence, the beatific vision. One could, however, lose this new supernatural state — through mortal sin. Mortal sin put one back into a flawed and insufficient situation, incapable of achieving the beatific vision. In such case, the sacrament of penance was needed, requiring true contrition and the confession of sin to a priest, who would assign *a penance* to do, completing the movement from the state of sin to the state of grace. In penance, sin was absolved and grace restored.

Grace was understood as a kind of metaphysical stuff — something we received at baptism, regained through penance, and accumulated through pious acts and good deeds, through participation in the sacraments and virtuous living. And the church was the mediator of this stuff, without which we were lost for all eternity. The church's authority and power were grounded in its capacity to "dispense" grace and, thus, to determine who would be saved and who would be lost. The individual's freedom was involved, to be sure, but freedom meant the capacity to obey: moral compliance with church teachings and regular participation in the sacraments. A story is told about the elderly monsignor who was confronted on an elevator by a zealous young woman who belonged to a born-again fundamentalist Christian group. "Have you received the Holy Spirit?" she asked the cleric. "Madam, I *dispense* the Holy Spirit," he declared, exiting the elevator without so much as a "good day" or a look back.

Reconstructing Grace Today

This understanding of grace began to be questioned and critiqued by European theologians early in the twentieth century. People like Henri de Lubac in France and Karl Rahner in Germany described grace experientially and relationally. Perhaps more significant, however, is that they discussed the supernatural as a fundamental dimension of all human existence. Most important of all, the dualisms (nature/grace, body/soul, history/eternity, world/church, secular/sacred) were declared to be "academic abstractions" that had no reference in real experience. They had a certain validity and value *as concepts,* allowing us to distinguish academically, but lived existence was seen as unified and whole. There was no such thing as an ungraced human nature in lived existence, no sacred realm apart from the space-time continuum we call secular.

Henri de Lubac was the energetic center of the creative Jesuit theological renewal at Fourviere in France in the 1940s and 1950s. His major books, *Catholicisme* and *Surnaturel,* lay the foundation for a new Christian humanism by arguing that, by virtue of creation — that is, simply on the basis of our being human — the human person is effectively called to community with God, the transcendent fulfillment of our longing for happiness. Such a perspective ultimately undoes every authoritarian and ideological approach to the fundamental question of salvation by suggesting that one is saved not by church membership or confessing right beliefs, not by conformity to ecclesial law or participation in sacramental ritual, but by the very way in which we are created as human beings and in our living out

that humanity in life. It is at the level of our humanity that we are
saved, and this salvation is worked out, not in some religious sphere
apart, but in our living of life. Our freedom, our capacity for love
and creativity, our ability to think and pursue questions — these are
expressions of grace built-in to the very nature of human being. The
dualisms that had previously divided religion and faith from everyday life by separating the supernatural from nature itself, are undone
in de Lubac's rethinking of grace as intrinsic to human nature itself.
Grace is far more universal than Christianity. Indeed, it is tied to our
experience of human existence itself.

No single Catholic thinker has done more to retrieve the insights
of Christian spiritual teaching for our time and to inspire reconstructing Catholicism than Karl Rahner, the German Jesuit who persisted
in integrating the insights from his experience of the Spiritual Exercises into a coherent revising of fundamental Catholic theology.[4]
Rahner's theology of grace, a major presupposition in many of the
Second Vatican Council's documents, yet largely hidden from the
popular church three decades later, needs a new hearing in the light
of today's cultural crisis and new spiritual quest. Rahner's theology
can properly be called "constructive or revisionary postmodernism."
He seeks to overcome the modern worldview by constructing a
postmodern worldview through revision of modern premises and
traditional concepts.[5]

Rahner's Starting Point:
Experience and Questions

The starting point in Rahner's thought is our shared human existence and the curiosity and wonder that attention to it prompts.
Rahner begins with *experience*.[6] God cannot be the starting point,
nor can Jesus or the Bible. These hold no immediate credibility; today's world has, in fact, come to understand them as part of the
problem. No, the starting point must be experience, fundamental
and universal human experience, what Rahner calls "unthematic
knowledge." Such knowledge emerges from our immediate experience, before it has been "thematized" in concepts and language. This
is knowledge acquired not from without, but from within, "original
knowledge" because it wells up from the origins of our own selves
in our lived interaction with the world. This knowledge seeks expression in concepts and words, but our efforts at expression never
completely capture the experience itself. We try to thematize our ex-

perience, seeking to understand it ourselves conceptually and to share it with others in words. But we continually recognize the limitations involved in this process, using terms like "you really had to be there" or "I can't put it into words — it was just incredible!" Thus, there is a continual interplay between our raw experience (unthematic knowledge) and our efforts to understand and communicate it (thematic knowledge).

In this way, Rahner moves initial human knowing back beyond rational concepts and language, beyond Descartes's starting point ("I think, therefore I am"). Here, Rahner finds a universal human experience of wonder and mystery: we are swimming in a sea of unappropriated encounters and have no words, *yet*, to name what we "know." This is where Rahner begins to build his postmodern understanding of the human person and our encounter with God: God giving God's self to us, not in concepts or words but in the immediate experience of gracious mystery that is fundamental to our "original knowledge." Rahner says we always carry this experience with us; it's always there, not only as backdrop from our past, but as an ongoing encounter in the present. We may try to ignore it, deny it, bury it under piles of concepts and words. In fact, we all do attempt to flee from this raw experience, because within it we are vulnerable and dependent and not in control. Yet we never really escape it. Further, this original knowledge emerges again and again into consciousness, becoming the source of our freedom, our transcendence, and our questions. We know ourselves to be immersed in mystery, a context of continual wonder and frightening dependency.[7]

This is the context, then, for our hearing of the Gospel. It is a story about Jesus of Nazareth that comes to us from our historical tradition through our scriptures, and yet it is *first* a story about our own experience, a story we already know unthematically. Jesus' liberating yes to God and his no to temptation, his radical trust in *Abba* and his reconciling compassion for others, his death and resurrection — this is the story form of our own original knowledge. And if it is our story, it is the story of all the earth, a universal story about gracious mystery as our source and destiny and the need to live by courage and trust. Yet this story is not an "answer" to our questions, as the fundamentalists would have it. Rather, the Gospel is the thematization of our experience of mystery, helping us make peace with our deepest questions by our acceptance of incompleteness, vulnerability, emptiness.

The Mystery We Call God

One of the great pieces of twentieth-century theological writing is Rahner's meditation on the word "God" in his *Foundations of Christian Faith*.[8] "God" is different from other words, which have clear referents in human experience. "God" doesn't point to anything concrete like "tree" or "table" do. The word "God" is without contour: "It says nothing about what it means, nor can it simply function like an index finger that points to something encountered immediately." But for this very reason, because its referent is so liquid and diffuse, "it is obviously quite appropriate for what it refers to."[9] For Rahner, "God" is "the nameless one... the silent one." "God" does not enter into the realm of our existence through an *active* process: "We should not think that, because the phonetic sound of the word "God" is always dependent on us, therefore the word "God" is our creation." No, we hear and receive the word "God." It comes to us in the history of language and in the story of humankind and through our own story. It is "our opening to the incomprehensible mystery."[10] This is the meaning of grace: that God, the incomprehensible mystery that is both source and destiny, gives us its very self — at the level of our unthematic experience.

We don't know God as an object "out there," nor is God simply the product of our imagination "in here." This is the Enlightenment's dualism (Kant). Our knowledge of God is not through empirical observation nor through rational deduction — the *only* ways of knowing in modernity. Rather, God emerges in the relationship between our questioning selves and the unexplainability of things. Our minds are driven toward coherence and meaning, and yet the focus of our thinking (the concrete, material world of things and persons) does not and cannot finally provide coherence and meaning — precisely the point! We are driven beyond the things in themselves to the mystery that they intimate. As Michael Buckley observes, "God is given as the orientation of the mind when it moves through nature in its drive for truth... moves towards reality and finds it is finally and radically mystery."[11]

God is "not a supreme being," whom we come to know like the person down the street or our office colleague. Nor do we come to know God by reading the Bible or studying theology. We come to know God not by undertaking the task directly (trying to know God), but experientially in our search for meaning and coherence in history and the world. We don't know God by turning away from the world (in otherworldly pursuits) but precisely by turning to the world. God is not another "thing," even a very big and powerful thing. God is first and always what we come to know by questioning things all the way, by wondering how they finally make sense, by pursuing the truth freely. When we simply ask the question "Why?" we are caught up in a process that leads ultimately to mystery, which is the ground and context for everything.

Grace as God's Self-Communication

Grace, then, is seen as God's self-communication to us: Absolute Mystery's coming into self-donating relationship with human persons.[12] The first movement of grace is that we are created as capacity for this gift: we have an incompleteness, an unfinishedness, an emptiness at the very center of our self. We are radically open to Mystery, driven there by our search for fulfillment. This is the great paradox: that our greatest gift is the hunger, the thirst, the desire, the persistent search for "more" and "beyond." This hunger can only be satisfied by our "yes" to Mystery. What makes us capable of receiving the divine into our very selves is the incompleteness that is integral to being human. I like to describe the human person in Rahner's theology as a donut, with an emptiness at our center. Just as there are no donuts without holes, there are no human beings that are not empty (and thus open). We find this emptiness unsettling, to put it mildly. We want to be complete *now* and seek quick and easy fulfillment in finite realities. Yet there is no satisfying this spirit-hunger with *things*. This is the way of addiction: the more we feed our emptiness with things, the more ferocious our hunger becomes. In order to be satisfied, we must make peace with our incompleteness and be open to Mystery. This is the way of grace.

Grace and Human Freedom: Our Lived Decisions

We are created incomplete and unfinished, internally driven toward the "more." But that doesn't mean that there's no role for human freedom in the dynamics of grace. Quite the contrary! Grace is also a decision. We can say no to Mystery's self-gift, stuff our emptiness with idolatrous spirit-substitutes, and seek to flee our radical incompleteness and dependency. We are created with a potential for God's self-gift; but this potential needs freedom's "yes" to be realized.

Perhaps the most insightful piece of Rahner's theology of grace is this: that our decisions about grace happen unthematically too. We don't sit down and thoughtfully choose to be open to Mystery's amazing self-gift, nor dispassionately say no to grace in favor of an alternative. Our choices are happening in the living of life, as we go about the normal processes of human activity. Here we encounter Mystery in thinking, loving, creating, hoping. Our "yes" to grace is in our relationships, our work, our leisure, our politics. Our "no" to God's self-gift comes as we shut down transcendence. We demand absolute control in seeking power, absolute security in pursuing wealth, and absolute certainty in creating and clinging to ideology. Making peace with our emptiness and living with openness before Mystery is challenging, particularly as we face this challenge every day and every hour, in interaction with self, others, social structures, nature, and economic and political realities.

Grace is universal as a possibility, built-in to the fabric of our humanity, and receives our free response quite apart from church membership or religious affiliation. Our "yes" or "no" to grace is in life. That is why not all those who cry "Lord, Lord" are saying *yes* to grace, nor are those who claim to be atheist or agnostic saying *no* to God's self-gift. Our openness to Mystery's self-disclosure and self-donation is embedded in the fabric of our lives and the processes that make them up — in our self-understanding, relationality, generativity, and integrity.

Redefining Church in the Light of Rahner's Thought

Vatican II's call for a renewed and reformed church seems clear in the light of Rahner's theology of grace. Nothing short of a revolution in pastoral practice — a reconstructing of Catholicism — will do. The church is not the broker for grace. Rather, it is *the people* (the Council used the term "People of God") who come together to confess and to celebrate the deepest meanings of their lives by reference to Jesus Christ and the Gospel. The church is the context for thematizing the unthematic, for bringing to consciousness and then to expression the dynamics of God's offer of grace and our freedom. The church is a support group for our everyday "yes" to Absolute Mystery's self-gift. As a community it is a laboratory for learning to make peace with emptiness and openness to grace, a situation in which we are mutually involved in learning the practice of transcendence and freedom. Church is where we gather to scheme together about global transcendence: the going beyond ideology and socio-economic structures that deny human dignity or attempt to prevent access to human fulfillment. The church is an instrument of personal and communal liberation and reconciliation, where we together remember Jesus' "yes" to grace and encourage one another and the world to live in solidarity with that "yes."

The interplay of personal self-understanding, interpersonal relationships, our mutual interdependence and responsibility before nature and society — these are at the very heart of being church and the Catholic spirituality of conversion. Retrieving grace in a postmodern world demands the radical redefining of church. In today's paradigm shift, something old is collapsing, but something new is coming to be. The continuity is deep and profound, nonetheless. We are simply rediscovering ancient truths and finding new language to describe what goes on in the adventure of human life — and that is the reconstructing of Catholicism.

The Psychospiritual Dynamics of Grace

Gerald May's book *Addiction and Grace* discusses the psychospiritual dynamics of sin and grace.[13] According to May, all human beings have an inborn desire for God, a desire that is, in fact, our deepest longing and most precious treasure. This yearning is seen as the essence of the human spirit, the origin of our highest hopes and noblest dreams, the very thing that gives meaning to human life. Yet in our lived existence, this desire is at times repressed and at other times focused on finite realities that are not God, and what was meant to be a desire for God becomes, instead, a flight from this desire through displacement and addiction. God creates us out of love, and this love draws us toward itself by means of our deepest desires.

Yet we are created with free will, and our freedom allows us to choose as we wish, for or against God, life, and love.

> The love that creates us may be haunting, but it is not enslaving; it is eternally present, yet endlessly open....Free will is given to us for a purpose: so that we may choose freely, without coercion or manipulation, to love God in return, and to love one another in a similarly perfect way. This is the deepest desire of our hearts.[14]

Still, our freedom is not complete. May sees the powerful force of addiction (not restricted to chemical addiction by any means, but a universal tendency to focus our desire in compulsive behaviors) working against it:

Psychologically, addiction *uses up* desire. It is like a malignancy, sucking our life energy into specific obsessions and compulsions, leaving less and less energy available for other people and for other pursuits. Spiritually, addiction is a deep-seated form of idolatry. The objects of our addictions become our false gods. These are what we worship, what we attend to, where we give our time and energy, *instead of love.* Addiction, then, displaces and supplants God's love as the source and object of our deepest true desire.[15]

The way out of this addictive enslavement is the process of *detachment,* which brings the liberation of our desire: "Detachment uncovers our basic desire for God and sets it free. With freedom of desire comes the capacity to love, and love is the goal of the spiritual life."[16] The key to detachment is not will power, as we are frequently led to believe, but grace. Will power is an active process that *we* control. Grace is an interactive process that is initiated by *God:*

> Grace is our only hope for dealing with addiction, the only power that can truly vanquish its destructiveness. Grace is the invincible advocate of freedom and the absolute expression of perfect love.... [It is] the dynamic outpouring of God's loving nature that flows into and through creation in an endless self-offering of healing, love, illumination, and reconciliation. It is a gift that we are free to ignore, reject, ask for, or simply accept.[17]

May gets to the predicament that is at the heart of our human condition when he points out that we are dependent upon grace for liberation from our addictions, but that those very addictions impair our receptivity to grace. In practical terms, the dynamic involves a "bottoming out" before we are desperate enough to surrender to God's love. We will never turn to God in loving openness as long as we are handling things well enough by ourselves. However, our most powerful addictions will cause us to defeat ourselves, bringing us to the rock bottom realization that we cannot finally master everything. This is the great paradox: in one sense, addiction is the enemy of grace, but in another sense, it can also be a powerful channel for the flow of grace — because it is addiction that brings us to our knees.

The way out is grace and the balance that the dynamics of surrender requires. Asking for help out of the experience of humility is the beginning of our surrender — what Augustine called "prevenient grace." Cooperating with God's love and rehabilitating our own freedom is a long process that involves patience and a continuing surrender, what Augustine called "following grace." And remaining steadfast in this surrender, refusing the tendency to attribute our growing sense of freedom to ourselves, will *bring us home* — what Augustine called "the grace of perseverance."

A Summing Up

The heart of Catholic spirituality is grace, understood as God's gift of God's self to us in loving relationship. Contemporary Catholic theologians understand this relationship as *universal* — that is, it is occasioned in every human life. To be human is to be invited to relationship with God. Further, this relationship is not limited by explicit faith: one need not be Catholic, or even Christian, or even religious, to participate in this relationship. Grace is God giving God's self to us as Mystery, and it is received, not as grace or as God, but as Mystery. We come to know and to relate to Mystery in living life — in our thinking, our loving, our hoping, our creating. It is here, in these everyday and fundamental human activities, that we encounter the Mystery that is God. *All* human beings are born with a desire for God, but we suppress that desire and direct it away from the Holy Mystery and toward spirit-substitutes (power, wealth, personal pleasures). This directing of our God-desire toward what is other than God is called "sin." We are all taught, in various ways and in various circumstances, to direct our God-desire toward "things" — to see even our self in this thingified way. But the hunger for God, and for ourselves open to and in union with God, never goes away. It burns deep within and makes everything else unsatisfying and incomplete. "Redemption" is what Catholic spirituality calls redirecting this God-desire to its proper goal. This happens in and through the practice of "detachment" and the life-long process of conversion. We withdraw our desire's attachment to things and to our thingified self, and we orient it again toward the Holy Mystery, understanding ourselves as dependent upon and flourishing only by participating in the dynamic life of this Holy Mystery. Jesus is *the redeemer* precisely because he shows us the way of this redirection and reorientation. To follow Jesus is to *die* to our falsely directed desires, and to *rise* to a new way of living that is grounded in and directed toward relationship with Holy Mystery. This is the meaning of baptism and participating in Christian community: the redirecting of our desire and our lives by following in the way of Jesus.

— Chapter 6 —

The Experience of
Sacramental Community

The sacramental principle means that the natural world is a sign of
God, not merely because God created it, not merely even because God
created it as good, but because God, somehow, actually is *in* it.
— Andrew Greeley and Mary Greeley Durkin,
How to Save the Catholic Church

The Catholic vision sees God in and through all things: other people,
communities, movements, events, places, objects, the world at large,
the whole cosmos. The visible, the tangible, the finite, the historical —
all these are actual or potential carriers of the Divine Presence. Indeed,
it is only in and through these material realities that we can encounter
the invisible God.
— Richard McBrien, *Catholicism*

In Catholicism the Jesus experience and the experience of gracious
Mystery working in human life and all of creation come together
in and through the experience of sacramental community. It is here
that Jesus is remembered and, in that grateful remembering, made
present. It is here that believers find interpretive clues to what is
happening in their lives and in the world around them. It is here
that the liberating experience of grace is thematized, made conscious
and explicit. Just as Jesus laid bare the spiritual depths of life for
those he encountered in Galilee, confronting them with decision, so
too does his risen presence in sacramental community lay bare the
depths of his followers' lives, the decisions we face, the issues of
love and justice that must be addressed today. People come to the
sacramental community with their spiritual hungers. They come to
be washed clean, to be fed, to be forgiven, to be healed, to celebrate
their love. And in the sacramental community these things really happen. They happen in life, and here in the sacramental community life

is thematized, its deepest meanings uncovered and celebrated in the transforming memory of Jesus Christ.

In thinking about the experience of sacramental community, the key words are "in and through" — not in the sense of a brokering function, but in the sense of *mediation* and *symbol*. Sacramental community mediates through symbolic communication, mediates the Jesus experience to the believers who make up such communities and mediates *basileia* through them (individually and collectively) to the broader community. Sacramental community is fundamentally about communication (seeing/hearing and responding, not so much verbally as nonverbally through holistic symbols): God communicating to us in and through symbols, members of the community communicating to one another in and through symbols, and the community communicating to the world in and through symbols. In all of this, Jesus is himself a symbol and the sacramental community a symbol as well.

The Meaning of Sacrament

The word "sacrament" comes from the Latin *sacramentum,* a term first used by Tertullian and later by Augustine in referring to baptism and Eucharist as sacred signs — visible signs of invisible realities. Other Christian writers use the Greek word *mystērion* in referring to the ritual celebrations that typified their gatherings. *Mystērion* was, no doubt, borrowed from the Greek mystery cults, which used it to refer to the special theophanies (divine revelations) that were central to their ritual practice. *Mystērion* was applied to baptism and Eucharist because these ritual actions were seen as celebrations of those ultimate mysteries that had been revealed in the life and death and resurrection of Jesus, mysteries that are realized in the challenge of living life. Jesus himself was, for Christians, the great theophany, and Christian rituals were focused on remembering him and on ecstatic experience of his risen presence. For the early Christians, Jesus was more than spirit person, social revolutionist, and teacher of wisdom. He was seen as *the embodied expression of God's wisdom and compassion.* In Jesus — his person, his healing, his boundary-breaking activity, even his tragic and grotesque death by crucifixion and the consequent belief that God had raised him — God was speaking to humanity. God was expressing Godself in Jesus' humanity.

Jesus as Primordial Sacrament

Marcus Borg points out that "the early layers of the movement's developing traditions portray Jesus not only as a teacher of wisdom, but also as intimately related to *the wisdom of God*...imaging Jesus as the emissary, child, and incarnation of the wisdom of God."[1] Interpreting their own experience in the light of the Jewish tradition of God *speaking* to God's people in and through persons and events, the early Christians spoke of Jesus as a revelation and incarnation of God's *Word*. Paul refers to Jesus as "the power and wisdom of God" (1 Cor. 1:24) and goes on, referring to "the hidden wisdom [*sophia*] of God which we teach in our mysteries...what scripture calls *the things that no eye has seen and no ear has heard*" (2:7, 9). The Gospel according to John presents Jesus as "the Word [*logos*] made flesh" (John 1:14), that which "in the beginning...was with God and...was God...[and] through whom all things came to be" (1:1–3) "was made flesh [and] lived among us" (1:14). And the First Letter of John begins thus: "Something which has existed since the beginning, that we have heard, and we have seen with our own eyes; that we have watched and touched with our own hands: the Word, who is life — this is our subject." The author of the Letter to the Colossians says, "He is the image of the unseen God" (Col. 1:15).

In these and in many other instances throughout the New Testament writings, we find the language of the invisible becoming visible, the divine transcendent becoming tangible, the sacred being enfleshed. Rahner would say that in Jesus the unthematic is being thematized. After Jesus' death, Christians continued to experience God in and through Christ. In their ritual gatherings, Christians continued to experience the invisible becoming visible and the divine made tangible. Numerous New Testament stories testify to this tangible experience of the risen Jesus in sacramental community: the story of the disciples on the road to Emmaus who recognized Jesus in the breaking of the bread (Luke 24:13ff.); the appearance to the disciples in the closed room (John 20:19ff.); the appearance on the shore of Tiberias (John 21:1ff.). Catholicism thus describes Jesus as "the primordial sacrament"[2] — the one in whom that which cannot be seen directly is made visible. This is the most basic meaning of "sacrament": something or someone, some event or some activity, accessed through our senses (seeing, hearing, tasting, smelling, touching), which communicates divine presence and activity. A sacrament is a created reality that discloses to us Uncreated Reality. "Sacrament" means sign or symbol — a visible sign, a perceptible symbol, of something invisible and sacred.[3] For Christians, Jesus is sacrament par excellence because he is the full and complete expression of God to us. Rahner states the Catholic understanding of Jesus as sacrament clearly and forcefully:

> The grace of God no longer comes...steeply down from on high, from a God absolutely transcending the world, and in a manner that is without history, purely episodic; it is permanently in the world in tangible, historical form, established in the flesh of Christ as part of the world, of humanity and of its very history. This is what we mean by saying that Christ is the actual historical presence in the world of the eschatologically triumphant mercy of God.... There is the spatio-temporal sign that effects what it points to. Christ in his historical existence is both reality and sign, *sacramentum* and *res sacramenti,* of the redemptive grace of God, which through him no longer...rules high over the world as the as yet hidden will of the remote, transcendent God, but in him is given and established in the world, and manifested there.[4]

The Early Christians' Experience of Community

The communities of Jesus' followers and devotees that formed in the first decades following his death understood their gatherings as his continuing presence. The wisdom and compassion of God continued to be embodied in these communities of "healed healers," who gathered for the breaking of the bread, continuing Jesus' table-fellowship and celebrating their ecstatic experience of his risen presence among them. Scholars who study the social world of early Christianity point to a deep and powerful sense of community as the most distinctive gift of Christianity to those attracted to it. John Gager, for example, describes "the radical sense of Christian community: open to all, insistent on absolute and exclusive loyalty, and concerned for every aspect of the believer's life."[5] In such communities, liminal people (people at the fringes of imperial society, people without status or position) made a home for one another, sharing their goods in common, giving and receiving hospitality and affection, resisting the hierarchies and boundaries all about them, sustaining each other in the face of persecutions, reaching out in compassion to those in need.

Because of the considerable mobility throughout the Mediterranean world fashioned by the Romans and because the Christian movement utilized a far-ranging network of synagogue communities already established by Judaism, Christians developed "a double sense of community: first, within the local community, which symbolized and reinforced their distinctive values; and, second, as part of an international network of communities, which served to counter- balance their sense of isolation in times of uncertainty or open hostility."[6] But unlike Judaism, which employed identified buildings (synagogues) for their meetings, "Christianity had no identifiable places of assembly for at least two hundred years." And unlike the various pagan cults, it had no distinctive priesthood.[7] These egalitarian communities met in members' homes to celebrate their "mysteries" in common, and the gathering, not the place, was sacred.

The Community as Sacrament

If Jesus is the primordial sacrament, making visible and tangible the invisible sacred, then the communities that remember him and make him present share in this sacramental role. Tad Guzie says:

> The mystery of Jesus is in fact the mystery of ourselves, and Christian- ity is truly bold in its belief that God has said everything [God] wants to say to us in the life of one of our own, who had to live out human existence in the same way that we do. The tendency to idealize Jesus in normal enough. There is no reason why we should not say wonder- ful things about the wonderful person who is Lord. But the wonder finally has to be brought home to ourselves, because it is in ourselves that we finally experience the mystery of Jesus.[8]

In Catholicism the church (understood as the body of believers) is a sacrament, making visible in history the compassion, mercy, and forgiveness of God.[9] If Jesus was divine love in a body, then the church is divine love in a community. The church discloses and makes accessible the hidden mysteries of *basileia* and *charis*, continuing the mission and ministry of Jesus in space and time.

Rahner describes the church as "the abiding presence of that primal sacramental word of definitive grace, which Christ is in the world, effecting what is uttered by uttering it in sign."[10] And Dominican scholar Edward Schillebeeckx puts it this way:

> The earthly Church is the visible realization of this saving reality in history [namely, Jesus]. The Church is a visible communion in grace. This communion itself...is the earthly sign of the triumphant redeem- ing grace of Christ....The inward communion in grace with God in Christ becomes visible in and is realized through the outward social sign. The essence of the Church consists in this, that the final goal of grace achieved by Christ becomes visibly present in the *whole* Church as a visible society.[11]

In sacramental community, we experience real communication with the divine: God speaking to us in sign and symbol; us responding to God in sign and symbol; God *in and through the community* speaking reconciliation, compassion, and justice to the whole of humanity. Such communication requires full awareness and heartfelt participation of the whole assembly, and it requires community leadership that can effectively facilitate such communication. Far from being passive observers of spiritual magic, the gathered community is an egalitarian assembly of active agents, attentively listening to God's dynamic word and responding from the heart and viscera. And the communication doesn't cease when the assembly disperses. The dismissal rite sends us forth as God's word to the world — the embodiment of God's compassion and wisdom in history.

Speaking Nonverbally

Learning to communicate with nonverbal symbols is sometimes challenging in a highly verbal culture. We are so given to the literal that the invitation to live by metaphor can be daunting. But Catholicism is about metaphor and nonverbal symbol — taking this communication much more seriously than mere words. Catholic spirituality demands attentiveness to symbolic expression.

Human beings communicate nonverbally all the time. We show affection and intimacy physically with our bodies, embracing, kissing, touching. We send flowers to *say* "We're sorry, we share your grief," or "Congratulations, we're happy for you!" We show up at our kids' soccer games — not so much to enjoy the athletic contest as to tell our children that we care. Hallmark Cards knows how important our symbolic communication is. So do advertising executives and politicians, both of whom spend great amounts of time and money focusing on *image*. The clothes we wear, the cars we drive, the decor in our homes, our bodily posture, the way we walk — all of these are nonverbal expressions of our values, our aesthetics, our very selves.

Making eye contact, our facial gestures, the way we sit — psychologists tell us that these frequently communicate more to the person we're with than any words we might say. We *say something* with touch: sometimes a touch is intrusive and offensive; at other times it's welcomed as a true expression of care or affection. When we send gifts, we usually want to *say* something to the receiver — and the gift selection is difficult precisely because it is *a gift*, and we want it to communicate exactly the right message.

We use symbols like stones and wedding rings, totems and flags and emblems, precisely because they *work* where logic or a sermon does not. Symbols, not discourses or discussions, do the most effective job of bringing into our awareness the realities of loving and being loved, living and struggling and dying together.[12]

God's message to us is Christ. Christ is our message to the world. Despite what fundamentalist Christians might think, we *speak* Christ nonverbally — the forgiving gesture, the warm smile, the angry protest, the value stand we take at work, the ballot we cast, the check we write, the time we spend and the care with which we spend it, the commitments we make. God *speaks* nonverbally, too. God speaks compassion and self-giving love in a person, and we receive that person in sacrament — in the sacramental community and in the mysteries of sacramental ritual.

Catholic Sacramental Rites

"The Lord be with you." "And also with you." This is the way we greet one another at the beginning of each sacramental rite. In this brief phrase, we speak the whole message. But what occurs thereafter is that same message expressed in ritual action, gesture, bodily activity, sensual contact. The message comes in fire and water, bread and wine, song and dance, colorful processions, the laying on of hands, anointing with oil, mutual embracing, silence, prostrations, incense. Words are spoken — probably too many words. But the words have a decidedly nonverbal context, and even the words are spoken metaphors: stories from the scriptures, ritual prayers, references to the cross, "This is my body, this is my blood."

The ritual environment (architecture, furnishings, the use of natural and electrical light, the way the space is structured and arranged, decorative ornaments, statues, and so on) sets a mood. At its best, it is warm and inviting, inspiring, comfortable, a place that facilitates communication and interaction between people. The *church,* however, is the people, the assembly, the community. The early Christians celebrated the mysteries in members' dining rooms. Some contemporary communities follow this same practice, though frequently choosing a living room. While church need not have a special building dedicated wholly to its liturgical activities, attention to the environment is, nonetheless, important. The space needs to provide an ambiance for a sacred encounter, and since the one remembered and made present is Jesus, overly lavish, expensive buildings seem oddly inappropriate as well. The gathered community, if it is true to its Lord, is dedicated to social revolution and radical egalitarianism, and the place of gathering should not be a garish contradiction of this mission.

The words of a traditional Hawaiian Catholic hymn say it all: "We come to tell our story. We come to break the bread. We come to celebrate our rising from the dead."[13] Sandra DeGidio expresses well the role of sacramental community:

> In sacraments, Christians gather to celebrate their belief in God and God's care through liturgical ritual. Liturgical celebration, or ritual, is a community's fullest expression of itself. Through story (the word) and symbolic actions, the art called ritual speaks to and of the whole person, the whole community. It makes tangible in symbol, gesture, word, and song the past, present, and future experience of our relationship with God, with others, and with the world.[14]

Baptism into the Lord

The most central Catholic sacraments are baptism and Eucharist. Baptism is the initiation rite that celebrates a threefold transition in the initiates' lives: the movement from sin to grace; a developing relationship of belonging and full participation in the community; and identification with Christ. The movement from sin to grace means recognizing those places in our lives where we are refusing the initiative of gracious mystery, where we are shutting down transcendence, and moving toward a heartfelt "yes" to the offer of grace. The movement toward belonging to community means establishing new relationships of friendship and support by sharing deeply the spiritual struggles we face in our life journey. Identifying with Christ means recognizing his story as our own and his openness to God as the path we choose. Since this sacrament is initiation, it is a prolonged process that takes place over several months, and can last as long as three years. During this process, which includes multiple public rites concluding with water immersion and an anointing with oil, the candidates reflect on their individual spiritual journeys, the events and circumstances in their own lives that draw them to Christianity, the movement of God's mysterious purpose in them. They engage the community in discussion about the Christian life and the particular ways in which this local community and its members are living that life. Each candidate develops a special relationship to a *sponsor* — a member of the community who serves as his or her mentor throughout the process. They are instructed in the traditions of Catholicism and learn to connect the central meanings and values with their own spiritual and moral struggles and issues and concerns in contemporary culture. They begin to participate in some community activities and the practical life of the church.

The final preparation for full initiation takes place during Lent, a season that lasts just over six weeks, beginning with Ash Wednesday and concluding with Easter. This time of forty days commemorates the Gospel accounts of Jesus' forty days in the wilderness at the beginning of his public ministry. Jesus prayed and fasted and faced down the temptations of Satan. During Lent the whole community engages in these practices with the initiates. It is a time of surrender to God (detachment) and a time of renewal and empowerment through retrieval of the spiritual center. It concludes with the celebration of the Easter Triduum: Holy Thursday, Good Friday, and the Easter Vigil.

The Easter Triduum

Holy Thursday commemorates the origins of Christian Eucharist in the bringing together of Jesus' table-fellowship, the Jewish traditions of Exodus and Passover, and his farewell to his disciples prior to his execution. The Gospels present a powerful story in which Jesus gathers with his disciples for a Passover seder the night before his death — "the last supper" or "the Lord's supper."[15] Jesus' death is interpreted sacrificially: he refuses to succumb to conventional wisdom and hierarchical dictates and surrenders instead to his *Abba;* he dies in order to effect the movement from slavery to freedom; he offers his body to be broken, his blood to be spilled. Jews celebrate Passover in the eating of the sacrificed lamb, a sacred meal that is shared with God. Likewise, Christians are to eat Jesus' body and drink his blood — a communion with him, a communion with God. Christians celebrate Jesus' passover from death to new life, identifying with him in breaking bread and sharing a common cup, in the eating and drinking, remembering his death and sharing in his new life.[16] A common Holy Thursday song is sung: "We remember how you loved us to your death, and still we celebrate, for you are with us here; and we believe that we will see you when you come in your glory, Lord. We remember, we celebrate, we believe."[17] The account of this event in the Gospel according to John narrates Jesus washing his disciples' feet, inviting them to do the same humble service for one another.

Most Catholic communities engage in mutual foot-washing on Holy Thursday as part of the celebration of this sacred night.

Good Friday commemorates Jesus' death. The Passion Story is read from the Gospel. The cross is venerated: "Behold, behold the wood of the cross, on which is hung our salvation. O come, let us adore."[18] The victims of oppression are remembered. Many Catholic communities spend part of the day in solemn public procession, visiting sites of pain and repression: prisons, AIDS hospices, public housing projects, military installations, and the like. At each site a comparison between contemporary suffering and the suffering of Jesus is made. Good Friday, like Ash Wednesday and all the Fridays of Lent, are days in which Catholics abstain from the eating of meat and take only a little food. It is a day of prayerful connection with the Jesus who was executed, but who was also vindicated by God in the resurrection. Connections are made to injustice and suffering today, in the confident hope that these, too, will be reversed by God's love and justice in and through the sacramental community's witness.

The Easter Vigil

Finally, the great day of Jesus' victory over death arrives in the celebration of *the Easter Vigil*. The night begins with the striking of a new fire in front of the gathering place. The paschal candle is inscribed and blessed: "Jesus Christ, the beginning and the end, the Alpha and the Omega. Jesus Christ, yesterday, today, and forever." The candle is lit, and the fire passed to the whole community with candles. The Easter "Alleluia" is intoned three times. The great prayer of thanksgiving and praise is sung: "The light of Christ surrounds us, the love of Christ enfolds us.... Let us fill every space with the sound of our joy, praising Christ, who is living among us. As this candle shines out through the darkness of night, may the love of Christ burn ever in our hearts."[19] Readings from scripture are proclaimed: beginning with the Genesis account of creation (because Easter is a new creation), continuing with the Exodus account of liberating passage through the Sea of Reeds (because Easter is a liberating passage), readings from the book of the Prophet Isaiah (because Easter is a return from exile), a reading from Baruch (because Easter is the revelation of Wisdom), from the book of the Prophet Ezekiel (because Easter is the gift of a new heart and a new spirit), from Paul's Letter to the Romans (because Easter is our baptism into his death and resurrection), and finally from the Gospel (because Easter is the good news of Jesus' resurrection).

The candidates for baptism profess their faith and are immersed in water: "I baptize you in the name of the Father, and of the Son, and of the Holy Spirit." They are anointed with oil (because they are one with the anointed one). They are clothed in a new garment (because they are a new creation). The whole community renews their baptismal vows: "Do you reject Satan?" "We do." "Do you believe in God? In Jesus Christ? In the holy catholic church?" "We do." The Easter Gloria is intoned: "Glory to God in the highest and peace to God's people on earth.... Lord, Jesus Christ, only Son of the Father, you alone are the holy one, you alone are the Lord, you alone are the most high... with the Holy Spirit in the glory of God the Father. Forever and ever. Amen." It is time to celebrate Eucharist — together with the new initiates.

The Eucharist

"Eucharist" means "giving thanks." It is the thankful remembering of Jesus and the grateful calling to mind of gracious mystery present in our lives and the world, transforming us and the world about us. Jesus was transformed by the Spirit. Bread and wine are transformed by the Spirit. The gathered community is transformed by the Spirit. The whole of creation is being transformed by the Spirit. *Transformation in and through grateful remembering* is the eucharistic action of the community, and this is symbolically dramatized in the breaking of bread, the sharing of wine — eating the body of Christ, drinking his blood, taking his life into ourselves. A life given for the *basileia* of God, a life received for the *basileia* of God. It is Jesus' table-fellowship continued in space and time. It is the Israelites' liberating exodus from slavery to freedom *now.* Jesus dies and is raised. We let go, surrender, only to receive the gift of numinous life, life in the numinous. The small ego is taken up into the corporate Christ, the compassionate one. *We become Christ* in the breaking and the sharing, in the eating and the drinking. We embody radical compassion to the world, in the world, for the world.[20]

"The Peace of Christ be with you." "And also with you." The community embraces one another as sign and symbol of radical reconciliation. The harmony that was intended from the beginning is realized ritually. All are one. Peace reigns. The community is committed to creating this reconciliation and peace everywhere. "Go in peace, to love and serve the Lord." "Thanks (eucharist) be to God."

Becoming Christ through the Liturgical Year

Every Sunday commemorates the day of resurrection. Every Sunday Catholics celebrate Christ's victory over sin and death. Every Sunday we gather for Eucharist — to eat his body and drink his blood, to become Christ for one another, radical compassion for the world. But every Sunday is different, because every Sunday throughout the year specifies remembering Christ and becoming Christ in a unique manner. The Catholic liturgical year begins with Advent, a time of waiting and hoping, commemorating the Israelites' longing for God's "Messiah" to appear, celebrating our own patient hope for the fullness of God's *basileia* in our lives and in the world. Advent begins just after Thanksgiving and is popularly understood as a preparation for Christmas, but it is much more: a season of remembering God's promises and God's fidelity to those promises, a season of longing and expectation for God's faithful action in history.

Hope for a Messiah

The Hebrew *messiah* means "anointed one," and it was applied to Israel's prophets and kings, who were anointed with oil as a sign of God's favor and God's authority operating in and through them. The great king in Israel's history was David. He united Israel's conflicted tribes and led them in battle against their common enemies. He created prosperity and justice among them and established them as a strong and independent nation. Israel saw God's deliverance and God's salvation mediated through David, particularly because the years after his death saw a return to internal conflict and division, social injustice, and eventually the end of the monarchy and their defeat and exile. The Jews longed for another David, one like David, a son of David — an "anointed one" sent by God to bring God's salvation to the people.

This longing for a messiah reached a fever pitch in the political dissonance experienced under Roman occupation. Apocalyptic consciousness merged messianism with a sense of cosmic struggle between the forces of evil (darkness) and the forces of good (light). God would send "one like David" to lead the forces of light in battle, in a dramatic final contest, to defeat forever the forces of darkness. The greater the dissonance, the greater the expectation for God's anointed one to come and to bring God's cosmic rule (*basileia*), vindicating God's people and vanquishing their enemies.

Into this highly charged religio-political atmosphere, first John the Baptist and then Jesus came proclaiming the nearness and presence of God's *basileia*. It is thus possible to see how Galilean peasants named him *messiah,* translated to the Greek as *Christos*. For them, this was God's anointed one, bringing God's salvation, conquering the demons, healing the people, establishing God's *basileia* in word and deed. When, after his death and the revelation of his resurrection, they developed a complete spiritual understanding of what God had done in Jesus, his birth was celebrated as the coming of the messiah. In him the promises of God were fulfilled, the hope of Israel realized, the victory over evil and darkness accomplished — and yet the struggle for the fullness of God's *basileia* continues until all oppression becomes compassion, until all conflict becomes peace, until justice reigns everywhere.

Advent, then, is a celebration of all this. It draws the community's focus toward hope for the rule of God mediated in and through one like David, God's anointed messiah. We remember Israel's hope, and that hope is cast into our longings for the future, recognizing the present dissonance, patiently waiting for compassion and peace, harmony and justice, to be fully realized everywhere.

The Birth of Christ

Christmas is celebrated at the winter solstice, where cold and darkness are everywhere in the northern hemisphere. It is a celebration of light, of the Light that comes into the darkness, bringing the radiant warmth of God's embodied compassion. Christmas means reconciliation for families, release of prisoners, compassion for the poor, peace. In the birth of Jesus, the messiah has come, and with him God's *basileia*. The longing of our hearts is given assurance: what we expect and hope for is certain and has already appeared in the birth of a child born in squalor, a child who would grow to heal and liberate, to proclaim the rule of God in word and deed and become himself the enfleshment of God's compassion. In the Christmas story, it is the poor (Joseph and Mary themselves, shepherds) and the spiritually wise (the magi) who recognize Jesus as the fulfillment of God's promises: messiah, Emmanuel (*God* with us). This messiah is a stark contrast to King Herod, who represents the fearful manipulation of power: the conventional wisdom of oppression and violence. Christmas celebrates the vulnerability of a poor child, and the spirit of God who comes among the lowly to save. It is sad irony that Christmas today for so many has become a materialistic orgy of buying and apolitical sentimentality — more darkness. In the sacramental community it is the joyful feast of God's promise enfleshed, acted out in surrender to the Light and compassion for the poor.[21]

The season of Epiphany follows: the Light that flickered dimly as hope in the Advent wreath has appeared and is made radiantly manifest. First Mary's and then Jesus' "yes" to God has occasioned the full self-communication of God to us. The incarnation of God in Christ is manifested. Jesus is presented in the Temple by his parents, and Simeon exclaims, "Your word has been fulfilled. My own eyes have seen the salvation which you have prepared in the sight of every people: a light to reveal you to the nations." (Luke 2:29–32). Epiphany recalls the prophet's saying from the book of Isaiah: "Arise, shine; for your light has come, and the glory of the Lord has risen upon you. For behold, darkness shall cover the earth, and thick darkness the peoples; but the Lord will arise upon you, and the glory of the Lord will be seen upon you. And nations shall come to your light" (Isa. 60:1–3). Jesus is baptized by John in the River Jordan: "I have baptized you with water; but one who is coming will baptize you with the Holy Spirit." Jesus calls the first disciples, who exclaim, "We have found the Messiah!" (John 1:41). Jesus rebukes the demon, who recognizes divine power manifest: "I know who you are, the Holy One of God." Jesus heals the sick and exorcises the demons, and Peter says, "Everyone is searching for you" (Mark 1:37).

Pentecost

After the celebration of Lent and Easter, the light made manifest in Jesus descends upon the disciples at Pentecost as tongues of fire. This was originally a Jewish feast, recalling the giving of the Law at Sinai and celebrating the first fruits of the harvest. Christians rethink this feast from the perspective of their experience of Jesus, celebrating the giving of the Spirit to them (replacing the Law) and the first fruits of their preaching to the nations ("That very day about three thousand were added to their number," Acts 2:41). The fire witnessed by Moses on Mount Sinai, which burned but did not consume, now resides as tongues of fire in the community of disciples, and the prophecy of Joel is recalled: "In the days to come...I will pour out my spirit on all mankind. Their sons and daughters shall prophesy, your young men shall see visions, your old men shall dream dreams. Even on my slaves, men and women, in those days, I will pour out my spirit" (Acts 2:17–18). And Jesus says, "I have cast fire upon the world, and see, I am guarding it until it blazes."

The sacramental community burns with the compassion of God, and we are enlightened by the Spirit of Wisdom. Called to become now a light unto the world, the empty and the lowly are filled with the same Spirit that animated Jesus' *basileia* mission. The breath of God (*pneuma*) that filled Jesus, making him Spirit-filled prophet, fills us, and we are called to be Spirit-filled prophets — a prophetic community, the *politeuma* (*polis* + *pneuma*). The sacramental community sings, "Send down the fire of your justice, send down the rains of your love; come, send down the Spirit, breathe life in your people, and we shall be the people of God."[22]

Reconstructing Sacramental Community

Pope John XXIII wanted Vatican II to ignite "a second Pentecost." The enthusiasm of those early communities would be recaptured today in a reformed and renewed Catholicism — a network of vital faith communities that would take the fire of Pentecost into their hearts and set the earth ablaze. The Council ordered the revision of the sacramental rites, focusing them on the community's transformation. Sacraments are meant to facilitate a communal experience of transformed perception: we see and understand ourselves and our world, our work and our relationships, the environment and the human in a radically different way — open to, and bearing within, the gracious, compassionate, and transforming mystery! In sacramental ritual, we reconnect with the divine mediated in creation and history, and we reenact the Great Story of Jesus' healing liberation — for ourselves and through us for the world. Social dissonance is ritually overcome, and we know the presence of God here and now. This is the font and source of our transforming and liberating work in everyday living.

A New Understanding of Church

A reconstructed Catholicism is located in renewed parishes and small faith communities.[23] Full awareness and participation in ritual and a genuine sense of belonging and mutual responsibility are characteristic of these gatherings, as well as a sense of mission to and for the larger community. Reconstructing church today requires a number of shifts, described here by Brazilian theologian Marcello Azevedo:

- A shift from clerical hegemony to the active presence of lay people in the work of the church;

- A shift from an overly spiritualistic approach to an evangelization of the whole of humanity — body and soul, individual and community, society and culture;

- A shift from the individual as the final *object* of evangelization to being the active *subject* of the evangelization of the world at large;

- A shift from a hierarchical protective church to one open to self-transformation;

- A shift from seeing transformation as something juridical and organizational to something operating from the bottom up, new patterns of social relations founded on participation and communion;

- A shift from the primacy of theoretical elaboration to paying attention to reality and experience as the starting point for all reflection.[24]

These shifts in the way we think about and structure church are retrievals from the Christian movement in its earliest years. The focus is on laity, the real issues and concerns of their everyday lives, mobilized for personal, social, and cultural change. Juridical consciousness located "church" in the authoritarian structures that emerged in Christianity's marriage with culture after Constantine. Today, however, we find *faith community* as the new definition of "church."

Cultural Deconstruction and the Need for Community

The loss of community is perhaps the most immediately felt result of today's deconstructed world. The Enlightenment's celebration of individualism has combined with dislocating demographic shifts from rural to urban environments and an alienating economic order that separates people from nature and from the products of their labor. The result is the loss of cultural moorings and personal meaning and a sense of isolation. Leonardo Boff contends that "modern society has violated the principles needed for the development of community, resulting in atomization and anonymity. Persons have become lost in the mechanisms of macro-organization. But there has been a reaction from the grassroots, where *communiogenesis* is taking place."[25] There is a hunger to belong, to connect, to find communal meaning in mutual bonding, shared purpose, and the intimacy of friendship. Catholicism is responding to these hungers differently in various parts of the world. For example, a recent study suggests that the *comunidades de base* movement (basic ecclesial communities, small faith communities) in Latin America is largely a response to "the shock of modernity" that produced wide-scale and rapid dislocation and uprooting, shattering the rural pattern of community that had previously sustained Latin Americans:

> Modernity and its cultivation of the autonomous individual came full force to Latin America only in the past two generations. The result has been the immediate and keenly felt loss of community. While Northern European peoples had more slowly over an extended period become used to, and even championed individualism, to the Iberians of Latin America this cultural change has come as a sudden shock. In the crisis resulting from this disrupted way of life, it has become incumbent upon these people to recapture community. And they have done this in a new form of church — the basic ecclesial community.... Today there are as many as 100,000 groups in Brazil alone. In the basic ecclesial communities, the people... relate the experiences in the Scriptures to the experiences of their day — wages insufficient to provide food, shelter, and clothing; no medical care; inadequate education; political brutality. This reflection and religious consciousness-raising call forth present response — action expressed politically, seeking a change in the oppressive political structure of *status quo*.[26]

The *comunidades de base* movement has become widespread in Latin America, in part, because of the impetus it was given in two sub-continental gatherings of pastoral leaders: in 1968 at Medellín and in 1979 at Puebla. At these two meetings Latin American Catholic leadership developed pastoral strategies designed to translate and contextualize the vision of Vatican II — something like a plan for reconstructing Catholicism. The result was a very conscious effort on the part of the Latin American church to create *comunidades de base* as the embodiment of Vatican II's new understanding of church.[27]

The deconstruction of society and culture is more subtle in North America and Europe, but no less real. And here, in contrast to the Latin American situation, church leadership has given very little attention to the development of small communities. Nonetheless, the small community movement, though less prevalent here, is clearly a direction that more and more Catholics are taking.[28] We find it particularly in affinity groups experiencing oppression from the dominant culture—groups such as Dignity (a network of faith communities made up of gay and lesbian Catholics) and Women-Church (feminist Catholics who gather for support and ritual prayer). Or groups in conscious and faith-based resistance to the dominant culture — groups like the Ploughshares communities (Catholic peace activists engaged in civil disobedience to protest militarism and weapons of mass violence) and the Catholic Worker houses (a movement founded by Dorothy Day as a response to poverty and human need). Small faith communities are emerging among those seeking recovery from addiction, blending Twelve Step principles with Catholic spirituality, and as faith-based support groups for the divorced, families grieving the death of a child, people who have tested positive to the HIV-virus, those battling cancer, parents of adolescents in crisis, people suffering from chronic physical pain, and on and on. In such groups the insights of psychotherapy combine with the deep currents of forgiveness and healing in Catholic spirituality and with explicit attempts to embody mutual compassion.

Small Communities Everywhere

But one can find small faith communities emerging in more mainstream places as well. Unlike Latin America, it is not political oppression, military violence, or massive poverty that challenges us to seek community. "The problem of *underdevelopment* is not the major concern of most of the us in the U.S. On the contrary,...the major motive for the quest for community on the part of many in the U.S. is *overdevelopment*. Overdevelopment entails ease of mobility, an often alienated lifestyle, the anesthetic effect of material goods, loss of rootedness, and the like."[29] Catholics in the U.S. seek community to overcome their sense of isolation, to find their true selves in relationship with other equals, to be liberated from the definitions given them by a ubiquitous economic consciousness.

Faith and work groups bring business executives together to share the dissonance of faith and business and to find ways to better integrate them. Occupational groups (health care workers, teachers, lawyers) share the insights of faith on issues and concerns common to their professions. Keep Lent groups form in mainstream parishes to pray together over the Lenten scriptures, sharing the themes and practices of this liturgical season. Pastoral initiatives such as RENEW, Christ Renews His Parish, Cursillo, and Marriage En-

counter, create small faith communities in which people find the
support of friendship in sharing their struggles to live the Gospel
faithfully today. Some parishes develop neighborhood communities
for the celebration of Eucharist in people's homes. Increasingly families understand themselves as the domestic church, spending time
together in prayer and reflection. The examples of small community experiments multiply each year, and as the numbers of ordained
clergy rapidly decrease, an increasing number of such communities
become bolder in their sacramental activity. Discussion and shared
prayer among lay people becomes symbolic ritual as the level of
trust grows and the hunger for such communal spiritual expression
is voiced. Catholics find their true spiritual home in sacramental
community, and only when the experience of sacrament and the experience of community combine do they experience their gatherings
as truly Catholic.

A caveat raised by many today is the need to maintain a balance
between two values in tension: *ecclesia* (large gatherings of Catholic
believers, most often experienced in the parish at weekend liturgies)
and *koinonia* (smaller units that gather around felt needs or some
other common bond to pray, share life experience, and reflect on key
meanings and values from the tradition).

> *Ecclesia* can be a heartfelt experience, a meaningful experience, if
> wedded to *koinonia,* genuine experiences, on a regular basis, of the
> essence of church....In *koinonia* there is both *accountability* and
> *responsibility* around the dynamics of word, prayer, service, and
> fellowship. In *ecclesia* there may not be that accountability or respon-
> sibility. Persons can literally hide, divorced and alienated from each
> other — anonymous to each other.[30]

A similar caveat is raised regarding the need to maintain balance in
the tension between local church and the global or universal church.
A popular misunderstanding frequently sees the local church as a
kind of "branch office" of the *real* church, which is the Vatican.
But theologians are quick to point out that the particular church is
the universal church concretized and historicized. "It is the universal
church happening," says Leonardo Boff.

> The universal church is wholly in the particular church. The universal
> church does not exist in the way things exist....It only manifests itself
> in the particular church. Rome is not the universal church, it is a
> particular church, though it is *the* particular church constituted as
> the sign of the unity of the universal church present in *all* particular

churches.... The particular church is the church wholly but not the whole church.[31]

Since local church as *ecclesia* and *koinonia* are part of a larger network of such gatherings, it is important that lines of communication (for both mutual support and critique) be established and maintained with other assemblies and communities. Such networking need not be bureaucratic and juridical; rather, a pastoral networking grounded in faith in the one Jesus and the one *basileia* and seeking fidelity to these can affirm a wide variety of diverse expressions of church. Symbolizing and celebrating the unity of these gatherings, an important Catholic value, can be accomplished best, not through juridically imposed compliance, but through communication and networking for common purpose. Both the local expressions of church and an effective pastoral networking, however, require able and visionary leadership today — a critical need in today's Catholicism.

Ministry and Leadership

Since Vatican II there has been a simultaneous decline in the number of ordained clergy and an explosion of lay ministry.[32] Many priests have resigned their ordination in order to marry or simply out of frustration with the juridical structures they no longer value. Fewer men are seeking ordination, and the Vatican continues to restrict women from ordained office. Meanwhile, the numbers of lay people who work professionally or as volunteers in ministry has expanded dramatically. In fact, at most gatherings of Catholic pastoral ministers, lay people outnumber the clergy, and women outnumber men. Lay people work as ministers in diocesan offices, in parishes, in hospitals, schools, universities; in religious education, liturgy, spiritual direction, pastoral care, administration, and social outreach. There is virtually no ministry in which lay people don't function, and increasingly as leaders — which explains why not everyone interprets fewer priests as "a shortage."

Some see the declining number of clergy as a problem, while others see it as an opportunity, interpreting the declericalization of Catholicism as a positive value. Nonetheless, there is a growing concern about *quality leadership* that is widely shared — by clergy and lay people alike. Will there be competent and skilled women and men of deep faith to lead the Catholic experience in the future? There is evidence that the number of lay people who leave the ministry (because of low salaries and poor benefits, or because of their own inability to work creatively and with agency in juridical structures that restrict their ability to influence decisions and effect change) is far greater than the number of resigned clergy. The issue of quality leadership for tomorrow's Catholicism leads us to the need to reconstruct ministry.

Reconstructing Ministry

The experience of vital sacramental community requires the reconstructing of Catholic ministry. We need people (women and men) who have caught the vision of reconstructing Catholicism to begin to assume the responsibility of leadership — at every level of church (small communities, parishes, the global pastoral network). The passive stance that lay people have assumed, waiting for clergy and hierarchy to take the lead and show the way, will simply not do, nor will a dependent looking to juridical structures. This is particularly the case as we look to this generation of young people and project the future of Catholicism. People of faith, young and old and in-between, must look to themselves and begin to recognize that *they are the church,* and its ministry and leadership is in their hands. Asserting their spiritual needs, creating and sustaining sacramental community, becoming Christ for the world — this is the challenge of leadership today.

Ministry is grounded in *charis.* From the earliest years of Christianity, *all* the faithful are called to ministry and mission, each according to his or her charism. It is according to the way that we have experienced grace that we are called to ministry. Each of us has gifts to bring to the ministry (the ability to listen compassionately, to speak with eloquence, to oversee, to inspire, to heal divisions, to create the worship environment, to make the liturgy come alive with music and song, to forge new initiatives to make justice and peace, and so forth). But our individual charisms are not just our talents. "Charism" refers also to the ways in which we experience brokenness and the need for God's radical compassion. What we bring to the ministry is not only our intelligence and eloquence, but also our particular form of emptiness (and therefore openness). The alcoholic brings his alcoholism. The couple who have lost a child bring that painful experience. The one who has suffered racism or sexism brings her anger to ministry. But all believers are called to full participation in ministry, each according to his or her unique and special charism.[33]

The ontological distinction between clergy and lay, active and passive, those who minister and those who are ministered to, is an unfortunate historical development in Christianity. It led to a double-standard of discipleship: those who were really called to follow Christ, to represent him, and to embody his ministry and mission; and the merely baptized, who are totally dependent on those who represent and embody Christ to broker their salvation. No such distinction can be found in the New Testament, nor is it worthy of a reconstructed Catholicism. Ordination is a community designation of ministry function and a celebration of the ordained's charism. It is a further specification of one's baptismal commitment. But it is *not* becoming "more than" or "higher than" or "over" other members of the community. And such commitment to function ministerially need not be forever. We need to rethink and reform ministry, not simply extend the present problematic orders to women and married persons. We need a diversity of ministries and, no doubt, a diversity of ordinations, many people designated to act on behalf of the community to effect and symbolize the *basileia* of God in Christ.

Gifts That Differ, a Variety of Ministerial Roles

Still, to say that all the baptized are called to full discipleship and thus to participation in ministry and mission leaves open the manner of such participation. Because we have different charisms, we have different roles, different functions, different responsibilities, different opportunities, different limitations. So there is great variety and diversity in ministry, and not all are called to leadership. Leadership is a particular charism, and those who have this gift need to come forward today to share it with the church. Certainly not all who hold the juridical office of leadership (pope, bishops, pastors) have this charism, and one simply cannot assume that those who hold juridical office will be able to lead. Leadership emerges from the dynamic interplay between the individual's self-understanding and the community's recognition of this charism, and ordination ought to celebrate this in the sacramental community. Thomas O'Meara identifies six characteristics that shape a definition of ministry: "Ministry is (1) doing something; (2) for the advent of the kingdom; (3) in public; (4) on behalf of a Christian community; (5) which is a gift received in faith, baptism and ordination; and which is (6) an activity with its own limits and identity within a diversity of ministerial actions."[34]

As leaders emerge to assume responsibility within the communities of faith, they will need support in developing their skills and knowledge, but the idea of ministry as a distinct profession, including the way one earns one's living, is an open question in a reconstructed Catholicism. Certainly not all community leaders will be financially supported by the church. They will need to exercise their leadership as paraprofessionals, earning their living as electricians, teachers, nurses, physicians, plumbers, and so on. If Catholicism is to flourish and prosper, however, we will need some full-time, paid leaders (bishops?), whose role as church leaders will constitute a lifetime commitment — people whose careers are in ministry. Finding ways of selecting and supporting such persons and defining their role is a formidable challenge in a Catholicism that emphasizes spiritual experience and full awareness and participation of all the faithful.

Beyond the Sacramental Community

Our focus in this chapter on the importance of sacramental community in the Catholic experience leads us beyond such an experience to the roles we play, individually and collectively, in the larger community. We are formed for mission in and through our experience of sacramental community, and we rely on its support and nurturance in doing *basileia*. But the church doesn't exist for itself; its mission is in and for the world. The *basileia* proclaimed by Christ does not end in a network of vital faith communities, but inspires them to transform and re-create the whole of existence beyond those faith communities. The gathered church is scattered, sent to love and serve the Lord. We need to look at the liberating role that individuals, the community, and the whole network of communities are called to play in the world.

— Chapter 7 —

The Experience of Liberation

If persons and communities follow Jesus and proclaim the kingdom
of God to the poor; if they strive for liberation from every kind of
slavery; if they seek, for all human beings, especially for that immense
majority of men and women who are crucified persons, a life in conformity with the dignity of daughters and sons of God...if, in the
discipleship of Jesus, they effectuate their own conversion from being
oppressor to being men and women of service...and if they do all
this in the following and discipleship of Jesus because he did all this
himself — then they believe in Jesus.... If they abide with God in the
cross of Jesus and in the numberless crosses of history; and if in spite
of all this their hope is mightier than death — then they believe in the
God of Jesus.

— Jon Sobrino, *Jesus in Latin America*

Over the last few decades, a real alternative in American religious
life has emerged.... A prophetic spiritual movement for social change
has been steadily growing and is making a difference in the institutions of both religion and society.... It relates biblical faith to social
transformation; personal conversion to the cry of the poor; theological reflection to care for the environment; core religious values to
new economic priorities; the call of community to racial and gender
justice; morality to foreign policy; spirituality to politics; and, at its
best, it transcends the categories of liberal and conservative that have
captivated both religion and politics.

— Jim Wallis, *The Soul of Politics*

The experience of Christ and grace in sacramental community is a
path toward liberation, the liberation of individuals from their enslavement to all that is not God and God's *basileia* through a lifetime
process of conversion, and the liberation of all creation from indifference, injustice, and violence through the patient witness of the
sacramental community in solidarity with the unloved, the poor, the
oppressed, the violated. These two dimensions of liberation go together: personal conversion and social transformation. One is set
free from one's small ego-encapsulated self and embraces the larger

self, the whole self, the self that is imaged in Christ. The experience of liberation is a turning to others in compassionate service, identifying with the marginated other in one's recognition of one's own marginated status.

Here we should recall what was said in chapter 4: that the origins of Christianity lie in a peasant movement for justice grounded in the compassion and wisdom of God active in life and history. Dominic Crossan's succinct historical insight is clear:

> [Jesus] had both a religious dream *and* a social program, and it was that conjunction that got him killed. The Roman Empire may have regularly abused its power, but it seldom wasted it. It did not crucify teachers or philosophers; it usually just exiled them permanently or cleared them out of Rome periodically. Indeed, if Jesus had been only a matter of words or ideas, the Romans would have probably ignored him, and we would probably not be talking about him today. His kingdom movement, however, with its healings and exorcisms, was action and practice, not just thought and theory.[1]

In the liberation experience, all that has been said about Jesus, about grace, and about sacramental community meets the concrete dynamics of history. Here, in a new and more powerful awareness, we recognize that Jesus really died, that his own solidarity with the poor and the oppressed led to his violent demise. Here, in a new and more powerful awareness, we see that the dynamics of conversion — of saying yes to God's offer of grace and no to sin — makes us vulnerable to the brutal power of human systems and their terrible violence, that entering into the *basileia* experience puts us in jeopardy with the powers that rule this world. Here, in a new and more powerful awareness, we understand that as the body of Christ in history the sacramental community is called to embody and act on the same compassionate love that animated Jesus, that going into the water in baptism and breaking bread in his memory, if these actions are truly authentic, also means suffering love for the oppressed and courageous moral action on their behalf. The eucharistic hymn sung by Christians today brings this home:

> *Pan de Vida, cuerpo del Señor,*
> [Bread of Life, body of the Lord.]
> cup of blessing, blood of Christ the Lord.
> At this table the last shall be first,
> *poder es servir, porque Dios es amor.*
> [power is for service, because God is Love.][2]

The Basis of Catholic Morality

This experience of liberation is the basis for the Catholic moral tradition. Catholicism calls the individual to a continuous process of moral conversion, seeking liberation from sin and complete surrender to God in Christ, growing in the patterns of love and justice; and it calls the church community to a continuous process of social transformation, seeking social structures and public policies that affirm and protect the dignity of every person. The experience of liberation — of being liberated oneself and of collaborating (conspiring) in the liberation of others — is simultaneously the most challenging and the most affirming dimension of contemporary Catholicism, the most daring and yet the most attractive aspect of pursuing the Catholic path. In liberation, we abandon whatever false selves we've created to win acceptance and approval and gain the courage to accept our own acceptance, to assert our own needs and our own dignity, to claim our human rights. In liberation, we find solidarity with every oppressed/repressed/suppressed person, helping others assert their dignity and claim their rights. In liberation, we become hungry for justice and seek after peace, passionately giving ourselves to the work of transforming the structures of poverty and oppression, codependency and addiction, violence and death, into God's *basileia* of loving compassion and radical egalitarianism.

This is a difficult struggle, because it means change and transformation, becoming vulnerable in solidarity with the most vulnerable, risking the safety and security of our present arrangements and identifying with those at the edge, the victims, the nobodies. Here we let go of other rules and give ourselves to the rule of God, let go of our own controlling and surrender to a compassionate God who loves the poor, the suffering, and the outcast. Liberation is a real dying, but it is a death that hope compels. It is also a real rising in which we transcend fear and the self controlled by fear, finding new vitality and new power in God's lifting up of the lowly. Again, Crossan helps us see the basis of all this in Jesus:

> The Kingdom movement was Jesus' program of empowerment for a peasantry becoming steadily more hard-pressed through insistent taxation, attendant indebtedness, and eventual land expropriation, all within increasing commercialization in the expanding colonial economy of a Roman Empire under Augustan peace and a Lower Galilee under Herodian urbanization. Jesus *lived,* against the systemic injustice and structural evil of that situation, an alternative open to all who would accept it: a life of open healing and shared eating, of radical

itinerancy, programmatic homelessness, and fundamental egalitarianism, of human contact without discrimination, and of divine contact
without hierarchy.[3]

Domination and Liberation in Latin America

Contemporary Catholicism draws its focus on liberation from the
poor's struggle to overcome economic and political domination in
Latin America in recent decades. That struggle became thematized
in the work of theologian Gustavo Gutiérrez (A Theology of Liberation, 1973), in documents emerging from meetings of Latin American
bishops (at Medellín, Colombia, in 1968; and at Puebla, Mexico,
in 1979), and now among a whole generation of Latin American
theologians.[4] The remote background for the contemporary Latin
American liberation movement is European domination and control
of that continent through political colonialism. The more immediate
background is North American domination and control through economic colonialism. The inspiration for making liberation a theme of
Christian thought and praxis is the Second Vatican Council, particularly its crowning document "The Church in the Modern World."
The Council's teaching was further clarified by the 1971 international
synod of bishops, which published a forceful statement, *Justice in the
World.*

Gutiérrez reflects on the contemporary focus on liberation in his
"Introduction to the Revised Edition" of his book *A Theology of
Liberation:*

> What we have often called the "major fact" in the life of the Latin
> American church — the participation of Christians in the process of
> liberation — is simply an expression of a far-reaching historical event:
> *the irruption of the poor.* Our time bears the imprint of the new
> presence of those who in fact used to be "absent" from our society
> and from the church. By "absent" I mean: of little or no importance,
> and without the opportunity to give expression themselves to their
> sufferings, their camaraderies, their plans, their hopes.[5]

The new presence of the formerly absent — because of their courageous assertion of their dignity, their needs, their demands for justice,
and because the retrieval of biblical faith has created solidarity with
them and their cause among Christians worldwide — this is the heart
of the liberation experience today. It is a reversal of long-standing
patterns of domination and exploitation, in which Christians had
abandoned the oppressed and the poor in a theology of conquest and

"just wars," a theology of religious exclusivity and worldly success, a theology of private and personal salvation in heaven, a theology of partnership with worldly rulers. All of this is tied to juridical consciousness and the merger of Christianity with imperial power in the fourth century. Reconstructing Catholicism means a theology of liberation — liberation from juridical consciousness and from the partnerships with power that had rendered the church power*less* in effecting the reign of God in history.[6]

In Latin America, Spanish conquest of indigenous peoples was followed by centuries of colonial exploitation, during which time the invaders appropriated the land, the wealth, and the power. In the nineteenth century, however, the indigenous and mixed populations began to wage wars of independence from European rule in a series of uprisings and revolutions. Nonetheless, political colonialism was followed by economic colonialism, a shift from overt control to covert control, with economic manipulators from abroad now joining forces with indigenous manipulators at home. The result was a society in which a few were very rich and powerful and the rest were very poor and powerless:

> Vast numbers of Latin Americans came to believe that the so-called help extended to them by the United States, Canada, and other developed countries only increased their economic and political dependency. It widened the gap between the few who were well off and the great majority who were pushed more deeply into poverty. What these Latin Americans demanded was independence from the international economic system with its center in the north. They wanted to develop a more self-reliant economy that would produce the foods and the goods needed by the people that would make use of simple, labour-intensive technology, that would offer employment to the masses. They called this liberation.[7]

Meanwhile, the church had become

> increasingly identified with the rich and the powerful, who saw that religion was a good thing, useful in keeping the masses submissive through promises of an eternal reward in heaven if they made no trouble on earth. And it went hand in glove with a theory of the divine right of rulers over subjects — a European legacy that also brooked no uprisings from below and assured divine sanction for the status quo.[8]

All of this began to change in the 1960s, when political agitation for liberation combined with a shifting religious consciousness to produce a growing sense that the situation of poverty and oppression had become morally intolerable and required radical transformation.

Key to this development were the social encyclicals of John XXIII
and the teachings of Vatican II.

Catholic Social Teaching

The dominant focus of Catholic doctrine in the past century has
been its social teaching. From the pontificate of Leo XIII, which began in 1878, up to the present, Catholic leaders have spoken boldly
about social, political, and economic problems and the implications
of Christian faith for public life. This growing body of Catholic social
teaching is about human dignity, human rights, and the responsibility of individuals and social institutions to insure that those rights
are honored; about the importance of the common good and the role
of government in protecting and promoting it; about the scandal of
modern war and of spending billions on weapons of mass destruction
and the critical need to address the widening gap between the rich
and the poor; about the excesses of individualism, private ownership,
materialism, and consumerism, and the need to put the needs of the
poor first; about the structures of social sin and the need to reconfigure global systems. Taken together it provides a radical critique of
modern society and a principled vision of transformation. Ironically,
it has also been used to critique the church's internal life, calling the
church to practice itself what it preaches to others.

While this body of teaching is sometimes called "our best-kept secret" (because so many people, including Catholics, know little about
it), many contemporary Catholics have sought to make it practical in
a wide variety of imaginative and creative programs and initiatives,
increasingly in concert with people of other faiths or no religious
stance who share our social concern and the underlying values that
prompt a vision of social transformation. Nonetheless, Catholic social teaching is a startling departure from much of Catholic history,
reversing centuries of church alignment with the rich and powerful,
with the process of colonization and the oppression of indigenous
peoples, with patriarchal sexism and the domination of women. It
overturns common assumptions about Catholicism and challenges
deeply inbred patterns of domination and submission that continue
to characterize so much of the church.

Modern Catholic social teaching begins with Leo XIII's encyclical letter *Rerum Novarum* (1891), a response to the Industrial
Revolution that insists that wages be determined not by economic
considerations alone, but by taking into account the basic needs of

individuals. Workers' rights must be respected and honored. Justice demands that the common good of the community take precedence over individual gain in determining economic policy. Ownership of property, while a legitimate right, is subject to social and moral constraints.

Forty years later, Pius XI published *Quadragesimo Anno* (1931) as a follow-up encyclical to that of Leo. Here we find the use of a new phrase, "social justice," to describe "the type of justice that demanded due recognition of the common good, a good which included, and did not contradict, the authentic good of each and every person.... This provided the foundation for the balancing of political and civil with social and economic rights."[9] In the midst of the Great Depression and on the eve of World War II, the pope appealed for a return to religious and moral authority as a way out of the crisis that Europe faced. He suggested structures of economic self-government modeled on the medieval guilds as an alternative to capitalism and socialism:

> These structures would bring workers and managers together in joint organizations to determine policy for the industry as a whole, with a council of industry representatives determining overall national economic policy. Based on the law of justice and infused with a sense of social responsibility and Christian charity... such a system would not simply be another method of social organization, but the *Christian social order.*[10]

John XXIII and Vatican II

Catholic social teaching took a giant leap during the pontificate of John XXIII (1958–63). His two major encyclicals, *Mater et Magistra* (1961) and *Pacem in Terris* (1963), reflect a new and flexible openness as well as an urgency in a world that was rapidly changing, made ever more dangerous by the nuclear threat posed by both sides in the Cold War. John emphasized two critical imperatives: (1) the need to bridge the widening gap between rich and poor in an increasingly interrelated world; and (2) the importance of disarmament through the building of mutual trust among nations. In addressing both of these urgent problems, he balanced the traditional church doctrine that authority is derived from God with a new appeal for individuals to assert claims against governments:

> Since the right to command is required by the moral order and has its source in God, it follows that, if civil authorities legislate for or allow

anything that is contrary to that order and therefore contrary to the will of God, neither the laws made nor the authorizations granted can be binding on the consciences of the citizens, since *we must obey God rather than men.* (emphasis added)

He goes on to quote Thomas Aquinas: "Insofar as it falls short of right reason, a law is said to be a wicked law; and so, lacking the true nature of law, it is rather a kind of violence."[11] This new, revolutionary focus on conscience is further underlined: "If any government does not acknowledge the rights of man or violates them, it not only fails in its duty, but its orders completely lack juridical force."[12] This teaching is tantamount to calling for civil disobedience and mass uprisings — both of which became important features of Catholic life in its aftermath in Catholic protests against the war in Vietnam in the U.S. and in growing revolutionary resistance among Catholics in Latin America.

Two quotes from *Pacem in Terris* illustrate a movement toward liberating innovation in John's teaching. In his discussion of human rights, both political and economic, John emphasizes the dignity of the human person and government's role in promoting, protecting, and maintaining the rights of all. But he adds this: "He who possesses certain rights has likewise *the duty to claim those rights as marks of his dignity,* while all other have the obligation to acknowledge those rights and respect them."[13] In his critique of the arms race, he points out that arms expenditures deprive individuals and nations of the economic goods necessary for social progress and causes people to live in constant fear. But, again, he goes further, alluding to "the terrible destructive force of modern arms" and "the horror aroused in the mind by the very thought of the cruel destruction and immense suffering which the use of those armaments would bring to the human family." And then this celebrated reversal of the broad assumption that wars are "just wars": "It is hardly possible to imagine that in the atomic era war could be used as an instrument of justice."[14] To suggest the claiming of one's rights as a moral obligation and the waging of war as morally impossible — these are radical shifts in Catholic teaching, and they created the context for Catholic participation in socially transforming activities. But John's greatest contribution in moving the church toward liberation was the Council he summoned and the leadership he provided it.

Vatican II represents real change for the Catholic tradition. It foreshadows reconstructing Catholicism in at least six important breakthroughs: (1) its emphasis on religious liberty and freedom of conscience (which signals an end to religious exclusivism and opens the church to selective Catholicism); (2) its new emphasis on the nurturance of mutual love as one of the purposes of human sexuality (which signals an end to the procreative ethic and opens the church to a more positive stance toward human sexual behavior); (3) its focus on the retrieval of origins (which turns the church toward Jesus and the beginning Christian experiences); (4) its mandate to "read the signs of the times" (which makes relevance and communication criteria for pastoral effectiveness); (5) its description of church as "the people of God" (which led to an egalitarian sense of church and opened the way toward lay participation and responsibility in mission and ministry); and (6) its focus on the whole church as sign and instrument of the kingdom of God (which turned the church outward, its mission focused on human rights, justice, and peace).

The crowning document produced by the Council is its *Pastoral Constitution on the Church in the Modern World* (1965). O'Brien and Shannon point to five elements that are central to the document: personalism, the social nature of the person, the relation between the church and the world, justice, and development:[15]

- *Personalism:* a doctrine of human dignity and individual rights that focuses on the person and validates the claim of the person over and against society.

- *Our Social Nature:* individuals, though centers of freedom and individual responsibility, are not solitary beings; they are social and interdependent, and can neither live nor attain their full potential by themselves.

- *Church in Service to Humanity:* the church is called to have a healing and elevating impact on the dignity of the person, to strengthen the seams of human society and imbue everyday activity with a deeper meaning and importance — to contribute toward making the human family and its history more human.

- *Justice:* the church is called to help examine the values of life, defend human dignity, promote human rights, and build up the human family — to pursue justice by seeking more humane and just conditions of life and directing institutions to guaranteeing human dignity.

- *Development:* the goal of complete human fulfillment of all people demands that wealthier nations help poor ones and that economic and social structures be reformed.

The spirit of this document — and of the Council itself — can be glimpsed in an extended quote:

Persons should regard their lawful possessions not merely as their own but also as common property in the sense that they should accrue to the benefit not only of themselves but of others. For the rest, the right to have a share of earthly goods sufficient for oneself and one's family belongs to everyone.... Persons are obliged to come to the relief of the poor, and to do so not merely out of their superfluous goods. If a person is in extreme necessity, such a one has the right to take from the riches of others what he or she needs.... According to their ability, let all individuals and governments undertake a genuine sharing of their goods. Let them use these goods especially to provide individuals and nations with the means for helping and developing themselves.[16]

The church in Latin America was led immediately to focus on liberation in their efforts to implement the Council's teachings.

Medellín and Puebla

In the wake of the Council, Catholics in Latin America began forming small base communities committed to social justice. They studied the scriptures, prayed together, supported one another, and initiated collective efforts to assert their rights. They organized village councils and labor unions, protested against oppressive practices, and developed projects to improve their lives (clean water, better housing, work co-ops). For these Christians, "liberation" had religious meaning: the God of the Bible was on their side, on the side of the poor and oppressed. The God who liberated Israel from Egyptian bondage, the God who spoke through the prophets against exploitation, the God who wanted justice instead of burnt offerings — this God was on their side, supporting them in their struggle for liberation. And they saw Jesus as continuous with this Hebrew tradition:

He called the poor blessed, not because misery was a good thing, but because he believed a radical transformation was about to take place.... These Christians recognized that Jesus was a threat to the established order. Like many Latin Americans who challenged the established order, he had been tortured and executed. Yet when God raised him from the dead, God vindicated all the victims of history.[17]

As these Christians were joined by priest-theologians, this understanding of a socially engaged liberation approach to faith was collected and systematized, eventuating in the beginnings of "liberation theology." The focus was less on personal sin and salvation and increasingly on social transformation:

What was new and startling in the Latin American reading of the Gospel was that the passage from sin to new life involved not only personal but also social transformation. In other words, the Christian Gospel has a political thrust. The religious message of Jesus has ethical and political implications. It condemns injustice and calls for a social order that reflects God's will for humanity. The Gospel is a subversive message.[18]

When the bishops of Latin America, who as early as 1955 had already founded CELAM (Consejo Episcopal Latinoamericano, the Latin America Episcopal Council), met in 1968 at Medellín, Colombia, they sought to implement the Council's teachings by turning to liberation theology and the base community movement. The Medellín documents *Peace, Justice, Poverty,* and *Education* present a revolutionary analysis of Latin American poverty and dependency and endorse the struggle for economic and political liberation as well as the *comunidades de base* as a means for converting the poor.

> Medellín has become known as the conference in which the church chose to stand with the oppressed, attacked the political and economic structures of Latin America as purveyors of injustice, pointed out the unjust dependency of Latin America on outside powers, and called for radical change across the continent. Medellín saw clearly that the present order guarantees that the rich will grow richer at the expense of the poor, with the inevitable result that the poor will grow poorer in relation to the rich. And the bishops refused any longer to bless such an order.[19]

The Medellín bishops, along with their counterparts from other Third World countries, were a strong influence at the 1971 international synod of bishops, which produced still another document, *Justice in the World.* Here working for justice and social transformation is seen as *constitutive of the church's mission:*

> Listening to the cry of those who suffer violence and are oppressed by unjust systems and structures, and hearing the appeal of a world that by its perversity contradicts the plan of its Creator, we have shared our awareness of the Church's vocation to be present in the heart of the world by proclaiming the Good News to the poor, freedom to the oppressed, and joy to the afflicted. The hopes and forces which are moving the world in its very foundations are not foreign to the dynamism of the Gospel, which through the power of the Holy Spirit frees men from personal sin and from its consequences in social life.... *Action on behalf of justice and participation in the transformation of the world fully appear to us as a constitutive dimension of the preaching of the Gospel, or, in other words, of the Church's mission for redemption of the human race and its liberation from every oppressive situation.*[20]

Eleven years after the Medellín Conference (1979), CELAM met again, this time in Puebla, Mexico, a meeting that coincided with John Paul II's visit to Mexico. Of particular note was his speech to indigenous people in Oaxaca and Chiapas, in which he declared, "There is always *a social mortgage on all private property,* so that goods may serve the general assignment that God has given them. And if the common good demands it, there is no need to hesitate at expropriation itself, done in the right way."[21] The Puebla conference again gave overwhelming support to the base community movement, calling it "the hope of the church." The bishops were relentless in condemning the philosophy of national security that had arisen to keep liberation movements in check. The key phrase echoing from the conference, however, was "the preferential option for the poor." Christians are called upon to read society from the perspective of its victims: "What the option for the poor asks of middle-class people is to abandon their own class perspective and read society from below, though the eyes of the people at the bottom and in the margin."[22] This perspective should lead to action and public witness, genuine solidarity with the poor in their struggle for justice:

> What is presupposed here is that the poor are to be the agents of their own liberation. Their struggle for justice will liberate Latin American society. All who love justice, therefore, of whatever class, must support the poor in their struggle for liberation. The Church itself, the Puebla Document declared, must be in solidarity with this struggle.[23]

The Spreading of the Liberation Movement

The connection between social liberation and Christian spirituality has spread rapidly from Latin America to other parts of the Third World, and it has spread to oppressed groups in the First World (women, racial and ethnic minorities, gays and lesbians, people with disabilities). With all of these, we find the previously absent asserting a new presence, the formerly silent finding their voices. And in all these, we find persons who are victimized by structures affirming themselves and one another, discovering a God who loves them and seeks their liberation. The message is human dignity, equality, mutuality, opportunity, access, participation, fulfillment, justice. The experience is awareness, community, support, risk-taking, self-esteem, anger, protest, resistance, empowerment, and change. And in all of these, the problems are structures and resistance to change, cultural addictions, social ideologies, our inability to see how the arrangements of people in systems favors some and not others, affirms some and negates others, creates opportunity and access for some and marginates others. Our excessive individualism prevents us from seeing our interconnectedness and interdependence and hides the fact that individuals are embedded in social arrangements, in economic and political patterns.

Liberation calls us beyond the personal and the interpersonal to the social and the political. We move beyond the private to the public, beyond the individual to the collective. This is an extremely difficult learning curve for North Americans, who have been steeped in individualism. Patterns of domination and discrimination are subtle and complex, deeply ingrained in our psyches as assumptions. Victims and their pain are hidden, out of sight; or their situation is "their fault," just as others' success, wealth, and power are "their fault." The experience of liberation is an experience of change, profound spiritual, psychological, and social shifts that are risky, requiring personal courage and difficult transitions. Key to this experience of liberation is reconstructing spirituality — discovering again Jesus and the reign of God calling us to conversion, recognizing that this is not liberation for some at the expense of others. Liberation from unjust and oppressive structures and the patterns of domination and submission is liberation for all.

Transcending Sexism, Racism, and Homophobia

Women's struggle for equality and justice in society and the church, which focuses on all-pervasive patriarchal and sexist life — in familial and social life as well as in economic and political structures — is also a liberation for men. Long-standing patterns of domination and submission affecting gender roles and expectations permeate almost all aspects of human life, rendering women victimized even when they are among the socioeconomic elite. But patriarchy and sexism victimize men as well. We are too closely interconnected for the pain of women not to affect male sensibilities. The specifics about physical and sexual abuse in families, about rape and sexual harassment, about lack of access to positions of power and influence, about less pay for similar work and glass ceilings, about subtle psychological facets of male-female interaction and relationship — all of these reveal a male as well as a female enslavement. Liberation of women is also liberation of men — from the hurtful and destructive patterns that enslave us all.[24]

The same is true of racism. People of color experience discrimination and violence against them, regardless of their talents and abilities or even their socioeconomic status. They are born into a world of pain and suffering, of being rebuffed and slighted, of lower expectations and fewer opportunities — solely on the basis of the color of their skin. Their access to quality education and economic success is severely limited. The likelihood that they will experience poverty, illiteracy, unemployment, imprisonment, even violent death is much higher than among whites. They will encounter racism, conscious and overt or unconscious and subtle, from individuals and from institutions, almost everywhere they go. Again, the patterns of racism run deep, passing from generation to generation, affecting both the dominant and the dominated. Who suffers from racism? We all do. The baggage of hate and discrimination is a heavy load. We all suffer, and our social fabric is radically diminished. Intelligence and talent go undeveloped, human ingenuity frustrated, lives wasted. Anger, crime, and violence fill the playgrounds, the schools, the streets. Fear and intimidation reign; friendship and community are grossly inhibited. Liberation from racism is liberation for all, not only for black, brown, red, and yellow, but also for white. Developing a truly multicultural society, where diversity is recognized as a value and an asset and where the patterns of racism are transcended, will enrich everyone's life and enhance our institutions. God creates diversity, and the *basileia* of Christ beckons all of us to conversion from racism.

Gay and lesbian persons seek liberation from their closets: from self-hatred and discrimination, from pernicious snickering and social contempt, from humiliation, mockery, scorn, and violence. They also seek liberation from oppressive structures that assume heterosexuality: schools, clubs, media, banks, insurance companies, government agencies — and churches. Heterosexism and homophobia run deep in most cultures. Gays and lesbians are labeled "mentally ill," "social misfits," and "immoral," and are perceived as a threat to family life. Yet today's scholarly consensus is that sexual orientation is mostly a matter of genetic make-up and body chemistry: some people *naturally* seek affection and intimacy in same-sex relationships and can find personal fulfillment only there. Again, fear is a heavy burden to carry, and discrimination is violence. Liberation from homophobia and heterosexism is liberation for all, liberation to find love and pleasure where our hearts lead us, without defacing human dignity. Reconstructing Catholicism means reconciliation with our gay brothers and our lesbian sisters and becoming allies in their struggle against homophobia.[25]

Psychological Liberation

Liberation takes place in the human psyche as well as in society. Removing external barriers and changing social structures are tied to removing *internal* barriers and seeking *internal* change. The destructive patterns that we find in society afflict our interiority as well: shame and guilt, fear, hatred, contempt, self-righteousness, judgmentalism, alienation. Self-esteem and esteem of others go together. Self-acceptance and openness to others, compassion toward self and toward others, recognition of our own dignity and the demands human dignity make for social justice — the liberation experience ties these together. Liberation is not only a social goal, but an exhilarating interior process that transforms the self. Liberation is a healing that restores self-esteem and self-confidence to individuals as they discover an inner center of authority. Persons who have interiorized external judgments and see themselves as defective come to see that the source of their self-hatred is in defective structures. This was the great insight that emerged from *Brown vs. Board of Education:* that racial segregation led children of color to despise themselves, to interiorize the racism of the dominant culture implied in segregated facilities. Women, whose self-esteem has been damaged by patriarchy and sexism, are empowered by interior healing as well as by changing social structures. Gays and lesbians find coming out within (being reconciled to their own sexuality and discovering their own center of sexual authority), a necessary prerequisite to confronting heterosexist structures in society.

People who belong to target groups aren't the only ones who can and do benefit from inner healing. White, male heterosexuals are discovering increasingly their need to be healed — their urge to dominate others and their fear of diversity are tied to their own self-esteem problems. Excessive aggression and competition and the need always to be in control are more and more felt as deficiencies that are grounded in one's own insecurity. Attitudes that are projected outward — toward racial minorities, women, and gays — are tied to inner doubts and uncertainties. Being driven to position, wealth, power, and prestige is related to inner anxieties and unresolved childhood experiences. Gloria Steinem's book *Revolution from Within* (1992) provides some examples of leaders whose unexamined early lives are then played out on a national and international stage:

> Think of such current examples as Saddam Hussein, a boy beaten and tortured daily by his stepfather, who grew up to enjoy the close-up torture of others; or [Romanian] President Ceausescu, whose police state normalized his own earliest years of living in one room with nine siblings and an alcoholic, sadistic father. Think also of Ronald Reagan, who seems to have learned endless cheerful denial as the child of an alcoholic father; or George Bush, whose biographers describe a well-to-do childhood with an aristocratic, religious father who used a belt for discipline, controlled every aspect of family life, and insisted his sons compete, win, and become leaders, whether they wanted to or not.[26]

One can draw parallels between our contemporary national and global society and a dysfunctional family. Change and healing involve everyone. The patterns of dominance and submission, of controlling external authorities and codependent groups can be found in the relationship of international cartels and multinational corporations to individual nation-states. The lack of any connection to their own inner centers of authority creates a need for healing interventions. Liberation movements — whether among Latin American peasants or inner-city neighborhoods; African-American, Hispanic, feminist, gay, or white-male — seek the healing of a deconstructed and violent society in crisis. The economic dissonance created by abject poverty and opulent luxury, by an all-powerful elite and the powerlessness of the masses, is creating an inner and outer tension. Today's victims are found in Harlem and on Wall Street, in *barrios* and wealthy suburbs, among the poorest and the richest.[27] We need liberation and healing, grounded in the only real authority, which is God. The liberation and healing of Jesus' *basileia,* mediated in sacramental communities of compassion and service, must make social justice and the politics of compassion central to their identity and their work. Here inner and outer healing go together as people discover *charis* as their center and *charism* as their vocation, experiencing forgiveness and mercy as personal empowerment through conversion, and compassion and justice as the empowerment of a transformed social order.[28]

Reconstructing Moral Discourse

The U.S. bishops demonstrated courage and creative moral teaching in their pastoral letters on peace (1983) and economic justice (1986). What is most interesting and helpful about these documents is not the content of their final drafts, though in many ways what they teach is very much in line with what we've been saying in this chapter. More significant is the *process* that they developed in writing these letters. It provides the church with a new model for discourse about morality and ethics.

The Challenge of Peace: God's Promise and Our Response (1983) was the result of a full review of the moral issues surrounding the arms race. The bishops consulted with a wide range of experts in preparing the first draft, which was made public for the feedback of all interested parties. The draft sparked a national debate within and beyond the church, a dialogue that continued through the second and third drafts. The whole church and the general public, including persons of particular expertise (scripture scholars, theologians, peace activists, historians, political scientists, government officials, military and weapons experts) participated in the conversations that ultimately resulted in the final draft, which was approved in November 1983. The result was that, while not everyone agreed wholeheartedly with the document, there was a kind of Catholic consensus on many aspects of this key moral issue, and both church people and the general citizenry were wrestling with moral and ethical issues on an important public policy issue.

While that letter was still in process, the bishops began another document and another process. *Economic Justice for All* (1986) was focused on moral issues related to the American economy. Here the bishops tried to apply Catholic social teaching to concrete problems in the United States: poverty, unemployment, trade, food, and agriculture. The document applies Catholic ethical principles to these issues and advances proposals for reforms aimed particularly at improving conditions for the poor. Again, multiple drafts were published after consultation with both those making public policy and those who were particularly affected by it, people whose expertise was directly relevant to identifying appropriate moral principles or the economic issues at stake. Feedback from the church, from business and labor, from government, and from poor people and agencies focused on addressing the needs of poor people provided a lively national debate about economic structures and their effects. The final draft was sharply critical of national values and practices and called for structural changes in American economic life.

O'Brien and Shannon comment on the significance of these pastoral letters:

> Together, the two letters mark a significant development in American Catholicism. Both letters make very clear the need to incorporate justice and peace into every facet of life in the church. They express a critical distance between the church and American society, as the church draws, from its own tradition, norms on the basis of which to assess national practice and determine its own responsibilities. At the same time, while valuing prophetic witness, the bishops take their stand within and not apart from American society, sharing responsibility for the problems that exist, avoiding for the most part judgmental and moralistic statements about their fellow citizens, and urging vigorous public efforts to clarify the moral dimensions of political and economic life and to move forward toward goals of equality, justice, security, and peace. Clearly the bishops wish to be, and wish their people to be, both faithful Christians and responsible citizens, and they recognize that achieving those two objectives can involve difficult choices.[29]

Reconstructing Catholic moral discourse means involving the whole church in dialogue about important aspects of personal and social liberation, making connections between the Gospel and its meaning today for lived existence, both personal and social. It means providing leadership for conversations, decisions, and actions that reflect the call to conversion and its implications for the way we live our lives. Such moral discourse must be well informed, open, and flexible, broadly consultative, cognizant of the moral center as God's *basileia,* always hopeful and compassionate in reaching out to liberate and heal persons and structures. The U.S. bishops took some notable steps in the 1980s, but have seemingly backtracked since then — in part because of the flak they took from people within and beyond the church, arguing that they had no business meddling in public policy issues, and in part because of further retrenchment and conservatism issuing from the Vatican. The reconstruction of Catholic moral discourse must be retrieved in the present *kairos,* but that can happen only by liberating the church itself.

Healing and Liberating the Church

Michael Crosby has written a book describing the institutional church as "dysfunctional."[30] Applying the insights of psychology and family systems theory to the church, he sees the central bureaucracy involved in denial and cover-up in its addiction to male clericalism and controlling power and authority, while pastoral leaders and lay people are afflicted with codependency, passively participating in the dysfunctional patterns of domination and submission. Utilizing the language of Twelve Step recovery programs, he calls for "an intervention" in which the bureaucracy is confronted with its addiction and Catholics deal openly with their codependency. "Recovery is for the addictive process what conversion is for the spiritual life. Both involve an alternative process of leaving something behind and turning to something else."[31] True recovery can begin only with an admission of addiction — something neither Crosby nor myself see as a likely scenario for the Vatican in the near future. This means the healing process must focus now on the codependency of pastoral leaders and laity, "those of us who have been caught up in the family disease but now want to become involved in recovery's two processes: to stop our participation in the controls of the addictive process, and to begin thinking, feeling, and behaving anew."[32]

Liberating and healing the church today means reconstructing Catholicism: turning our energy toward following Jesus and living the *basileia* in and through sacramental community, giving ourselves to the conversion process and working to transform society through compassion and justice. Crosby calls this "a change of objects of our heart's thinking and consideration, its feeling and desires, and its behavior."[33] This new thinking, feeling, and behaving is tied to stopping our participation in the controls of the addictive process, letting the Vatican's obsession with controlling power sputter away, while we do church. Crosby, following the Twelve Step program, makes a series of recommendations: moving from "the lie" to truth and faith, from fear to freedom and courage, from attachments to detachment and commitment, actively seeking the kingdom and letting it seek us. While we continue to challenge the bureaucracy's addiction to controlling power, confronting it openly when appropriate, we need also to simply move on with embodying the Gospel vision emergent today. In this way, the church will be liberated to be again what it was called to be — by Jesus in Galilee hundreds of years ago. Jesus confronted the juridical consciousness of his own world and healed the people from their clinging to it. Turning again to this Jesus and to his *basileia* will set Catholics free, heal them, to be again his community of disciples. A lovely poem by e. e. cummings comes to mind:

we can never be born enough,
we are human beings
for whom birth is a supremely
    welcome mystery,
the mystery
    that happens
    only
    and whenever
we are true to ourselves.

These themes of continuous birth, mystery, and being true to ourselves expand dramatically as we move to the final part of this book. Here we will see that liberation and healing are more than sociopolitical and personal. Indeed, as Catholicism moves toward a third millennium, its challenge becomes increasingly planetary, even cosmic, liberation and healing.

Part Three

CATHOLICISM IN A RECONSTRUCTED UNIVERSE

❄

Challenges and Possibilities from the New Cosmology

THE TRANSITION FROM MODERNITY to postmodernity involves a major paradigm shift, a shift in the way we perceive almost everything. This change in perception begins with the physical universe (physics), with the Earth (seen from space), and with nature (ecology). Our understanding of the physical universe has changed dramatically and rapidly in the twentieth century, triggered mostly by the insights of Albert Einstein and our ability to observe both the macro (through telescopes) and the micro (through particle separators). Space travel has provided us with a mirror image of the Earth as a wonderful blue and green jewel that hangs in the blackness of space. For the first time we can see the planet as a whole. The ecological crisis has caused us to rethink our relationship to nature, and we are beginning to recognize ourselves as part of an intricate, interdependent web of life, more radically connected to and dependent upon the natural world than we had previously thought. The new physics, NASA, and the ecological dangers we now face are combining to change our perception of reality, our self-understanding, and the meaning and value of human activity. As Brian Swimme says,

> In our century, the mechanistic period of science opened out to include a science of mystery... the dawning recognition that the universe and the Earth can be considered living entities; the awareness that the human person, rather than a separate unit within the world, is the culminating presence of a billion-year process; and the realization that, rather than having a universe filled with things, we are enveloped by a universe that is a single energetic event, a whole, a unified, multiform, and glorious outpouring of being.[1]

In this final section of the book, we will explore this shifting sense of the universe and the human, attempting to reconstruct Catholicism in response to contemporary understandings.

This is both familiar to Catholicism and an extraordinary challenge to our tradition. It is familiar because ancient Israel developed a creation myth that tied the emergence of the natural world to the God who led them forth from Egypt. The Earth, the sun, the stars, the cycle of seasons, the power of fertility — all were seen as the handiwork of the same God who had liberated Israel and brought Judah back from Babylonian exile.

It is familiar, also, because early Christian traditions began to connect Jesus of Nazareth with the unseen wisdom of God (*sophia*), who was responsible for creation. We get images of a cosmic Christ in the Pauline and Johannine writings as well as in the book of Revelation: "He is the first-born of all creation, for in him were created all things in heaven and on earth...all things were created through him and for him" (Col. 1:15–16). The *basileia* proclaimed by Jesus in word and deed is universal, encompassing everything there is.

It is familiar, also, because Christian thinkers throughout the past two thousand years have explored the connections between creation and redemption, between what we know about universal reality and our faith in Jesus. Plato's understanding of the universe undergirds Augustine's theology. Aristotle's description of the physical universe is the basis for Thomas Aquinas's thought. Christian mysticisms celebrate the unity of all things in God. Catholic figures like Francis of Assisi, Hildegard of Bingen, and Meister Eckhart saw all of creation suffused with spirit. Only in recent centuries does Christianity reflect a split understanding of the natural universe (phenomena) and the sacred (noumena). So retrieving an integrated understanding is familiarly Catholic.

But the new paradigm is also a profound challenge to many of our assumptions and previous understandings. Copernicus and Galileo, in challenging previous understandings of the universe, were condemned by Rome, beginning a prolonged conflict between science and religion. That conflict intensified with the Enlightenment, during which reason and empiricism were seen as the tools of science in the exploration of the universe and society, and revelation and faith were diminutized, given over to the sphere of the private individual and the interior life of belief and value. One could choose either science *or* faith for an integrated understanding, or one could choose both science and faith, but in a bifurcated reality. Our newly emergent sense of the universe and nature shatters that separation and opens up new opportunities for an integrated understanding that brings faith and science together, but not without challenges. There has also been within the Christian tradition generally a locating of revelation in history rather than nature, a focus on time rather than place. Recovering a sense of the revelatory character of the cosmos and seeing the physical (matter and bodies) as the location of salvation is a daunting challenge, given our history of being influenced by dualisms in which the physical universe was perceived rather negatively.

Environmental damage, the extent and intensity of which we are only now beginning to glimpse, is tied to problematic patterns of perception — attitudes grounded in long-standing assumptions and beliefs — as well as the anti-nature behaviors that flow from them. Christianity, as it has developed over the centuries, is part of the problem. Some (Lynn White, for example) would say it is *the* problem behind our ecological crisis. We have focused almost exclusively on the human, and seen the rest of creation as there *for us*. We have focused on human purpose as salvation from this world — in a heavenly realm beyond space and time. We have seen matter, the body, the physical world in a pejorative way, emphasizing "control of" and "transcendence from." Our dualisms have led us to see the spiritual, the soul, and true human purpose above and beyond the earth, the universe, and physical reality. With these attitudes, it is no wonder that we are now witnessing pollution of air and water, destruction of the great rain forests, and the extinction of millions of plant and animal species. To the extent that we have embraced hierarchy, patriarchy, and dualism, Catholicism is a hidden culprit in the ecological devastation we are now facing.

Reconstructing Catholicism today means listening to the voices of physics, as well as to the beliefs and values expressed in the religions of indigenous peoples. It means listening to the voices of the Earth and her many creatures, who cry out for relief from the human assault. It means recognizing that the rule of God comes long before Jesus of Nazareth and that the meaning disclosed by him is ultimately cosmic and universal. Reconstructing Catholicism today requires that we perceive the reconstructed universe disclosed in the new physics, that we see the human and the Christian in the larger context of 15 billion years of cosmic evolution. It means that we find a creative integration of Christian faith and the harmony and balance that nature requires. Reconstructing Catholicism is about more than human liberation and human healing. It is about cosmic liberation and cosmic healing — connecting human creativity to the wondrous music of the universe.

— Chapter 8 —

Reconstructing Cosmos

When we look at the planets and stars and galaxies and subatomic particles, we see evidence from every direction that the universe is all of a piece, and that it began as a single seed, smaller than an atom. In a very real sense, you and I were there. Every scrap of matter and energy in our blood and bones and in the synapses of our thoughts can trace their lineage back to that point.
— Timothy Ferris, *The Creation of the Universe*

Now this is what we believe. The Mother of us all is Earth. The Father is the Sun. The Grandfather is the creator who bathed us with his mind and gave life to all things. The Brother is the beasts and trees. The Sister is that with wings. We are the children of Earth and do no harm in any way. Nor do we offend the Sun by not greeting it at dawn. We praise our Grandfather for his creation. We share the same breath together—the beasts, the trees, the birds, the man.
— Taos Pueblo Prayer

Perhaps the single most important spiritual issue of our time emerges in the global ecological crisis we face. The vast devastation that human beings have visited on the Earth in modernity poses profound threats to the survival of all life forms on the planet. Pollution of the land, air, and water has introduced life-threatening toxins into the food chain and our bodies. Depletion of the protective ozone, global warming, alarming increments in human population growth, and the killing off of millions of plant and animal species — all of these suggest a grim future devoid of natural aesthetics and a radically diminished existence, if, indeed, we can survive at all. The source of these problems is not superficial. It has to do with our self-understanding and our relationship to the natural world. We are alienated from nature, estranged from the elegant magnificence that is all about us and within us. Growing awareness of this alienation and estrangement challenges our fundamental meanings and values.

The Ecological Crisis

On June 13, 1992, scientists, government officials, and community leaders from all over the world came together in Rio de Janeiro to create global strategies aimed at preventing the Earth's environmental death. Never before had so many heads of state gathered together, nor seemed so united in a common concern. The Earth Summit, held on the twentieth anniversary of the first United Nations Conference on the Environment, demonstrated global distress about the state of the environment and an increasing desire to make dramatic and far-reaching changes, together. In his discussion of *Agenda 21,* the conference document that details a global plan to address the critical economic and ecological problems facing humanity on the eve of the twenty-first century, Daniel Sitarz describes the present situation with lucidity:

> Humanity is at a crossroads of enormous consequences. Never before has civilization faced an array of problems as critical as the ones now faced. As forbidding and portentous as it may sound, what is at stake is nothing less than the global survival of humankind. The effects of human impact upon the Earth have been accelerating at a rate unforeseen even a handful of decades ago. Where once nature seemed forever the dominant force on Earth, evidence is rapidly accumulating that human influence over nature has reached a point where natural forces may soon be overwhelmed.... The equilibrium of the planet is in jeopardy, as judged by forces as profound as the global climate and the atmospheric protection from the Sun's damaging rays. Major changes in the ecological balance of the world are occurring very rapidly, more rapidly in many cases than humanity's ability to assess the dangers.[1]

Sitarz's views reflect a growing consensus among environmental experts who have studied the immense devastation carried out by the human species in the last two hundred years:

> There is strong evidence from the world's scientific community that humanity is very, very close to crossing certain ecological thresholds for the support of life on Earth.... The global scientific consensus is that if the current levels of environmental deterioration continue, the delicate life-sustaining qualities of this planet will collapse. It is a stark and frightening potential.[2]

The specifics of the ecological crisis have been described elsewhere. One of the clearest and most readable accounts of ecological devastation is Al Gore's *Earth in the Balance,* in which the author provides well-documented explanations of global warming, stratospheric ozone depletion, the effects of radical deforestation (particularly the loss of tropical rain forests at the rate of 17 million hectares per year), pollution of the global water system, soil erosion and toxins affecting agriculture and the food-chain, and the problem of solid waste disposal.[3] What is most valuable in Gore's description of the growing environmental threats, however, is his ability to see linkages between them. Ecological problems reinforce each other in complex feedback loops. For example, there is solid evidence that global warming and depletion of the protective ozone reinforce each other:

> Global warming increases the amount of water vapor throughout the atmosphere and traps infrared heat in the lower part of the sky which would otherwise radiate back out to space, passing through the stratosphere. As a result, the stratosphere actually cools as the lower atmosphere warms. A cooler stratosphere with more water vapor means more ice crystals in the ozone layer, especially in the polar regions, where chlorofluorocarbons (CFCs) mingle with the ozone in the presence of the ice, thus depleting the ozone at a faster rate. The thinner the ozone layer, the more ultraviolet radiation strikes the surface of the earth and all the organisms living there. The ultraviolet radiation strikes vegetation that normally absorbs vast quantities of CO_2 through photosynthesis and seems to seriously disrupt its ability to do so. As the vegetation absorbs less CO_2, more of it accumulates in the atmosphere, causing still more global warming—and still more stratospheric cooling. The cycle is reinforced and magnified. It feeds upon itself.[4]

Overpopulation and Fossil Fuel Usage

Among the major factors contributing to the ecological crisis is the huge jump in human population. Over the past seventy years the human population has nearly tripled, growing from 1.8 billion to 5.3 billion, and the growth goes on:

> Currently the world's population is growing faster than ever before. Each year, 90 million people are added to our numbers, the demographic equivalent of another Mexico....If drastic declines in human fertility (or very large increases in mortality) occur over the next five years, it would be possible to stabilize the human population at about 12 billion within a century.[5]

Gore describes the startling surge in human population by reference to human history and his own lifetime:

> From the beginning of humanity's appearance on earth to 1945, it took more than ten thousand generations to reach a world population of 2 billion people. Now, in the course of one human lifetime — mine — the world population will increase from 2 to more than 9 billion.[6]

These numbers are staggering and point to the enormous impact the human species is having on the earth's ecological systems. By adding the equivalent of one China to the world's population every ten years, we are stretching earth's resources to the limit.

Sheer numbers of human beings are, indeed, a major factor in shaping the current crisis, but the situation is exacerbated by the rapid acceleration of the scientific and technological revolution, "which has allowed an almost unimaginable magnification of our power to affect the world around us by burning, cutting, digging, moving, and transforming the physical matter that makes up the earth."[7] Fossil fuels continue to be the dominant energy source for the human assault on nature. The burning of oil, gasoline, and coal pours billions of tons of carbon into the atmosphere each year. Petroleum-based pesticides and fertilizers are spread over agricultural lands, eventually being washed into fresh-water sources and then into the oceans. Approximately 600,000 tons of oil enter the oceans each year as a result of normal shipping operations, accidents, and illegal discharges. Meanwhile, wetlands are endangered, marine plant and animal life are suffocating, fresh-water sources are polluted. Fossil fuels are used to build miles and miles of superhighways, turn fertile farm land into shopping malls and housing subdivisions, destroy millions of acres of forest, and create thousands of solid-waste dumps to store garbage, much of which is products themselves made from fossil fuels.

Controlling human population growth and shifting from fossil fuels to renewable energy sources (solar, wind, thermal, water) would go a long way toward resolving the urgency of the present crisis and creating a *sustainable* human society. Sitarz suggests that "curbing the global appetite for fossil fuels is the single most important action" that can be taken to reduce the current ecological risks. *Agenda 21* contains a series of proposals designed to bring about a rapid change "to a pattern of energy production and consumption that relies more heavily on efficiency and environmentally sound energy systems, particularly clean and renewable energy sources."[8] The Rio document also contains sweeping measures that promote human fertility control and socioeconomic improvements likely to favorably affect demographic patterns in developing countries. The Millennium Institute, likewise, calls for the creation of "the religious, social, and economic conditions necessary to stop the growth of human population," and conversion "from carbon-dioxide emitting energy sources to renewable, non-polluting energy sources"[9] as two important steps required in saving our planet from impending doom. But such measures, radical though they may be given present patterns and trends, are still insufficient. Real change means major shifts in our attitudes and values, in the way we understand ourselves in relation to nature. As Gore says, "The more deeply I search for the roots of the global environmental crisis, the more I am convinced that it is an outer manifestation of an inner crisis that is, for lack of a better word, spiritual."[10] According to Lynton Caldwell:

> The environmental crisis is an outward manifestation of a crisis of mind and spirit. There could be no greater misconception of its meaning than to believe it to be concerned only with endangered wildlife, human-made ugliness, and pollution. These are part of it, but more importantly, the crisis is concerned with the kind of creatures we are and what we must become in order to survive.

In a celebrated article entitled "The Historical Roots of Our Ecological Crisis," Lynn White, Jr., speaks more pointedly:

> The present increasing disruption of the global environment is the product of a dynamic technology and science which were originating in the Western medieval world. . . . Their growth cannot be understood historically apart from distinctive attitudes toward nature which are deeply grounded in Christian dogma. . . . Since the roots of our trouble are so largely religious, the remedy must also be essentially religious, whether we call it that or not. *We must rethink and refeel our nature and destiny.*[11]

Roots of the Crisis: Otherworldly Religion and Controlling Science

We need to stand back from the present crisis and assess why things are so amiss. What are the underlying reasons for today's threatening situation? The answer, of course, is the human species. We are what has thrown the natural world into such imbalance. But is the human species *intrinsically* the problem? Are we a mistake of nature, inevitably drawn to behaviors that are destructive to the planet as a whole? A closer look suggests that the underlying problem is not the human species as such, but the human species of the past two hundred years — and more precisely, the human species in the Western hemisphere and north of the equator during the past two hundred years. It is *modern Eurocentered humanity* that has plundered nature and wrought such destruction to the planet. Thomas Berry suggests that the underlying problem is twofold: otherworldly religion and controlling science; religion that denigrates the natural world and sees it as at best neutral and at worst our spiritual enemy, and science as conquest that seeks to conquer and subjugate the world of nature. Transcending nature through religion and overcoming nature through science — these prevailing attitudes combine to create a human species that devastates the natural world, perceiving itself as separate from, and even alien to, nature. Berry traces the problem back to the fourteenth century, when Europe experienced the plague known as the Black Death. Between 1347 and 1349, the plague is said to have killed off as much as one-third of Europe's population. Almost half of the people of Florence died within a three-month period. "In response to the plague and to other social disturbances of the fourteenth and fifteenth centuries, two directions of development can be identified — one toward a religious redemption out of the tragic world, the other toward greater control of the physical world to escape its pain and to increase its utility to human society."[12] What ultimately came forth was a new exhilaration in the human power to dominate the natural world. "This led to a savage assault upon the Earth such as was inconceivable in prior times. The experience of sacred communion with the Earth disappeared."[13]

Otherworldly religion is *not* biblical. Both ancient Israel and the Jesus movement were thematically oriented toward the transformation of individual and society. Salvation was transformed existence, not existence in some other, ethereal realm. This should be clear from what we said earlier about the Jesus movement in chapter 4. Jesus was about healing and liberation. The otherworldly focus of Western religion is tied to Gnostic and Platonic influences, which saw the world of material creation as either the product of an evil demigod (Gnosticism) or a shadowy intimation of the real world of ideas (Plato). After Constantine, Christianity lost its socially transforming urge in its ties to empire and culture, focusing increasingly on a spiritual realm beyond the material, temporal realm as the source and destiny of humankind. Salvation became the soul going to heaven. Thomas Aquinas brought Christianity back to earth somewhat in his development of an Aristotelian theology grounded on the framework of nature's movement upward, but the focus remained ultimately on transcendence from matter and time in eternity, the beatific vision. Lynn White calls the victory of Christianity over paganism "the greatest psychic revolution in the history of our culture." In destroying pagan animism, Christianity created a human monopoly on spirit in this world. "The spirits *in* natural objects, which formerly had protected nature from man, evaporated." And humanity was provided religious rationale for the exploitation of nature.[14] After the Enlightenment, this anthropocentric spiritualism became even more individualized. The Catholic spiritual path was saving one's soul by going to heaven. Such otherworldly orientation saw this world, the world of space and time, as a veil of tears that one suffered through, being tested by temptation, toward fulfillment in the afterlife of heaven.

It is the combination of individualistic, anthropocentric, otherworldly religion and the emergence of rationalistic scientific technology that seems most responsible for the unleashing of massively destructive forces that today threaten the planet. The problem is not the human species as such, but a human species that seeks salvation in escape from matter and time, limits spirit to humankind, and becomes enthralled with the rational control of nature that is the root problem.

Native American Spiritualities

Contrast modern Eurocentered humanity with Native American indigenous people. Native Americans were *at home* in nature, which was seen as the source of sacred power. To live in harmony with the natural world, taking and giving back, recognizing and accepting a dependency — this was the goal of Native American spiritualities. While there is no word for "religion" among the diverse Native American nations, nearly all of them reflected a diffuse sense of sacred power or divine energy, which they experienced as all about them. Native American "God" is usually translated today as "Great Spirit," but such translation misses this sense of diffuse sacred power and divine energy that was seen as present *within* the natural world. Native peoples, in general, perceived the natural environment "as a sensate, conscious entity suffused with spiritual powers."[15] This spiritual energy/sacred power was given various names: *wakan* (Siouan), *orenda* (Iroquoian), *manitou* (Algonquian), or other names. Charlene Spretnak comments that "its translation as *the Great Spirit* seems to have been influenced by Christian contact. Many Indians maintain that an adjectival form more accurately conveys Indian usage: the Great Holy, or the Great Mysterious."[16]

Native Americans understood themselves as connected to nature, part of a larger cosmic whole, which included the Earth with all its plants and animals, the sun, the stars and moon. Such a perspective is central to the Native American worldview. To live in balance and harmony within this sacred whole was their spiritual aspiration. For example, the Hopi term *navoty* expresses the concept of being in perfect harmony and balance with the laws of the universe. *Navoty* implies that human communities are a cooperative part of the order and rhythms constituting this world. Spretnak points to the Lakota spiritual teacher Black Elk, who explained that peace lives in human minds "when they realize their relationships, their oneness, with the universe and all its powers, and when they realize that at the center of the universe dwells *Wakan-Tanka,* and that this center is really everywhere; it is within each of us."[17]

Indigenous peoples from other parts of the globe (Africa, Australia, South America, European pagans) reflect a similar sense of connectedness with nature's sacred powers and, likewise, pursue a pattern of harmony and balance. And non-Western world religions (Hinduism, Taoism, and Buddhism), while strikingly different from each other and from indigenous spiritualities in many respects, nonetheless seek a harmony and balance within nature as their spiritual goal. The roots of the ecological crisis seem peculiarly connected with a Western worldview that separates the human from a despiritized nature, and with social values that emphasize domination, conquest, and competition.

Shifting Paradigms

Linking the ecological crisis and social deterioration to common underlying causes has become increasingly popular. Analysts are making root connections between the dangers that beset the planet's natural environment and those that tear at the social fabric. Capra, for example, suggests that "whether we talk about cancer, crime, pollution, nuclear power, inflation, or energy shortage, the dynamics underlying these problems are the same."[18] Health problems (physical and mental), drug and alcohol addiction, dramatic increments of violent crime and suicide, economic anomalies (rampant inflation, massive unemployment, a gross maldistribution of income and wealth), and environmental devastation — all are interrelated. These problems, he writes,

> are *systemic problems,* which means they are closely interconnected and interdependent. They cannot be understood within the fragmented methodology characteristic of our academic disciplines and government agencies. Such an approach will never solve any of our difficulties but will merely shift them around in the complex web of social and ecological relations. A resolution can be found only if *the structure of the web itself is changed,* and this will involve profound transformations of our social institutions, values, and ideas.[19]

The structure of the web is, in fact, already shifting, because, says Capra, of the confluence of several transitions that will deeply affect our social, economic, and political systems: (1) the slow and reluctant but inevitable decline of patriarchy; (2) the decline of the fossil-fuel age; and (3) a profound change in the thoughts, perceptions, and values that have formed our particular vision of reality. Today the paradigm that has dominated our culture for several hundred years, shaping our modern Western society (and significantly influencing the rest of the world) is shifting. "This paradigm comprises a number of ideas and values that differ sharply from those of the Middle Ages," according to Capra.

> They include belief in the scientific method as the only valid approach to knowledge; the view of the universe as a mechanical system composed of elementary material building blocks; the view of life in society as a competitive struggle for existence; and the belief in unlimited material progress to be achieved through economic and technological growth.[20]

This global "turning point" is a shift from an exclusively rational, analytic way of thinking to the recovery of intuitive awareness; from linear and goal-oriented approaches to reality to nonlinear and holistic thinking. The shift is from aggressive and competitive behaviors to nurturing and cooperative ways of acting, from hierarchies to circles, from male domination to feminist mutuality. The emergence of a new paradigm is expressed in a rising concern with ecology, the recognition that there are limits to growth, and a new focus on harmony and balance — in the self, in society, and in the ecosystem. Capra calls this "ecological awareness," an intuitive wisdom that surfaces in such disparate expressions as nonviolent conflict mediation, corporate quality circles, the growth of feminist consciousness, and, of all places, the new physics!

The Mechanical Universe

From the seventeenth to the twentieth centuries, the physics of Isaac Newton dominated the scientific world. His genius lay in his ability to pull together the revolutionary, postmedieval insights of people like Copernicus, Kepler, Bacon, Galileo, and Descartes. These men provide the background to Newton's image of a mechanistic universe made up of solid objects permanently governed by absolute laws of motion. Together these men brought to a close the medieval notion of an organic, living, and spiritual universe, replacing it with a grand rational system of mathematic-like analysis of the material world meant to yield human certitude and control. Copernicus put forth the theory that the earth was not the center of the universe, but merely one of many planets circling a minor star at the edge of the galaxy. Kepler formulated empirical laws of planetary motion. Galileo directed the newly invented telescope to the skies, establishing scientific observations to validate the Copernican theory. He wanted to describe nature mathematically, to measure and quantify by focusing on shapes, numbers, and movement. Bacon developed a patterned inductive procedure: experiments, general conclusions based on them, further experiments testing those conclusions. His violent imagery in describing the purposes this method could pursue betray the ecological devastation that it would ultimately yield: "Nature, in his view, had to be *hounded in her wanderings, bound into service,* and made a *slave.* She was to be *put in constraint,* and the aim of the scientist was to *torture nature's secrets from her.*"[21]

Descartes, often seen as the founder of modern philosophy, wanted to create a science of certitude. He experienced an illuminating vision when he was only twenty-three years old: "He saw a method that would allow him to construct a complete science of nature about which he could have absolute certainty; a science based, like mathematics, on self-evident first principles."[22] In his reach for certitude, he rejected "all knowledge which is merely probable," and advocated belief in only those things "which are perfectly known and about which there can be no doubts."[23] Descartes's method became radical doubt: "He doubts everything he can manage to doubt — all traditional knowledge, the impressions of his senses, and even the fact that he has a body — until he reaches one thing that he cannot doubt, the existence of himself as a thinker."[24] His famous maxim, "I think, therefore I am," led Descartes to see the essence of human nature as *thought.* Clear and distinct concepts and analytic thinking (breaking up thoughts and problems into pieces and arranging them in their logical order) are the keys to certain truth. Like Plato, Descartes saw thought as more real and certain than matter, and the two as quite distinct. Cartesian dualism is the separation of mind and matter, the priority of mind, the reduction of the human to mind and everything else to *merely matter.* "To Descartes the material universe was a machine and nothing but a machine. There was no purpose, life, or spirituality in matter. Nature worked according to mechanical laws, and everything in the material world could be explained in terms of the arrangement and movement of its parts."[25] Capra's interpretation of Descartes's influence is to the point:

> The whole elaboration of mechanistic science in the seventeenth, eighteenth and nineteenth centuries, including Newton's grand synthesis, was but the development of the Cartesian idea. Descartes gave scientific thought its general framework — the view of nature as a perfect machine, governed by exact mathematical laws.... The Cartesian view of the universe as a mechanical system provided a *scientific* sanction for the manipulation and exploitation of nature that has become typical of Western culture. In fact, Descartes himself shared Bacon's view that the aim of science was the domination and control of nature, affirming that scientific knowledge could be used to "render ourselves the masters and possessors of nature."[26]

Isaac Newton (b. 1642) completed the mechanical universe by providing a consistent mathematical theory used to formulate the general laws of motion governing all objects in the solar system, from stones to planets. Newton saw the universe as an absolute space, an empty container independent from the physical phenomena occurring within it. Changes in the physical world were described in terms of time, seen as a separate dimension, which again was absolute, "having no connection with the physical world and flowing smoothly from the past through the present to the future."[27] Material objects were seen as solid and indestructible, made up of homogeneous atoms. Physical phenomena were reduced to the motion of material particles, caused by their mutual attraction, the force of gravity. Capra's interpretive summary provides a clear picture of Newton's universe:

> In the beginning God created the material particles, the forces between them, and the fundamental laws of motion. In this way the whole universe was set in motion, and it has continued to run ever since, like a machine, governed by immutable laws. All that happened had a definite cause and gave rise to a definite effect, and the future of any

part of the system could, in principle, be predicted with absolute certainty if its state at any time was known in all details. This picture of a perfect world-machine implied an external creator, a monarchical god who ruled the world from above by imposing his divine law on it. The physical phenomena themselves were not thought to be divine in any sense, and when science made it more and more difficult to believe in such a god, the divine disappeared completely from the scientific worldview, leaving behind the spiritual vacuum that has become characteristic of the mainstream of our culture.[28]

Einstein: Luminous, Expanding Space-Time

At the beginning of the twentieth century, a young German physicist named Albert Einstein initiated revolutionary trends in scientific thought. His thinking focused on three areas: (1) the mystery of light; (2) the mystery of the little (microphysics); and (3) the mystery of the complex, seen as inherently unpredictable. Einstein revolutionized the ideas of space, time, and motion, rewrote Newton's theory of gravity, and initiated the scientific search for harmony and unity in the universe. Between his twenty-fifth birthday (1904) and his thirty-eighth (1917), he rebuilt the universe in his mind, from which emerged his famous field equations suggesting that the universe was expanding. The initial insight was so stunning that Einstein himself doctored his equations to project a more stable universe. But when Edwin Hubbel saw the expansion in his telescope and showed it to Einstein, the latter was forced to return to his original equations. Subsequent scientific investigations have shown that we actually live in a universe very like that which Einstein described: a curved and expanding universe of space-time characterized by interactive processes, unpredictability, and astonishing, wondrous mystery.

Einstein's "special theory of relativity" and "quantum theory" shattered all the principal concepts of the mechanical universe, undermining the notions of absolute space and time, of elementary solid particles, of fundamental material substance, of a strictly causal nature of physical phenomena, and even of an objective description of nature. From Einstein's perspective, "The universe is no longer seen as a machine, made up of a multitude of objects, but has to be pictured as one indivisible, dynamic whole whose parts are essentially interrelated and can be understood only as patterns of a cosmic process."[29] Colorado astronomer J. McKim Malville describes Einstein's radical shift in physics this way:

The old Newtonian view of the separability of the world into is-
lands is no longer valid. Our reality has become an uninterrupted
flow...composed of a complex hierarchy of smaller and larger patterns of flow. The so-called "things" of the world are thus features
of the flow, like candle flames and water cascades, where flow lines
converge and then diverge. Our world is filled with processes, not
things, and these processes are all interconnected — a world tapestry
in which particles and people are merely regions in which there are
higher concentrations of world lines....As matter moves through it,
the structure of space-time changes like an ocean which lifts and
falls....In the vicinity of matter, space-time is positively curved, as
a sphere is positively curved. As matter changes location, space-time
flows from one shape into another.[30]

Einstein saw that time is not the same but different. There is no absolute time. Rather, time depends on other factors (on the position of
the observer, on the distance between the observer and what is moving, on how fast the observer is moving in relation to how fast the
thing that is being timed is moving). Time is relative. Einstein found
light more interesting than time and saw it as the secret of everything.
Nothing else travels as fast as light (300,000 kilometers per second),
making everything else relative to the speed of light. Light travels —
not in straight lines, but in a curved projection — in a space-time
continuum that is not three- but four-dimensional. To the three vec-
tors of Euclidian geometry (length, breadth, height), Einstein adds
time: space and time are one. There is no space without time, and
there is no time without space. Matter is not a stuff, but maps telling
space-time how to bend and curve. The whole universe is bent and
curved, dictating the lines on which light travels, an interrelated web
of mysterious curvatures. The universe is not *in* anything. Everything
there ever is is universe and is curved space-time. The universe has no
center, no closedness, but is open, expanding.[31]
   Einstein looked for a unified theory of the universe. He once said,
"I want to know how God thinks; the rest is details." He wanted
to get to the bottom, to the beginning, to the fundamental basis for
everything that is. What he found in probing the micro was radically mysterious. Electrons that jumped from one orbit to another;
the observer's participation in perceiving what is there; light acting
like wave and like particle; profound limits to even the most accurate measurements; probability rather than certainty; spontaneous
nature that cannot be predicted. His work opened up far more questions than it answered, initiating a sense of humility and wonder

among scientists. What Newton had all figured out had now become a radically puzzling mystery.

Evolution and the Origin of the Universe

Einstein's theories opened up the question of origins for new speculation. Newton's universe assumed a distant, clock-maker creator who set all things in motion and laid down eternal laws by which the universe was governed. As the clock image became discredited, however, the clock-maker fared no better. Meanwhile, the new physics made a literal reading of the biblical account of creation more incredible than ever. Genesis read as cosmic history was already caught up in the debate about evolution that Charles Darwin had spawned, and scripture scholars' utilizing historical-critical methods raised their own critique to those who would seek factual knowledge about the universe's beginnings from the Bible. Like the adult who discovers that she was adopted as an infant and now searches for her birth-parents, thoughtful and educated Christians wondered from whence all this had come. Somehow, some way, something must be responsible for the universe's origins. The universe and all its creatures had to have come from someplace. This question of origins is perennial among human beings. Brian Swimme suggests that our desire to know where it all came from, where it began, is recurrent and somehow *necessary:* "We want to know so we might live."

The notion of evolution first emerged from geologists, whose studies of fossils had led them to the idea that the present state of the earth was the result of a continuous development caused by the action of natural forces over immense periods of time. However, it was a French biologist named Jean Baptiste Lamarck who was the first to propose a coherent theory of evolution, according to which all living beings were seen to have evolved from earlier, simpler forms under the pressure of their environment. Several decades later, Charles Darwin presented massive evidence supporting biological evolution in the publication of his *On the Origins of Species by Natural Selection* (1859). Alfred Russel Wallace drew similar conclusions from independent research at the same time. Life scientists had been moving in the direction of evolutionary theory at least since Lamarck's work, but Darwin and Wallace were the first to suggest *how* it happened (adaptation through individual characteristics to environmental changes) and to provide irrefutable empirical support for the theory. Physicists were forced to surrender the Cartesian conception of the world as a machine that had emerged fully constructed from the hands of its Creator. Increasingly, the universe as a whole had to be pictured as an evolving and ever-changing system in which complex structures developed from simpler forms. Einstein's revolutionary theories about the nature of the universe expanded evolutionary theory from the life sciences into the larger context of universal origins. The entire universe, it appears, is evolving, developing, coming out from a single point, billions of years ago.

Both practical astronomy and mathematical and astrophysical theory point to one model of the evolving cosmos and its origins: the universe began in a fireball of light, "the Big Bang." George Gamow, the originator of this theory in the 1940s, discusses its development in his autobiography, *My World Line*.[32] Today there is a scientific consensus that says everything that is the universe emerged from the almost infinite density and energy of a single primordial atom. Everything there is — trillions of galaxies, each containing an estimated 100 billion stars, each galaxy perhaps 100,000 light years across — expands from a single point no larger than an atom! "The whole universe grew in a flash from a *seed*, known to mathematicians of the process as a singularity. Not only light and heat, and later matter, emerged from this seed but also space and time."[33] Indeed, all the creative energy that went into fashioning the stars and the planets, the creatures of Earth, the human and all that we imagine and create, goes back to a point, where structure did not yet exist, only an immensely dense and intensely hot numinous energy. The scientific explanation of the Big Bang is complicated, but documented by credible hypotheses. Four strains of evidence, in particular, suggest the validity of this model:[34]

1. *The flight of the galaxies:* Observation that the galaxies are speeding away from each other in an expanding universe logically suggests that at an earlier time everything was closer and closer together, ultimately in a single, tightly compacted seed that exploded.

2. *Heat radiation in the universe:* 3^0K microwave radiation, predicted by theory and measured in experiments, floods space and can be detected in every direction. The existence of such radiation and its probable source in the cosmic fireball 12–15 billion years ago was most recently confirmed by the NASA COBE satellite. This radiation is cosmic dust left over from the Big Bang.

3. *The ratio of hydrogen and helium in the universe:* The percentages of hydrogen and helium that would have emerged in the

flaring forth of the fireball is consistent with the percentages of those elements in the universe today (75 percent hydrogen, 25 percent helium).

4. *The calculation of the age of the universe:* Scientists calculate the age of the universe, based on the Big Bang, at 12–15 billion years. There is no incongruence between this figure and what can be determined by measuring the rate of disintegration of uranium in measuring the age of the planet.

According to the Big Bang theory, there is no previous cause — nothing previous to the exploding seed: no time, no space, no energy, and no matter. All of these emerge in and with the Big Bang itself. The earliest thing is a vacuum: no matter or mass, but incredible energy. A fluctuation of the vacuum created the Big Bang — like a bubble filled with energy and the bubble bursting. From this emerged what scientists call "virtual realities," tiny realities that were actual but incredibly short-lived. They appeared, then were annihilated, reappeared, then were annihilated again. These tiny realities were extremely numerous, imaged as a kind of a "space foam," but only one little spin-off developed into the cosmos. One little bubble happened to get a huge burst of energy and inflated immensely, bursting forth with an ocean of micro-particles in twos: matter and anti-matter self-destructing. And only one in one billion of these particles escaped the self-destructive process and survived: a photon, one quantum of light. From this comes everything there is; the whole expanding process emerges from nothing, developing forth from a quantum soup into galaxies of first-generation stars, then into second-generation stars and planets, and so forth.[35] This evolutionary history of the cosmos is best described today as "a story," a story of 15 billion years of creative transformations.

The New Story

"It's all a question of story," writes Thomas Berry. "We are in trouble just now because we do not have a good story. We are in between stories. The old story, the account of how the world came to be and how we fit into it, is no longer effective. Yet we have not learned the new story."[36] Berry sees the traditional story as "dysfunctional," unable to serve the highly diverse peoples of today's global civilization and overly focused on the human and on revelation narrowed to a particular tradition. The greatest revelation, he says, is the universe itself. To see nature and the cosmos is to behold a wondrous and evocative revelation of God. All other revelations are subservient to the natural world. The story of the universe — from its wondrous emergence billions of years ago to the unlikely development of planet Earth and the precise conditions suitable to bring forth life in elegant diversity — this is the new story that must become our common story. The new story of the universe is a global creation narrative — one that can serve diverse human cultures by putting them *within* the larger framework of evolving cosmos.

"Story provides a pattern of meaning, coherence, and unity. The story is the primary vehicle for revealing who we are," writes James Conlon in *Earth Story, Sacred Story.* "A good story rings true, uniting us to what is sacred. It reminds us of our roots and challenges us to consider our destiny. It increases our capacity for reflection and empowers us to engage more fully in life."[37] The same is true of sacred image or symbol. An effective symbol reveals us to ourselves and draws us into a profound and life-giving dynamic. The image of the Earth as seen from outer space is just such a symbol — a new icon to go with the new story of the universe. Our global pathologies, the discoveries of science, and the image of Earth from space — these combine to gift us with a new revelation and a new story.

"The new story," says Berry, "is about a living universe. We have failed to understand that the universe is alive. The best way to get in touch with the immense notion of a living universe is through story. In this way we come to see that the universe story is, in fact, our story."[38] The story of the universe is the story of the emergence of a galactic system in which each new level of expression emerges through the urgency of self-transcendence. Hydrogen in the presence of some millions of degrees of heat emerges into helium. After the stars take shape as oceans of life in the heavens, they go through a sequence of transformations. Some eventually explode into the stardust out of which the solar system and the earth take shape. Earth gives unique expression of itself in its rock and crystalline structures and in the variety and splendor of living forms, until humans appear as the moment in which the unfolding universe becomes conscious of itself. The human emerges not only as an earthling, but as a worldling. We bear the universe in our beings as the universe bears us in its being. The two have a total presence to each other and to that deeper mystery out of which both the universe and ourselves have emerged.[39]

Berry and Brian Swimme have, in fact, authored a book entitled *The Universe Story*. In its introduction, they point out that the story of the universe has been told in many ways by various peoples throughout human history. Such stories give meaning to life and to existence itself. "It has provided guidance and sustaining energy in shaping the course of human affairs. It has been our fundamental referent as regards modes of personal and community conduct. It has established the basis of social authority."[40] Today's situation, they suggest, calls for a new type of narrative, a narrative that combines history and science with a poetic sensitivity for the sacred. Such a narrative is needed, not to provide additional data to what scientists have already presented, but to help us understand the *significance* of the data we already possess. What the scientists have found has not yet been sufficiently assimilated to bring about a new period in our comprehension of ourselves and of the universe itself. Indeed, we continue to live in the Cartesian-Newton mechanical universe. But Swimme and Berry suggest that "we are now experiencing that exciting moment when our new meaning, our new story is taking shape. This story is the only way of providing, in our times, what the mythic stories of the universe provided for tribal peoples and for the earlier classical civilizations in their times." For them, the final benefit of the universe story as it has now emerged might be to enable the human community to become present to the larger Earth community in a mutually enhancing manner. "The urgency of our time is that the story become functionally effective."[41]

The new story of the universe (or better, the new sense that the universe *is a story*), together with the image of the Earth hanging in the blackness of space like a precious jewel, might bring about a radically new sense of the human as integral to everything else that is. In doing so, it might foster a sense of humility and gratitude, a recognition of our dependence on everything that came before, everything that now sustains, and a profound sense of the integrity and elegance of nature. It might reawaken a sense of awe and mystery, a genuine consciousness of sacred universe, worthy of reverence and deep respect. The new story of universe might provoke a new spirituality among global humanity and a new spirit of community with all of nature, opening us to the wondrous bond that is love. Were we to rediscover cosmic love, the present crisis with all of its dangers would be overcome.

Sallie McFague suggests that the possibilities for understanding both God and human existence are radically different from what was found in the monarch/realm worldview that dominated Christian consciousness for so long: "Such a perspective does not diminish either human beings or God; in fact both are enlarged." While human beings are "de-centered as the point and goal of creation," we are "re-centered as co-creators of it." God is "de-centered as king of human beings and re-centered as the source, power, and goal of the fifteen-billion year history of the universe."[42] Since we who are now alive are the first human beings who really know this story, our responsibility is enlarged. Our aesthetic response (awe and wonder before the elegance of this continuing evolutionary process) must be accompanied by an ethical response: helping the creative process to continue and thrive on our planet. The reconstructed universe in no way diminishes how we think about God. "To think of God as creator and continuing creator of this massive, breathtaking cosmic history," she writes, "makes all other traditional images of divine transcendence, whether political or metaphysical, seem small indeed." In fact, the passing notion of God as king is by comparison "domesticated transcendence." A genuinely transcendent model would insist that God is the source, power, and goal of the universe; but a source, power, and goal that works *within* its natural processes; hence, this model, while genuinely transcendent, is also profoundly immanent"[43]

Gaia Consciousness

Transcendence and immanence come together in the image of the ancient Greek Earth goddess, Gaia, rediscovered today as symbol for the Earth as a single living organism. The "Gaia hypothesis" was originally put forth in the mid-1960s by James Lovelock and Lynn Margulis, whose research in planetary biology suggested to them that the planet as a whole was functioning like a single living organism, self-regulating its various systems in a manner similar to a human body. Their research for more than a decade produced voluminous data that demonstrated that the Earth "keeps the environment constant and close to a state comfortable for life" by defining and maintaining the conditions necessary for its survival.[44] Two centuries earlier a Scotsman named James Hutton saw something similar. He likened the Earth to the human body, alive and pumping. Writing in the eighteenth century, he described the planet as a kind of superorganism, whose proper study is "planetary physiology." Like a human body, which is fragile yet capable of self-repair, the Earth, he thought, is continually repairing itself, wasted in one place yet restored in another. A century later, an American named Matthew Fontaine Maury doing pioneer work in the study of ocean currents saw the planet as a living being whose breath is the wind and whose blood is the sea. Hutton and Maury are but two of the many scientific minds whose images predate the Lovelock-Margulis hypothesis. What is unique about their hypothesis is the evidence they put forward to support such a viewpoint, particularly their work in cybernetics and the atmosphere.[45] Studying the atmospheres of other planets for NASA, Lovelock reasoned that the gases in a planet's atmosphere should react according to the laws of chemistry and physics to form stable compounds and settle into a lifeless equilibrium. However, he found that the Earth's atmosphere defies this natural expectation. In Earth's atmosphere, gases coexist when they should combine, and elements and compounds appear as gases when they should remain settled as solids on the surface. Struck by the vast amounts of free oxygen in Earth's atmosphere, Lovelock wondered why this highly volatile gas did not react with other elements, such as carbon, to form stable compounds like carbon dioxide. Other planets' atmospheres have carbon dioxide as a dominant gas, yet it accounts for only three-hundredths of one percent of Earth's atmosphere. He was curious about what keeps Earth's oxygen at 21 percent despite extreme differences in the globe's chemical composition. If it shifted a few points higher, fires would burn out of control, and at lower than 12 percent, most organisms would die. He wondered what kept the oceans' salt content constant at 3.5 percent by weight, why the Earth's average surface temperature has remained relatively constant (between 50 and 68 degrees Fahrenheit), even though the sun's output of energy over the past 3.5 billion years of life on Earth may have increased as much as 30 percent. A mere two percent increase in solar output would ordinarily cause the seas to boil. He concluded after many years of experimentation that the Earth plays a self-regulatory, self-organizing role, maintaining optimal conditions for life.[46]

In the thirty years since the conception of the Gaia hypothesis, the name "Gaia" has become synonymous with the concept of an integrated, self-organizing, self-regulating, living planet of which we are an inextricable part. "Physically and spiritually," writes Elizabeth Roberts, "we are woven into the living processes of the planet itself. Together with the sea, air, sunlight, and other life forms, we take part in a planet-sized living system....The closest analogy to the biosphere of the Earth is that of a single cell. We are an integral part of this living cell sustained by its currents of energy and patterns of organization."[47]

It is no surprise, given everything we've said in this chapter, that the ancient Greek Earth goddess returns to us as a symbol in our time. Just when the world as secular had seemingly triumphed, we see the Earth as *sacred*. When the planet's future is threatened with extinction through ecocide, we see the Earth as *alive*. In a time when everything is broken down into its individual composite parts and reality is atomized, individualized, we see the Earth as *one*. *Gaia* means the Earth as *sacred living unity*.

"Gaia consciousness," then, is a new perception, a new way of seeing. Lovelock himself came to this new understanding, in part, by attending to the photos of earth sent by the astronauts from outer space. "The vision of that splendid white-flecked blue sphere stirred us all," he writes.

> We now see that the air, the ocean, and the soil are much more than a mere environment for life — they are part of life itself. The air is to life just as the fur is to the cat. For life on Earth, the air is our protection against the cold depths and fierce radiations of space. We are all, creatures great and small, from bacteria to whales, part of Gaia.

Seeing the Earth as the astronauts did gives us perspective, and this perspective provides a new perception, something there but not seen before. Where we had seen only the without, we now also see a within. Where we had seen things in their separateness, we now see them as parts of a larger and interdependent unity. Where we had seen reality as objects, we now see spirited subjects. Where we had seen nature as there for us, we now see it in its own integrity, possessing its own meaning and value. Where the dominant image of the universe's source had been male monarch, it is replaced with life-giving and nurturing woman.

A feminist performing artist, Rachel Rosenthal, has put together a dramatic performance that seeks to recapitulate popular attitudes toward our planet. It is her attempt to return to theater's ancient religious functioning in enacting publicly the myths of the community. Her performance of *GAIA* puts the issue of decision squarely before us. Imagine her as Gaia: her bald head, noble and beautifully formed, her eyes burning with a searing intensity. She stands, feet apart, knees bent, arms spread wide, exhorting, raging, cajoling, vilifying her audience, who she says is hell-bent on destroying her:

You know me...I'm the one you never bothered to name

earth, with a small e
I, the first and most powerful of the Gods.
Even after you saw my loveliness from up there...
my comely blues and wisps of clouds,
the generosity of my life-
giving waters...Even then you didn't
name me.

I had a name once.
In this culture's genesis I was Gaia.
...
I am a cosmic body born out of cataclysm and catastrophe
I was seeded and, alone among the Bodies, was willing
I nurtured the seed in my awesome womb....

In the end, survival is up to us.

I am sorry.
...
I am sorry for you, I am sorry for me.
But then it's the same thing, isn't it?
For now *you* have the power and with the power,
the responsibility. If you cripple me beyond
repair, I will retreat back into the muds forever
and you will find yourselves my masters at last.
But you will be masters of a dead Spaceship

Earth, and at the same time its slaves. For you
will need to put all your technological resources
to work to maintain your life-supports, a task
that I willingly performed for eons.

And yet the ultimate irony is ours.

Willy-nilly you have reintegrated the Feminine.
For you yourselves are now in the role of the
dreaded and hated Great Mother with all her
powers of selection between Eros and Thanatos!
The choice is yours!

In healing me you heal yourselves.
...Embrace me...I am you...*You* are Gaia now.[48]

A Numinous Universe

The reconstructing of cosmos and the imaging of Earth as Gaia are
breathtaking transitions, holding great promise in a time of epic dan-

ger. What is particularly remarkable as we look at the billion-year process of unfolding cosmos, however, is the miracle of it all. Scientists describe how improbable is the existence of a universe capable of harboring life. There seems to be no reason why the laws of physics and the constants of nature could not have been slightly different from what they are. Gravity could be a little stronger (or a little weaker) than it is, or the rate of expansion in the universe could have been just a fraction greater (or smaller). There is no apparent fundamental reason why the mass or charge of the electron should not be a little greater than it is, or the mass of the proton a little less. Yet if any of these changes were made, even the slightest alteration from the patterns that, in fact, exist, a lifeless universe would almost certainly be the result. Richard Morris has commented in *The Edges of Science,* "It appears that, unless there is some mysterious principle at work, life is the result of a series of remarkable coincidences."[49]

It is easy to see how, without positing anything like predestination or even the slightest impingement on human freedom, one could easily be led toward seeing in all of this a compassionate divine purpose at work. Indeed, the diminutized God of an earlier epoch is now seen as cosmic dynamic reaching far beyond the human, operating within the wondrous evolutionary process. Spirited matter and energy are everywhere in the universe, and from the beginning. Catholicism's juridical consciousness appears even more limiting than we had previously thought. God is acting in and through cosmogenesis, and faith means recognizing the universe's unfolding as divine process, finding our role in healing and liberation as a cosmic compassion. The whole universe, from the micro to the macro, is shot through with gracious mystery. Teilhard de Chardin could not resist calling cosmogenesis a "divine milieu."

The Thought of Teilhard de Chardin

Pierre Teilhard de Chardin was a French paleontologist and a Jesuit priest. Writing in the 1920s and 1930s, Teilhard was already then fully aware of the unity of the cosmos: "The stuff of the universe, woven in a single piece according to one and the same system, but never repeating itself from one point to another, represents a single figure. Structurally, it forms a Whole."[50] One cannot understand the Whole by its parts, according to Teilhard. But in seeing the Whole, all the parts become comprehensible. Seeing the Whole means grasping the magnificence and the elegance of the numinous, active *within* the universe. As a paleontologist whose study of fossils put him on the cutting edge of evolution theory development during its most controversial period and as a Jesuit priest deeply committed to Catholicism, Teilhard's passion was a unified vision of faith and science. He interpreted the evolution of the universe as the unfolding of divine love. Perceiving the "heart" of matter, the "within" of all things, the "urge toward centreity" continuously operative in the evolutionary process — such seeing is what faith is all about for him. All matter is spirit-matter, and the trajectory of evolution is a spiritual journey.

Teilhard sees cosmogenesis as the dynamic process of evolutionary change and transformation: matter evolves, from the simple to the complex and toward greater and greater unity. As matter complexifies externally, from atoms to molecules to organisms, there is an intensification of what Teilhard calls "the within of matter." This is the law of complexity-consciousness: the elements of matter are linked together in more and more complex patterns, and consciousness, which exists in a primitive form even in the prelife stages of evolution, becomes increasingly intense. Corresponding to "the without" and "the within" of matter, there are two distinct components of physical energy: tangential energy, which links the body with others of the same order, and radial energy, which moves evolution upward, toward greater centreity.[51]

This process of "complexity-consciousness" doesn't happen automatically, as though predetermined from without. Rather, it happens in and through what Teilhard calls "groping." The trajectory of evolution hasn't been determined from the beginning, nor does it progress by totally random chance. Groping is testing tracks through experimentation, a trial and error process in that spirit-matter pervades everything so as to try everything, trying everything so as to find everything (like millions of sperm which grope their way toward the ovum). As tracks are tested, eventually one track emerges as *the* track, and then a new process of groping begins, new experiments on many tracks, and then again *the* track emerges.

As evolution progresses, it moves toward goals or thresholds. The first of these is the advent of life in the development of the cell, which represents genuine novelty, consisting in its ability to organize a large amount of matter in a single unit and in certain internal changes toward greater centreity. Teilhard notes that "life no sooner started than it swarmed," filling what was probably a shoreless ocean with innumerable, microscopic cells that are closely interrelated and form a living film on the earth: the biosphere. Now *living* matter becomes more and more complex in its forms and increasingly intense in its consciousness, developing from vegetation to animal life, from arthropods to vertebrates, from less complex mammals to primates. As more complex creatures are formed by the union of less complex elements, the range and variety of the creatures' activities are extended, the integration of their various faculties and operations is improved, and their capacity to respond to the presence of alternative possibilities is increased. Consequently, the ability of successive creatures to focus their behavior is heightened, and the precursor forms of self-possession and purpose appear. And then a second threshold is reached: consciousness becomes reflexive, conscious of being conscious, and we have the advent of thought in the appearance of human beings. As human beings spread to inhabit the globe, a layer of thought now covers the Earth: the noosphere.

Throughout the billions of years of cosmic evolution, numinous presence and divine energy are operative. The gradual unfolding of the universe is a divine process. The world of matter is the world of spirit. The space-time continuum in which creation continues is a divine milieu. Teilhard sees God, not above this world, out of this world, or beyond this world, but *present in* the universe from its inception as the energy that drives evolution forward and as the center of attraction that is the goal toward which we move. We will explore Teilhard's thought further in the final chapter of this book.

Seeing the Numinous

Seeing the numinous universe and being drawn into its dynamic of freedom and love — something religious mystics, including a great many Catholic mystics, have known and written about for centuries — is a possibility for global humanity as we move toward a new millennium. The fact that we don't see the elegance that is right in front of us, that we don't notice the beauty within and without, points to a peculiar pathology of modern humanity. Given this pathology, however, such perception ultimately will demand the courage to take great risks in the transformation of civilization. But the alternative is a frightening path of alienation, isolation, and ultimately ecocide, the death of all life forms. Teilhard wrote this about "Seeing":

> We might say that the whole of life lies in that verb — if not ultimately, at least essentially. Fuller being is closer union...[and] union increases only through an increase in consciousness, that is to say in

vision. And that, doubtless, is why the history of the living world can be summarized as the elaboration of ever more perfect eyes within a cosmos in which there is always something more to be seen. After all, do we not judge the perfection of an animal, or the supremacy of a thinking being, by the penetration and synthetic power of their gaze? To try to see more and better is not a matter of whim or curiosity or self-indulgence. *To see or to perish* is the very condition laid upon everything that makes up the universe.[52]

Emily Dickinson is said to have written about heaven, "What awaits us is the unfurnished eye." To see, oh, to see. Yet seeing, really seeing, is dangerous business: "They have eyes but see not, ears but hear not." Sometimes we fail to see because we know, at another level, that what we see will change us. Hence the passage in the Gospel (Matt. 13:13–15) in which Jesus explains why he speaks in parables:

> Because they look without seeing and listen without hearing or understanding...the prophecy of Isaiah is being fulfilled: "You will listen and listen again, but not understand, see and see again, but not perceive. For the heart of this nation has grown coarse, their ears are dull of hearing and they have shut their eyes, for fear they should see with their eyes, hear with their ears, understand with their hearts, and be converted and healed by me."

In the next chapter, we explore the impact of the numinous universe on the human — the implications a vision of a reconstructed universe has for redefining human persons.

— Chapter 9 —

Reconstructing the Human

We now experience ourselves as the latest arrivals, after some 15 billion years of universe history and after some 4.5 billion years of earth history. Here we are, born yesterday. We need to present ourselves to the planet as the planet presents itself to us, in an evocatory rather than dominating relationship. There is need for a great courtesy toward the Earth.

— Thomas Berry, *The Dream of the Earth*

When we reflect on the creativity and forgiveness, the Wisdom, insight, and perdurance required of humans in our moment of crisis, we understand the need for the tremendous power of the universe for our work, our survival, and our celebration of life. To become fully mature as human persons, we must bring to life within ourselves the dynamics that fashioned the cosmos. We must become these cosmic dynamics and primordial powers in new human form. That is our task: to create the human form of the central powers of the cosmos.

— Brian Swimme, *The Universe Is a Green Dragon*

Cosmogenesis as it is now understood suggests a new anthropology, a new understanding of what it means to be a human being. Seeing the universe as luminous process and numinous unfolding opens up radical new vistas for the meaning and purpose of the human. The sense of a mysterious design in the universe's evolution toward us suggests a new notion of what the uniquely human role might be. The age-old question, "Why am I here?" is beginning to find a new answer. The definition of human being is not "producer/consumer" as our culture tells us, nor "rational animal" as Thomistic Catholicism emphasized, but rather *reflexive consciousness of the universe* itself. The human is to be *that part of the whole that sees the whole,* the mirror in which nature and cosmos look back at themselves and reflect upon themselves. Human beings are the ones who are present to, who notice, who listen to and pay attention to, who reflect and celebrate the splendor and beauty of creation. This reflexive consciousness was activated by the universe millions of years ago and developed gradually toward communities and cultures, in which the wonder and awe that gripped human consciousness led to artistic expression, celebration, and worship. The pathology of modern culture is the decline of this reflexive capacity, and the challenge of reconstructing humanity today is its retrieval. What is most needed today in cosmogenesis is for human beings to recover their original vocation: awareness and celebration. The first step toward the realization of this vocation of human being, however, is to retrieve a sense of our connectedness to nature and cosmos.

Our Unity with Earth and Cosmos

The human is not apart from nature, the Earth, the cosmos, but intimately connected. The human comes forth *from* the Earth, is creatively fashioned, physically and spiritually, by the genius groping of spirit-matter in cosmogenesis. Western understandings of the human, particularly those of recent centuries, have described the human as mind and spirit, possessive of an eternal soul, emphasizing our rationality and our distinctiveness from other life forms. Human being is seen as from another realm and destined to return to another realm. We see ourselves as visitors *to* space-time, pilgrims *on* Earth, wayfarers *in* history. Our true home is elsewhere. The notion that we are *of the Earth,* that we *are* the Earth, that our shape and form and capabilities are gifts to us from the creative genius of earlier life forms — this is a new way of understanding the human. John Seed and Joanna Macy provide us with a graphic sense of who we are in their "Gaia Meditations":

> What are you? What am I? Intersecting cycles of water, earth, air and fire, that's what I am, that's what you are.
>
> WATER — blood, lymph, mucus, sweat, tears, inner oceans tugged by the moon, tides within and tides without. Streaming fluids floating our cells, washing and nourishing through endless riverways of gut and vein and capillary. Moisture pouring in and through and out of you and me, in the vast poem of the hydrological cycle. You are that. I am that.
>
> EARTH — matter made from rock and soil. It too is pulled by the moon as the magma circulates through the planet heart and roots such molecules into biology. Earth pours through us, replacing each cell in the body every seven years. Ashes to ashes, dust to dust, we ingest, incorporate and excrete the earth, are made from earth. I am that. You are that.

AIR — the gaseous realm, the atmosphere, the planet's membrane. The inhale and the exhale. Breathing out carbon dioxide to the trees and breathing in their fresh exudations. Oxygen kissing each cell awake, atoms dancing in orderly metabolism, interpenetrating. That dance of the air cycle, breathing the universe in and out again, is what you are, is what I am.

FIRE — Fire, from our sun that fuels all life, drawing up plants and raising the waters to the sky to fall again replenishing. The inner furnace of your metabolism burns with the fire of the Big Bang that first sent matter-energy spinning through space and time. And the same fire as the lightning that flashed into the primordial soup catalyzing the birth of organic life.

You were there, I was there, for each cell of our bodies is descended in an unbroken chain from that event.... We have been but recently in human form.... In our long planetary journey we have taken far more ancient forms than these we now wear. Some of these forms we remember in our mother's womb, wear vestigial tails and gills, grow fins for hands. Countless times in that journey we died to old forms, let go of old ways, allowing new ones to emerge. But nothing is ever lost. Though forms pass, all returns. Each worn-out cell consumed, recycled...through mosses, leeches, birds of prey....

Beholding you, I behold as well all the different creatures that compose you — the mitochondria in the cells, the intestinal bacteria, the life teeming on the surface of the skin. The great symbiosis that is you.[1]

To think of the human as a constellation of basic elements, as process, or better, as sub-process of a much larger process, as interdependent process, expression of the great flaring forth of the fireball, descendent of the great supernovas, outcome of the steadfast efforts of cells and organisms, creatures of the Earth — such is a great contrast to the prevailing sense of ourselves. Francis of Assisi had it right when he spoke of Brother Sun and Sister Moon. These are not simply figurative ways of speaking. We are *related* to the rocks and the hills, the flowers and the trees, the insects and the birds, the fish and animals. This is the first movement in describing the human: we are process within process within process, fruit of the Earth, brother and sister to the creatures that surround us. We are as much animal as any of them; they, too, are spirited subjects. Together we are the universe, still becoming, mapping energy with inventive originality, bringing forth variety and diversity, magnificence and beauty.

Our relationality and connectedness to everything else cannot be emphasized too greatly. We need to sit with this sense of ourselves and let it permeate our consciousness. Our isolated separateness and need to be other than all of nature is a tragic misunderstanding. This is our home, our origin, our destiny. We can be released from nature-phobia, relax in our embodiedness, smell the ground. We are part of all this; all this is part of us. We must put down our shields and our weaponry, embrace the stars. Though we are born and die, we never came from anywhere else, nor are we going anywhere from here. We are home. This is our family. The universe is trembling with anticipation and ready to embrace this long-lost and alienated brother and sister. This should not be dismissed as romanticism, mysticism, flaky academic ramblings. This is who we are, more real than the embattled individualism that has segregated us from our environment and turned us into the planet's bully. We are integral to an expansive, vibrating, life-giving, processive cosmos and one with the Earth and all her creatures.

The Universe's Reflexive Consciousness

Yet the human is unique, different as a species from any other life form. Though we have descended from others and continue to be radically interdependent with others, we are original and seemingly have a unique role to play in the larger purpose of the universe. Indeed, the human is an extraordinary creation imbued with ingenious creativity and capable of inventive problem-solving. The appearance of the human was characterized by a new faculty of understanding, a new mode of consciousness typified by its sense of wonder and celebration as well as by its ability to refashion and use its exterior environment as a instrument in achieving its own ends.

In the development of human being, we find unique physical transformations, including an increase in brain size, an upright posture and bipedal walking, frontal focus of eyes and countenance, development of the arms and hands for increased capacity in grasping, shaping, and manipulating. Upright posture freed the arms and hands as well as the jaws to develop new roles. The unique abilities of the human in hand usage and the refinement of throat, tongue, teeth, and lips — eventually leading to human speech — combined with enlargement of the brain to shape an original creature that would develop significant new powers of awareness.[2]

It is here, in the dramatic breakthrough to reflexive consciousness, that the universe finds a way to turn back upon itself in conscious self-awareness. The human not only sees the beauty and elegance of the universe and wonders at it, but is aware that it is seeing and won-

dering and finds celebrative participation in story, ritual, music and
dance, a plethora of artistic expressions, and in conscious relationship with the sacred source and center. This capacity to behold and
be present to the great drama of cosmogenesis, micro and macro, its
terror and excitement, its beauty and elegance, its coming to be and
ceasing to be, is the uniqueness of the human.

The Development of Human Consciousness

Anthropological studies tell us that the development of human consciousness doesn't happen in an instant, not even in a generation or a
century. Rather, human development takes place over hundreds of
thousands of years — from the primordial emergence of hominids
four million years ago to the appearance only two hundred thousand years ago of *Homo sapiens*. During this time, gradual physical
transformations are accompanied by dramatic psychic shifts and the
extension of new skills and abilities. Scientists date the emergence
of *Homo habilis* at 2.6 million years ago. *Homo habilis* exhibits
uniquely human characteristics in the shaping and handling of tools,
in an enhanced understanding of plant and animal life in gathering
and hunting, in the development of keen perception (seeing, hearing,
and scent), and in the beginnings of feeling for aesthetic beauty. There
is evidence of remarkable skills in working with stone and a uniquely
human artistic sense in artifacts that have been discovered from this
period. Swimme and Berry tell us that the more significant foundations for the human mode of being were established here in these
transition years. They note that during the period of *Homo habilis*
human consciousness was taking shape in multiple ways:

> The sense of time and space was developing; imagination was receiv-
> ing the impress of its most powerful images; the stock of primordial
> memories that would influence all future generations was being devel-
> oped; an intimate rapport between the human and the natural world
> was being established, a rapport that was filled with both the terror
> and the attraction of the surrounding wilderness.[3]

These psychic developments shape consciousness toward awareness
and celebration: the ability to notice and to reflect, to remember, even
imaginatively to make present.

More than a million years later (1.5 million years ago), *Homo
erectus* flourished throughout Africa, eventually migrating first
throughout Asia and then to southern and western Europe. *Homo
erectus* made further refinements in stone and wooden tools, began

wearing animal skins for clothing, and discovered the controlled use of fire for warmth and food preparation. Controlling fire brought with it a significant psychic advance, giving to the human a sense of power as well as an increased sense of human identity in distinction from other living beings. "With the fire in the hearth a communing with mythic powers takes place, social unity is experienced, a context for reflection on the awesome powers of existence is established."[4] This sense of communing and reflection continues in our experience of candles, bonfires, camp fires, and the fireplace. Fire helps shape the development of human consciousness.

Only after these many millennia of evolutionary development does the human reach the new level of conscious awareness in which we recognize ourselves. It was a mere two hundred thousand years ago that *Homo sapiens* appeared in north-central and east Africa. If the time of the universe from the first instant of cosmogenesis up to today were reduced to twenty-four hours, *Homo sapiens* doesn't appear until minutes before midnight. In terms of the big picture of cosmic evolution, two hundred thousand years ago is only yesterday. The most remarkable new development in the early stages of *Homo sapiens* is the consciousness of death and the development of elaborate burial practices. A heightened sense of the coming to be and passing away of things dramatically affects these first ancestors of ours, much as it does us in our experience of it. Death is such a profound mystery — when we notice it. We don't really notice death until someone very near us dies. Then the great mystery of the arising and ceasing of all things invades our consciousness, as it did many millennia past with early *Homo sapiens*. Here we find early attempts to integrate the human process with the larger processes of the universe in the first attempts to interpret existence:

> The entire range of natural phenomena impinged on human consciousness at this time with a wonder that easily turned into ritual celebration. The transition moments of the cosmological order evoked awe and reverence and invited participation. That all of this was related to danger, to the struggle for survival, to death, provided the challenge and excitement that is itself, perhaps, an imperative deep within the entire cosmological process. The universe was a dramatic reality, filled with powers and voices, constituting the Great Conversation that humans participated in through daily and seasonal rituals as well as through rituals associated with birth, maturity, and death.[5]

It seems that the kind of creature the human was coming to be necessitated awareness of and contact with the sacred. Beyond the increased capacities for tool making, finding shelter, identifying food sources, and utilizing fire, we find in *Homo sapiens* a psychospiritual need for the numinous: "The human needed a rapport with the all-pervasive spirit powers which were manifested throughout the phenomenal world," and thus began to evoke the numinous presence — perceived as the origin, support, and final destiny of all that exists — by engaging in symbolic rituals.[6]

Freedom and Cultural Coding

From the first hominids to *Homo sapiens,* a journey of over 3.5 million years, human consciousness is refined and the capacity for reflexive awareness expands, through the attentive shaping of stone, through the discoveries of the mysteries of fire and death. Understanding and communication, human emotional and feeling capacities, artistic and spiritual acuity — these psychic functions emerge from spirit-matter's groping and take shape for the first time in the development of the human. Parallel to these developments is the notable lack of specialized functioning found elsewhere in evolution. The drama of evolution unfolds in a series of particular new functions (e.g., birds flying, fish swimming, horses running, trees blossoming). These specialized functions are advantageous in their immediate efficacy, but they are also limiting in a larger perspective. In the human, no such specialized physical function appears. Rather, the human is open to an extended range of possibilities:

> To have fins or wings is not to have hands with the immense range of possibilities open to such an organ, which can embrace or repel, bring life or death, build a sand castle or a cathedral, paint the Sistine chapel or play a Mozart concerto. Such an unlimited range of possibilities resides in hands that are freely directed by the human mode of intelligence. Even so there has been a price to be paid for this liberating mode of the human: loss of the instinctive, almost infallible, guidance that is available to the nonhuman species in their various activities.[7]

Lack of specialized function and expansion of possibilities creates the human quality of *freedom,* a leap beyond whatever freedom could be ascribed to spirit-matter in its previous forms. The capacity to select between alternative possibilities, to determine from within and consciously what activity to pursue, takes a giant step in the human. Such freedom necessitates something beyond the genetic coding that guides other life forms in their specialized functions, which operate instinctively. Humans need to learn a great deal more than the survival skills quickly passed on by other animals to their young. This period of learning (training for expanded freedom) is occasioned by still another unique aspect of human existence: a prolonged period of physical helplessness and vulnerability in infancy and childhood. This extended period, needed to activate both physical and psychic capacities, provides time for the extensive mental and emotional development that freedom demands.

> A long acculturation period was needed for arriving at a truly human maturity, for the learning of language, for initiation into the rituals whereby humans coordinate their own activities within the cosmological order, for adjusting to appropriate roles within the social order, for acquiring artistic skills, for learning the stories, the poetry, the songs and music of the community.[8]

Whereas other life forms depend almost completely on genetic coding to receive their guidance, the human depends heavily on this extensive period of acculturation after birth. In such an extended acculturation process, the human recapitulates the long process of human development, compressing millions of years into less than two decades, learning hand-eye coordination and skillful manipulation, discovering the mysteries of fire and death, finding meaning in coordinating with the cosmos. Such recapitulation can only happen in and through human cultures.

> The human is genetically coded toward further transgenetic cultural codings, which in their specific forms are invented by human communities themselves in the various modes of expression. These distinctive cultural inventions are not simply the work of individuals or even a single generation. They are the work of a people over the generations.[9]

In human being, society and culture emerge as part of the evolutive process, carrying psychic developments forward from generation to generation, allowing new groping to work off the breakthroughs of previous human creativity. Genetic coding and cultural coding collaborate toward further cosmic development.

Modernity's Dysfunctional Cultural Coding

However, over the past several hundred years, particularly in the developed nations of the West, human cultural coding has become increasingly dysfunctional, creating dissonance with the genetic coding operative in cosmogenesis. In other words, modern culture is educating human beings for alienation, isolation, conquest, and domination, and we are losing our ability to survive. Thomas Berry says:

> Our cultural coding has set itself deliberately against our genetic coding and the instinctive tendencies of our genetic endowment are systematically negated.... We must go back to the genetic imperative from which human cultures emerge originally and from which they can never be separated without losing their integrity and survival capacity.... We must invent, or reinvent, a sustainable human culture by a descent into our pre-rational, our instinctive resources.[10]

Ecological devastation threatens our physical survival, but survival in a human mode of being is also threatened. Our alienation from nature has cut us off from the source of our psychic and spiritual powers, which originated in the wonder and awe with which reflexive consciousness beheld the beauty of nature. Further, patterns of domination and excessive individualism in modernity have decimated human community. Berry describes the situation well:

> We have before us the question not simply of physical survival, but of survival in a human mode of being, survival and development into intelligent, affectionate, imaginative persons thoroughly enjoying the universe about us, living in profound communion with one another and with some significant capacities to express ourselves in our literature and creative arts. It is a question of interior richness within our own personalities, of shared understanding with others, and of a concern that reaches out to all the living and nonliving beings of the earth, and in some manner out to the distant stars in the heavens.[11]

We have become autistic rather than aware, unable to notice the beauty of trees and flowers, snowflakes and thunderstorms, the flight of birds, the playful interaction of squirrels. The majesty of mountains and the forests' dark mysteries no longer inspire or enchant us. We hardly notice the unique and wondrous beauty of other human beings, whom we seldom contemplate but frequently covet or dismiss solely according to their physical attributes. We are autistic because there's diminished connection between our inner world and the outer world. We are concerned with the human order, but have no perspective on the larger world of nature or cosmos. Our spiritual and psychic abilities (sensitivity, empathy, the capacities of understanding and intimacy, artistic perception) are blunted. This is because the outer world is absolutely necessary to activate the inner world: if we lose contact with the soaring birds, we begin to lose music and poetry. The grandeur and majesty, the terror and wonder of nature is the basis of our interiority. We would have no depth or internal power — no soul — were it not for our contact with the beauty of nature. That is the very essence of reflexive consciousness, mirroring the external. The uniquely human consciousness, fashioned for billions of years by the cosmos and for millennia by the cultures of human communities, is losing its reflexive abilities, caught up in addictive patterns of production and consumption. When human beings report that they're "surviving," what they mean is that they're desperately trying to survive, at least in a human mode of consciousness.

The irony today is that, in the face of such dysfunctional cultural coding, we need to discover again our genes. "Our cultural resources have lost their integrity," writes Berry. "They cannot be trusted. What is needed is not transcendence but *inscendence,* not the brain but the gene."[12] We need to listen to the groping tendencies that lie deep inside our psyches. The hunger for beauty, for connectedness with nature, for community with one another, for contact with the sacred powers of the universe — these cry out to us. Like the lungs of a smoker hacking and coughing, begging for relief, for air, our psyches search for a way beyond the present addictions, groping for the healing of attentive consciousness: to awaken from our cultural pathology, to become aware again, to be able to notice, to wonder, and to celebrate.

Looking to Nature and Cosmos

Reconstructing the human today means retrieving the lost human, connecting again with the forces that created the human many millions of years ago. We must look to nature rather than culture; we must reform cultures in the image of nature. As the first generation to be informed by an empirical view of the origins of the universe, we must look to the forces of cosmogenesis to find our way back to ourselves as human and to our unique role in the universe's creative purpose.

Thomas Berry claims that there is reason to believe that "the earth was never more resplendent than it was when human consciousness awakened in the midst of the unnumbered variety of living forms that swim in the seas and move over the land and fly through the air."[13] While the human impact in recent centuries has tarnished that resplendence and thereby diminished our own interiority, imagining that moment in cosmogenesis and trying to discover the mysteries that lie behind it is a strategy that only we — from the perspective of our view of the whole cosmic process — can pursue.

Such a strategy, were it to draw the fascination of people everywhere, could evoke the awakening of consciousness we desperately need. It would facilitate what is today required: the reinvention of the human — as a species *within* the community of life species, shifting our sense of reality and value from an anthropocentric to a biocentric norm of reference. Getting back to emergence and origins, to the budding forth of reflexive consciousness in the human amid a wild and untamed Earth community, would also help us see the unrepeatability of that process. Getting back to that birthplace of the human spirit, according to Edward O. Wilson, "seems harder every year. If there is a danger in the human trajectory, it is not so much in the survival of our own species as in the fulfillment of the ultimate irony of organic evolution: that in the instant of achieving self-understanding through the mind of man, life has doomed its most beautiful creations."[14] Our emergence, like everything in cosmogenesis, is novel and original, unique, unrepeatable, irreversible. It cannot happen again. There are no second chances. Yet the human moment, though threatened in serious ways, is not over. In some sense, it has only just begun. The challenge we face, that the universe faces in us, is daunting but not beyond us. Our response, however, must be resourced by a return to origins and a relearning of cosmic wisdom. Nature can teach us how to survive, indeed, how to prosper in delight and celebration, which is our true vocation.

Berry's analysis finds that there are three basic laws of the universe that identify the reality, the values, and the directions in which the universe is proceeding. Understanding these laws of cosmogenesis and integrating them into human cultures are today's critical tasks. These laws are identified as differentiation, subjectivity (or *autopoiesis*), and communion — the governing themes and basal intentionality of all existence.

> The universe arises into being as spontaneities governed by the primordial orderings of diversity, self-manifestation, and mutuality.... Indeed, the very existence of the universe rests on the power of this ordering. Were there no differentiation, the universe would collapse into a homogeneous smudge; were there no subjectivity, the universe would collapse into inert, dead extension; were there no communion, the universe would collapse into isolated singularities of being.[15]

Differentiation: The universe is structured for diversity, from elementary particles and atoms to galaxies and planets and throughout the vast array of patterns in the biosphere. This is so from the beginning (with the breaking of cosmic symmetry) and continues up to the present, where we find it in human fingerprints and in snowflakes, in the vast number of life species (somewhere between 10 million and 100 million), and in the great variety of human languages and cultures.

> In the universe, to be is to be different. To be is to be a unique manifestation of existence. The more thoroughly we investigate any one thing in the universe...the more we discover its uniqueness. Indeed, all fifteen billion years form an epic that must be viewed as a whole to understand its full meaning, This meaning is the extravagance of the creative outpouring, where each being is given its unique existence. At the heart of the universe is an outrageous bias for the novel, for the unfurling of surprise in prodigious dimensions throughout the vast range of existence.[16]

Yet modernity has spawned patterns of conformity and homogeneity and a great fear of diversity. Human creativity is shackled by the compulsion to sameness. Boring and deadening routine characterizes industry, business, education, and the professions. True novelty is suspect. The creative impulse of young people atrophies as they are socialized into modern cultural prisons of conservative expectations and demands. Students' economic security becomes the primary outcome sought by schools and educators. Fast-food chains, discount department stores, shopping malls, supermarkets, and suburban subdivisions mirror, not the creativity and variety of nature, but a treadmill existence of cultural cloning. No wonder the young dye their hair purple and blue and seek new body-piercing locations. No wonder they find schools boring and want to extend adolescence rather than settling into careers and family life. Their rebellion is genetically grounded in a groping toward variety, differentiation, uniqueness, creativity — as is the emotional torment and mental illness of their elders. We need to reinvent human cultures for creativity and diversity, honoring imagination and the unique gifts of persons and subcultures, nurturing variety and differences.

Subjectivity: The Enlightenment saw subjectivity as a quality of human existence, but referred to everything else in the universe as objects. Yet what ultimately finds expression in human consciousness is present from the beginning and everywhere in the universe. There is a source of spontaneity, a self-manifesting power, a functioning self, within all things (living and nonliving). Galaxies, stars, the Earth, living organisms, atoms — each reality has a dynamic of organization centered within itself. "Even the simplest atom cannot be understood by considering only its physical structure or the outer world of external relationships," write Swimme and Berry. "Things emerge with an inner capacity for self-manifestation."[17] Interiority and sentience are qualities of the cosmos and all its expressions, including of course the human.

In our objectification of everything else in our imaging of a mechanical universe, we have ironically reified human being as well. The loss of human interiority and feeling is perhaps most notable in what happened to human sexuality in modernity. The reduction of sex to genital stimulation; the focus on physical appearance as the source of sexual attractiveness; the neglect of an internal, self-manifesting dynamic in sexual interaction; the eclipse of celibacy and abstinence from intercourse as acceptable sexual patterns — all typify modern attitudes, not just about sex, but about ourselves. Likewise, in the modern revulsion of contemplative practices and the compulsion toward physical activity. We are out of touch with our interior center and with our sentient capacities, unfeeling and increasingly incapable of feeling, without awareness of our own and others' subjectivity. We need to reinvent human cultures with a renewed sense of depth. "Our immediate challenge," says James Conlon, "is to awaken our interior sensitivities to experience more fully the beauty, mystery, darkness, and dynamic balance of Earth. From these recesses of human self-awareness will flow the organization and action to heal the wounds of Earth and the people of Earth.... The reinvention of humanity will flow from the experiences in the recesses of their being."[18]

Communion: Cosmogenesis is governed by differentiation, by subjectivity, and by communion.

> In the very first instant when the primitive particles rushed forth, every one of them was connected to every other one in the entire universe. At no time in the future existence of the universe would they ever arrive at a point of disconnection.... The universe evolves into beings that are different from each other, and that organize themselves. But in addition to this, the universe advances into community — into a differentiated web of relationships among sentient centers of creativity.[19]

This web of interconnection is everywhere in nature: the community within the atom, the interrelatedness of Earth's spheres (ice, sea, life, air, fire, rock, thought), the interdependence of life species, planetary and galactic relationships. So, too, with the human: our connection to and interdependence with one another and everything else in the universe is scientific fact.

Yet modernity is characterized by alienation, a sense of separateness and isolation. Human community and our communion with the natural world is sundered by fear and conflict. We not only perceive ourselves excessively as autonomous and separate individuals, but our self-consciousness is characterized also by an overagainstness. We compete, compete, compete — seeing our success as the demise of others. Psychologists analyze human interaction in "win-lose" patterns. Winning, however, is increasingly a lonely and even terrifying place to be. It goes against our deeper, genetic coding:

> The loss of relationship, with its consequent alienation, is a kind of supreme evil in the universe. In the religious world this loss was traditionally understood as an ultimate mystery. To be locked up in a private world, to be cut off from intimacy with other beings, to be incapable of entering the joy of mutual presence — such conditions were taken as the essence of damnation.[20]

Reinventing the human and human cultures means a radical new sense of our interconnectedness and mutual dependence, our need for community and communion.

When we look to nature and to cosmos, we find the qualities needed to refashion the human, qualities such as sensitivity, creativity, risk-taking, generosity, and celebration. These qualities characterize spirit-matter in its groping activity from the beginning and at every stage of development. Today the universe is urging them on humanity by a return to the central characteristics of nature: differentiation, subjectivity, and communion. Allowing these characteristics to shape ourselves and our cultures is key to our survival and our prosperity. They can become in the human the cardinal virtues of global humanity in the twenty-first century.

Toward the Ecological Self

Awakening from our cultural pathology through retrieval of awareness is the great spiritual challenge of our time, the key to connecting again with the riches of human genetic heritage. Reconnecting with nature and cosmos is tied to practicing awareness. Buddhism's analysis of the human predicament and the solution it offers appears directly on target: the problem is mind, and its solution is mindfulness; the problem is craving, and its solution is cooling our thirst through detachment; the problem is distraction and noise, and its solution is quiet attentiveness; the problem is the ego-self (the substantial self), and its solution is Buddha consciousness (awareness of reality as flow, as process). The problem is the small self ("the skin-encapsulated ego"), and its solution is the eco-self (coextensive with other humans, all life forms, the planet, the cosmos).

Buddhism sees the self as a metaphoric construct rather than as a hard description of reality. It is our way of structuring human identity and agency, the hypothetical piece of turf on which we construct our strategies for survival, the notion around which we focus our instincts for self-preservation and our needs for self-approval, the boundaries of our self-interest. The substantial self becomes the source of suffering because it denies or hides the true, processive nature of who we are. It masks the interdependent flow of our coming to be and our cessation. Like Einstein's description of the universe as cosmogenesis, it is better (truer) to see the self as an energy map in constant flux, like the flame of a candle or the tide of the ocean. Where is the "river" in the flowing water? Where is the "flame" in the burning candle? Where is the "self" in life's journey? The substantial self is our effort to step out of process, to stop the flow, to be rather than to become. But the human being is better described as the "human becoming" — emergent from the union of sperm and egg and genetically programmed from ancestral origins, dependent on the ingesting of energy from the sun translated into green plants through photosynthesis and, perhaps, from thence into the muscle tissue of animals, dependent, too, on water and oxygen, the warmth and acceptance of others' love. The human becoming is embryo, infant, toddler, child, adolescent, young adult, midlifer, senior citizen, corpse. Where is the self? Which set of cells? Which psychic state? Each image of the self is a snapshot that images the energy map at a given time, but the process is flowing, coming to be, constantly changing, ceasing to be.

Alan Watts called the self "the skin-encapsulated ego." Gregory Bateson referred to it as "the epistemological error of Occidental civilization." In modernity it serves as conceptual support for a narrow individualism, an isolated separateness, an overagainstness, a threat to our survival — a very self-absorbed ME.

In a compelling essay interpreting Buddhism in the context of ecological crisis, Joanna Macy discusses the arising of "the ecological self" as replacement for the conventional self. Today we experience a widening of identity and self-interest due to three converging developments: (1) the dangers that are threatening to overwhelm us and a loss of certainty that there will be a future; (2) the emergence of the new paradigm in science, replacing the old assumptions about a distinct, separate, continuous self with a processive "self" seen as open, self-organizing system whose principal functions arise in interaction with its environment; and (3) the resurgence of nondualistic spiritualities, blurring or even undermining categorical distinctions between self and other.

An expanded self is emerging, arising in the grief, the anger, the fear we experience before the decimated eco-system and our deconstructed world. Several weeks ago when I was watching the evening news, the report of two boys throwing a third child out the fourteenth-floor window of a public housing project was too much for me. I wept spontaneously as the reporter told how the boy had been dangled for minutes while his older brother pleaded with the two other boys to save him. But he was dropped to his death because he had refused to steal candy for the older boys. The news was so stunning in its tragedy, I didn't know who I felt more compassion for, the boy who had been killed or his killers, the older brother whose pleas were ignored or those who ignored the desperate attempts to save his brother. I wept. I sobbed. What kind of society does this to its children? The graphic and tragic news seemed like a metaphor for our larger world. I felt a depth of pain, not because it had been inflicted on my body or even on someone with whom I had a personal relationship. It was more an experience of a larger, extended self, a broadened self-interest, that grieved — for us all.

I had much the same response to the movie *Schindler's List*. Did I feel more compassion for the Jewish victims of Nazi murder and terror, or for the German perpetrators who had lost all sensitivity and compassion, their very souls? That was forty-eight hours of mourning — again, weeping for us all. Awareness of and presence to planetary devastation can and does evoke feelings of sadness, anger, and fear. "When we mourn over the destruction of our biosphere," Macy writes, "it is categorically distinct from mourning over our own death. We suffer *with* our world — that is the literal meaning of compassion." An extension of identity comes, not through efforts to be noble or altruistic, but simply by being present to and owning our pain.[21]

The larger eco-self is arising, too, from the world of science. Life is seen as dynamically composed of self-organizing systems, patterns that are sustained in and by their relationships (cybernetics). The notion of the separate self, distinct from the world it observes and acts within, is undermined by the findings of twentieth-century science: the self's perceptions are shaped by its changing position in relation to other phenomena (Einstein); the very act of observation changes what is observed (Heisenberg). Macy observes:

> There is no logical or scientific basis for construing one part of the experienced world as *me* and the rest as *other*, because as open, self-organizing systems, our very breathing, acting, and thinking arise in interaction with our shared world through the currents of matter, energy, and information that move through us and sustain us. In the web of relationships that sustain these activities, there is no clear line demarcating a separate, continuous self.

The *process* that decides and acts cannot be neatly identified with the isolated subjectivity of the individual or located within the confines of the skin. The total self-corrective unit that processes information is a system whose boundaries do not at all coincide with the boundaries either of the body or what is properly called "self." Seen in this way, the self is a false reification of an improperly delimited part of a much larger field of interlocking processes. It is a metaphor that we can decide to limit to our own skin or broaden to include family, organization, species, planet, the universe.[22]

The resurgence of nondualistic spiritualities offers us hope in the reactivating of awareness and through such awareness an expanded self-interest. Buddhist meditation heals the mind through the discipline of attentiveness. Being present to our breathing, body posture, the flow of consciousness — over a long period of time — brings mindfulness. We become present to the now, open to the other, freed from internal preoccupations and aware of the external, even when it threatens or pulls at our desires. We are aware that we are frightened, attentive to our desires, but recognize that reality is neither our fears nor our desires. We become one with the flowing, and through expanded compassion give ourselves to it. Self is expanded from identification with the individual body-mind to family, circle of friends, nation, race, human race, all living things, planet, all that is. A nondualistic Catholicism similarly offers practitioners healing and liberation, retrieval of presence to and participation in the flow, a way of compassion. We will explore all of this in greater detail in chapter 10.

— Chapter 10 —

Catholicism Green and Cosmic

> Let us not forget that nowhere are the elements of a complete "evo-
> lutive energy" better recognizable and more advanced today than in
> a well understood Christianity: that is to say, in the flaming percep-
> tion of a Universe which is neither cold, nor closed — but which
> irreversibly converges (Matter and Spirit altogether) on a loving and
> lovable Center of intense personality.
> —Teilhard de Chardin, *Building the Earth*

> Being rooted in love for our real communities of life and for our com-
> mon mother, Gaia, can teach us patient passion, a passion that is not
> burnt out in a season, but can be renewed season after season. Our
> revolution is not just for us, but for our children, for the generations
> of living beings to come. What we can do is plant a seed, nurture a
> seed-bearing plant here and there, and hope for a harvest that goes
> beyond the limits of our powers and the span of our lives.
> —Rosemary Radford Ruether, *Gaia and God*

Catholicism, like other human cultures and communities, must
undertake its reconstruction today in light of what we now know
about the universe and the unique role of humanity in cosmogenesis.
We need to rethink and refeel what it means to be Catholic according
to the great cosmic themes of differentiation, subjectivity, and communion. The challenge is to reconfigure this great spiritual tradition
in the light of new vision, bringing together its centuries-old wisdom
with a radically changed context. Catholicism must be made green
and cosmic.

Charlene Spretnak has written, "The core teachings of the great
wisdom traditions live in an enduring present. They are relevant,
powerful, and accessible. The insights that arise from their core practices yield a paradigm of resistance, creativity, and profound renewal
for our time."[1] I believe this to be true of the wisdom traditions in
general, and in particular of Catholicism. There is a premodern richness in Catholicism that, when retrieved and seen with postmodern
eyes, can resource our healing, reactivate reflexive consciousness, and

inspire creative energies for envisioning and shaping harmony and balance between the human and our larger cosmic context. Catholicism need not be seen solely as part of the problem, but can play an important and creative role in our groping toward a solution. Indeed, there are spiritual riches in Catholicism that can help to bring about a new renaissance in human cultures and a sustainable global society.

In this final chapter, we will revisit the key themes of Catholicism developed in Part Two (Jesus, grace, sacramental community, and liberation) with the image of a reconstructed universe in mind. How to image Catholicism green and cosmic, how to refashion the Catholic experience as access to and celebration of numinous universe, how to reconstruct Catholicism by connecting again with our genes — these are the questions we bring to the core aspects of our tradition. Sallie McFague comments:

> Christians have often not been allowed to feel at home on the earth, convinced after centuries of emphasis on otherworldliness that they belong somewhere else — in heaven or another world.... But what if we were not only allowed but encouraged to love the earth? What if we saw the earth as part of the body of God, not as separate from God (who dwells elsewhere) but as the visible reality of the invisible God? What if we also saw this body as overlain by the body of the cosmic Christ, so that wherever we looked we would see bodies that are incorporated into the liberating, healing, inclusive love of God?[2]

Reconstructing Catholicism — refashioning this particular wisdom tradition for a new generation and for generations to come — means retrieving an organic sense of the cosmos and perceiving its sacred character, recognizing that Jesus' call to conversion is an appeal to heal human freedom, drawing human beings into the universal and cosmic rule of God. Catholicism is about helping us reclaim our vocation to become aware again and to become present and responsive to the numinous universe.

The Experience of the Cosmic Christ

The Jesus experience has been interpreted from the beginnings of Christian tradition as a cosmic event. Christ is seen as the cosmic manifestation of God, appearing both as the immanent divine source and ground of creation and its ultimate redemptive healing, Christ as both creator and redeemer of the cosmos. In Jesus, the creative powers that brought all things into being are made manifest. In Jesus, the tragic catastrophe of human freedom gone awry is healed and humanity is made new. In Jesus, the hidden design active in creating the heavens and the Earth and all life including the human, that which sustains and nurtures everything in the universe, reveals its mysterious purpose as reconciling love. The *basileia* proclaimed by Jesus in word and deed is that harmony and balance and generous compassion that was always present from the beginning. The twofold evolutive movement of God generously giving Godself to creation and creation groping toward its fulfillment in openness to Godself meet in the divine outpouring that fills Jesus. And in his "yes" to that divine force that shapes the universe, creation itself is revealed as "the body of God."

"Even as the life-giving breath extends to all bodies in the universe," writes Sallie McFague, "so also does the liberating, healing, and suffering love of God. The resurrected Christ is the cosmic Christ, the Christ freed from the body of Jesus of Nazareth, to be present in and to all bodies.... The liberating, inclusive love of God for all is alive in and through the entire cosmos."[3] This sense of the cosmic Christ, present from the first centuries of Christian faith, sees salvation as the direction of creation and creation as the place of salvation: "The entire fifteen-billion-year history of the universe ... is seen to be the cosmic Christ, the body of God in the Christian paradigm. Thus, the direction or hope of creation, all of it, is nothing less than what I understand that paradigm to be for myself and for other human beings: the liberating, healing, and inclusive love of God."[4]

Human freedom, expressive of genetic coding but developed and given direction in cultural coding, had become conflicted and problematic. The design of cosmogenesis was being frustrated by human pride and greed. Reflexive consciousness was languishing in human self-absorption. Humans had eyes but could not see; they had ears but could not hear. Their minds were closed and their hearts had hardened. Jesus, in his rejection of conventional wisdom (the result of cultural coding), opens himself to the ancient wisdom of Jewish covenant and sees it as universal. The God of creation and the God of liberation reflect a singular compassion, revealed in the trust of Abraham and the gift of progeny, the vision of Moses and gift of desert sustenance, the prophets' oracles and the gift of purified survival. Divine *sophia*, agent of creation and liberation, finds in Jesus her incarnation and in his rhetoric and activity her supreme manifestation. The problem of human freedom is healed in Jesus' obedience to God's wisdom and compassion. Cosmogenesis is reconciled to its design. This is the meaning of redemption.

Redemption and Creation

Throughout much of Christian history, redemption has been mis-
interpreted. Drawing on Gnostic and Platonic thought, Christian
thinkers sometimes saw creation itself as the problem. Matter and
body were seen as intrinsically evil and, thus, to be transcended.
The erotic urges of creation were condemned. The world was to be
overcome toward a purely spiritual realm. Redemption became liberation from creation, because creation itself was seen as "fallen."
The real problem — human freedom's frustration of nature and humanity out of sync with cosmic purpose — was eclipsed in a dualistic
understanding of reality that saw nature and cosmos as evils to be
overcome. The result has been an exacerbation of the real problem:
human freedom's further alienation from cosmic purpose. But the
redemption that Christ brings heals human freedom and draws humanity into a deeper communion with matter and energy, with Earth
and cosmos. The mystery of Christ is the union of God and cosmos. The liberation of Christ heals human blindness and reactivates
vision. It heals hardened hearts and unleashes our passionate love
for creation. The Christ drama is a return to genesis and a retrieval
of primal human consciousness, setting us free from dysfunctional
cultural coding.

> God, in the model of the universe as God's body, makes her home
> in the universe (and in our planet) and gives us, we believe, in the
> story of Jesus of Nazareth some clues as to how we should live in our
> home. The most basic clue is to *love it,* for that is what the liberating
> parables and healing stories, and the eating practices in different ways
> suggest.[5]

Reconstructing Catholicism means recognizing continuity between
creation and redemption. The mysterious generativity that activates
cosmic fluctuation and energizes the groping of the universe's evolution now seeks to heal the human, to liberate us from fear and
untrust, to make us humble and grateful, generous and creative.
Christ is a critical moment in the reactivation of human consciousness. Is it any wonder that those first Christians turned to the
language of creation to tell of their redemptive experience?

> He has taken us out of the power of darkness and created a place
> for us in the *basileia* of the Son that he loves, and in him, we gain
> our freedom, the forgiveness of our sins. He is the image of the un-
> seen God and the Elder Brother of all things created, for it was by
> him and in him that all things were created, whether here on earth in

the sensible world or in the world beyond the horizon of our senses which we call heaven.... All things were created through him, by him, in him. But he himself is before all things; in him they consist and subsist.... He is the New Beginning, the First-born of the dead.... For it was [God's] good pleasure that in Christ all fullness should dwell; it is through him and in him that all things are to be reconciled and reharmonized. For he has removed the contradiction and made peace by his own blood. So all things in the visible earth and in the invisible heaven should dwell together in him. That includes you, who were once alienated, enemies in your own minds to God's purposes, immersed in evil actions; but now you are bodily reconciled in his fleshy body. (Col. 1:13–21)[6]

Being taken out of the power of darkness, gaining our freedom, being born anew from death, reconciling all things — these are the result of revisiting creation, tapping into the immense power of genesis, drawing from the source. Redemption is the universe retrieving the creative powers of cosmogenesis through the healing of human freedom.

Christ as Incarnation

Human freedom is healed in Christ and reflexive consciousness is reactivated, but this healing and reactivation do not come from *outside* the cosmos. Rather, Jesus emerges from *within* the process of cosmogenesis. He is the manifestation of divine Mystery, present from the beginning and active in evolutive groping, but emergent in conscious self-reflexive awareness and concrete personal manifestation only in this new moment that is Jesus Christ. The incarnation is not about a divine being external to the evolving universe suddenly breaking into the material realm. Again, such an interpretation is tied to dualism's influence on Christian thinking. The incarnation is the emergent manifestation in human being, in the energy map that is Jesus of Nazareth, of the immense Mystery present, and active within, from the beginning. The author of the Fourth Gospel describes the incarnational event this way:

In the beginning was the Word [Greek *Logos*]: the Word was with God and the Word was God. He was with God in the beginning. Through him all things came to be.... All that came to be had life in him, and that life was the light of humanity.... The Word was made flesh, and he lived among us, and we saw his glory. (John 1:1–14)

Teilhard's Christology

Teilhard de Chardin, whose thought about numinous presence within the process of cosmogenesis was discussed briefly in chapter 8, is an important resource in revisioning Catholic tradition in the light of a reconstructed universe. Just as the advent of life in the development of the cell and the advent of thought in the development of reflexive consciousness in the human are threshold breakthroughs in evolution's journey, so too is Jesus. In Jesus, according to Teilhard's view, evolution pushes forward in the advent of compassionate consciousness. He is "the new human" that humanity has been groping toward, the track that emerged from centuries of experimentation. In Jesus, radial energy reaches its peak and the love that is destined to unite all of humankind and through them the whole universe breaks forth from within the Earth.

Cosmogenesis, which in the advent of life is biogenesis and in the advent of thought is noogenesis, now becomes "Christogenesis." Humanity is called to a new unity in "the body of Christ," and to "live in Christ" is to become a new creation, to inhabit the "theosphere." To become a Christian, in Teilhard's view, is not so much a matter of language or ideology; rather, it is the experience of a new consciousness, characterized by seeing the Whole and by loving it. It is in cosmic compassion that we affirm our unity with the whole of humankind and freely choose at-one-ment with all things. To follow Jesus means to pursue the track he represents — onward and upward, with additional experimentation. To become this new humanity has little to do with explicit, confessional belief. It has everything to do with groping. Jesus' *basileia* of healing and liberation is groping, now in human systems.

This sense of groping toward a new future of harmony and balance shifts the focus of hope for the future from heaven to Earth, from an otherworldly goal to the transformation of cosmos. Teilhard's understanding points us toward "the Omega point": the goal that the universe is pursuing, the end in which God will be all in all. He sees Christ as the disclosure of this goal, the one in whom the divinization of cosmos dawns. Compassionate consciousness is, then, the cutting edge today of evolution's journey. True compassion is grounded in mystical insight: that the gradual unfolding of the universe is a divine process. God is present in the universe, from its inception, is the energy that drives evolution forward, and is the center of attraction that is the goal toward which we move. Christogenesis in the incarnation is the manifestation of this energy and the appearance of this center of attraction.

Grace As Radial Energy

From our discussion in chapter 8, you may recall that in Teilhard's law of complexity-consciousness, matter complexifies externally, and correspondingly there occurs an intensification of the within of matter. Corresponding to the without and the within of matter there are two distinct components of physical energy: tangential energy, that links the body with others of the same order, and radial energy, which creates internal bonding. The Third Insight in Redfield's novel *The Celestine Prophecy* provides a popular understanding of this when it describes the human discovery of a new energy which forms the basis of and radiates outward from all things, including ourselves:

> The basic stuff of the universe, at its core, is looking like a kind of pure energy that is malleable to human intention and expectation in a way that defies our old mechanistic model of the universe — as though our expectation itself causes our energy to flow out into the world and affect other energy systems.[7]

In human beings, psychic development is toward conscious love, which Teilhard describes as the strongest, the most universal, and the most mysterious of cosmic energies.

> Essentially, it is the attraction of each element of the universe by the universal term of evolution, Omega; it is the primitive and universal psychic energy, existing at all levels of the universe. In its most rudimentary forms it is practically identical with molecular forces; later in the evolutionary process it takes the form of reproductive drives; in humankind, love has entered the realm of reflexive consciousness, of the spiritual.[8]

The significant mutations now taking place are not in anatomical and physiological patterns, but in patterns of thinking, knowing, feeling, desiring, choosing, willing. Evolution today progresses at the level of human volition — in our capacity to freely choose love. Teilhard sees the ultimate meaning of cosmogenesis as a process of "amorization." As tangential energy decreases and the external universe experiences entropy, radial energy increases, and we experience divinization. This process is guided by intuited faith, which sees the integrity of all things in God. Intuited faith extends evolution's curve in the direction of community and compassion — an explosion of radial energy linking us to one another and pulling us upward toward a collective consciousness. Love is the higher form of human energy, the higher and purified form of an inner universal attraction, and it is love alone that is capable of carrying the personalization of the cosmos to its term by reconciling opposites without allowing one to be destroyed by the other, and by bringing together extremes in the pursuit of both union and distinction to their limits. Freely chosen love, grounded in an intuition of cosmic unity: this is what has emerged in Christ, the track on which evolution now proceeds. Teilhard writes,

> The phenomenon of Christianity seems to have been obscured by the way in which men have often tried to define it by certain characteristics which are only accidental or secondary to it. Simply to present the teaching of Christ as an awakening of man to his personal dignity or as a code of purity, gentleness and resignation, or again as the starting point of our Western civilization, is to mask its importance and make its success incomprehensible by ignoring its characteristically new content. The essential message of Christ is not to be sought in the Sermon on the Mount, nor even in the drama of the cross; it lies wholly in the affirmation that God, a personal being, presents Himself to man as the goal of a personal *union*.

In this sense, Jesus is the disclosure of the goal that had been intimated but never explicitly known. What cosmogenesis is striving for is nothing less than personal union with the divine. The religious groping of human beings had drawn near the idea that God, a spirit, could only be reached by spirit, but in Christianity this becomes explicit: "The gift of the heart in place of the prostration of the body; communion beyond sacrifice; God as love, and only to be finally reached in love; this is the psychological revolution."[9]

Ewert Cousins comments on Teilhard's vision of grace as radial energy and connects it with a broader Catholic theological tradition focused on the immanence of the Spirit:

> What Teilhard sees as the immanent love energy of the cosmos, the theological tradition saw as the action of the transcendent Spirit, who is the love of the Father and the Son. Both Teilhard and the theological tradition affirm absolute immanence and transcendence. Although the transcendent is immanent in all levels of the cosmos — even in a speck of dust or an atom — the transcendent is not present in all levels in the same way, but according to the perfection of the level. The Spirit works in the plant kingdom as the ultimate source of vital energy, but is not present in his full personal reality because the plants are not persons and do not have the power to receive or give a personal response.... However, human beings can respond in a per-

sonal way since they are images of the Trinity. Finally, on the level of grace, the Spirit is present to human beings in a most personal way, transforming them into likeness of the Trinity.[10]

Locating grace within spirited matter, seeing it as a component of physical energy, shatters previous dualisms. Grace is not at odds with nature; grace is the heart of nature. Personal union with God is not found in a flight from matter and body, but precisely in turning toward, and embracing, the physical universe. Opening oneself to divine love means opening oneself to the drama of existence — to the pain and the violence, to exhilaration and the sublime, to life and death and new life. One does not — indeed, cannot — find God apart from creation; and whoever looks deeply at creation will see God. But such looking and seeing is never as an observer from afar; rather, it is the contemplative seeing, the mystical vision, that draws one into communion.

The Mysticism of Francis of Assisi

Francis of Assisi (1181–1226) exemplifies this mystical connection to nature and can serve as a representative of Catholic nature mysticism. He has been rediscovered as a spiritual model in our time and has become the patron saint of the ecology movement. Matthew Fox reports that Francis follows the cosmic or creation-centered tradition of Hildegard of Bingen (1098–1179) and of the Celtic tradition that flourished in both the Rhineland and in northern Italy, where Francis lived.[11] Celtic spirituality emerged from the marriage of Christianity and pre-Christian religions. "In pre-Christian Celtic religion," writes Sean McDonagh, "powerful spirits were associated with the forces of nature. The ancient Celts recognized water as the first principle and source of life.... Trees and sacred groves were also seen as abodes of the spirits. In the transition to Christianity, monastic churches, like that of St. Columcille in Derry, were built in a clearing within a sacred grove."[12] Thus, the nature mysticism that Francis reflects is quite broad in Catholic tradition. Its eclipse in the Enlightenment and modernity is due largely to the contradictory attitudes that nature mysticism represents vis-à-vis rationalistic dualism. Seeing God in nature and sensing a loving connection to the Earth, the elements, the diverse creatures, is not alien or foreign to Catholicism. Francis is representative of a long and broad Catholic tradition that celebrates creation as numinous and experiences the unity of self, nature, and God. "For Francis, every creature in the world was a mirror of

God's presence," writes Sean McDonagh. "What emerges here might be called a *fellowship approach* to creatures...a kinship with, and deep insight into the heart of all creation."[13]

Ewert Cousins says, "St. Francis gave expression to a holistic spirituality that finds resonance in primal peoples and in the global spirituality of the future....Because he felt himself part of the family of creation, he did not exploit or dominate nature, but rather humanized nature and naturalized the human."[14] He sees Francis's attitude toward nature and his mysticism as even more relevant to the twentieth century than to the thirteenth:

> In the Middle Ages and into modern times, Westerners did not listen seriously to his *Canticle.* They failed to call water their sister and air their brother. In the global environment of the twentieth century, we have no choice. We must listen to Francis' *Canticle* — and sing its melody along with him — or we will perish from the earth.[15]

The Canticle of Brother Sun, written in 1225, about a year and a half before his death, is the most celebrated legacy of Francis. It is similar to expressions one finds among primal peoples, Native American spirituality for example, in its attitudes toward the wonders of nature:

> Most high, all powerful, all good Lord!
> All praise is Yours,
>   all glory, all honor and blessing.
> To You, alone, Most High, do they belong.
> No mortal lips are worthy
> To pronounce your name.
> All praise be Yours, my Lord,
>   through all that you have made,
> And first my Lord Brother Sun,
> Who brings the day;
>   and light You give to us through him.
> How beautiful is He,
>   how radiant in all his splendour!
> Of You, most high, he bears the likeness.
> All praise be Yours, my Lord,
>   through Sister Moon and Stars;
> In the heavens You made them, bright
>   and precious and fair.
> All praise be Yours,
>   my Lord, through Brother Wind and Air.
> And fair and stormy, all the weather's moods,
> By which You cherish all that You have made.
> All praise be Yours, my Lord, through Sister Water,

So useful, lowly, precious and pure.
All praise be Yours, my Lord, through Brother Fire,
Through whom you brighten up the night.
How beautiful He is, how gay!
Full of power and strength.
All praise be Yours, my Lord,
    through Sister Earth, our mother,
Who feeds us in her sovereignty and produces
Various fruits and coloured flowers and herbs.[16]

This canticle exemplifies Francis's sense of organic relationship between nature, the human, and God.

For him nature was not something separate from God and human beings: an autonomous given, standing on its own apart. Nor was it humanity's footstool on which they could lift themselves above, trampling and exploiting nature in the process. For him nature was sacred, an expression of God himself; it was divine gift which bore God's imprint.[17]

Such awareness and connectedness is the fruit of a habit of prayer, something Francis practiced through his lifetime. Prayer is key to transforming our consciousness, opening our minds and hearts to numinous presence, teaching us both humility and gratitude.

Contemplative Prayer

Prayer is energy. It is opening ourselves to the divine energy that creates and sustains the cosmos. It is directing that energy toward other energy maps: persons, situations, events, circumstances. Prayer draws us into the very center of the dynamic of cosmogenesis, where numinous, personal compassion mysteriously reconciles and harmonizes. Effective prayer requires our maximum attention and focus. Distractions from without and within must be noticed, but set aside, as we concentrate fully on the sacred Source who is love itself. Prayer requires effort, because we are so self-absorbed, so preoccupied with our fears and desires, so distracted by our concerns, petty and large. In prayer, we give ourselves and our field of influence over to this personal source of perfect compassion and open our consciousness with all its psychic powers to the great Mystery that rules the universe.

Prayer is a deeply personal encounter with the personal presence that permeates everything. Like all personal encounters, it moves gradually and with much hesitation toward trust and genuine openness, demanding in turn self-revelation, self-acceptance, self-confidence, self-assertion, self-surrender. Prayer leads us from alienation and distancing toward intimacy and communion. In the process, we give over our efforts to dominate and control, gradually yielding and finally surrendering. We are drawn out of ourselves and into the divine milieu, enlarging our field of vision, recognizing ourselves as part of an immensity, a flow, a great mystery, an intricate web of interaction. Some mystics compare it to a dance, a wondrous, music-drenched dance, where movement and personal presence cause our self-consciousness to melt and our awareness of everything around us to be heightened. Prayer leads us to awareness: alert noticing and empathy.

Thomas Merton reminds us that the love of God, which seeks us in every situation and seeks our good, also seeks our awakening. It is in and through prayer that we are awakened and our freedom reconnected with the purpose within the universe:

> Since this awakening implies a kind of death to our exterior self, we will dread His coming in proportion as we are identified with this exterior self and attached to it.... The mind that is the prisoner of conventional ideas, and the will that is captive of its own desire cannot accept the seeds of an unfamiliar truth and a supernatural desire. For how can I receive the seeds of freedom if I am in love with slavery and how can I cherish the desire of God if I am filled with another and an opposite desire? God cannot plant his liberty in me because I am prisoner and I do not even desire to be free. I love my captivity.... I must learn therefore to let go of the familiar and the usual and consent to what is new and unknown to me. I must learn to "leave myself" in order to find myself by yielding to the love of God....
>
> For it is God's love that warms me in the sun and God's love that sends the cold rain. It is God's love that feeds me in the bread I eat and God that feeds me also by hunger and fasting. It is the love of God that sends the winter days when I am cold and sick, and the hot summer when I labor and my clothes are full of sweat: but it is God Who breathes on me with light winds off the river and in the breezes out of the wood. His love spreads the shade of the sycamore over my head and...it is God's love that speaks to me in the birds and streams....
>
> If these seeds would take root in my liberty, and if His will would grow from my freedom, I would become the love that He is, and my harvest would be His glory and my own joy. And I would grow together with thousands and millions of other freedoms into the gold of one huge field praising God, loaded with increase, loaded with wheat.[18]

Praying for others is directing this focus on divine love outward toward other energy maps, sending our openness and our yielding to circumstances and situations external to ourselves. It isn't asking God to change her mind, nor is it a magical effort to control according to our own desires and fears. It is reflecting radial energy, focusing it with our psychic powers, communicating compassion. We send peace and harmony and love toward others to become part of the dynamic process affecting their energy field. The power of prayer is the power of radial energy communicated in and through the capacities of our own consciousness.

In Catholicism, as with Christianity generally, we pray *in and with* the risen and cosmic Christ. In his complete and total surrender to God in life and in death, Jesus has been swept up in the compassion of God that rules the universe. This is the meaning of the tradition that he is now "sitting at the right hand of God." He has given himself over to the radial energy that seeks to reconcile all things and harmonize the cosmos. He is in complete communion with the creative force that brings everything into being and nurtures life and thought and love. In consciously joining ourselves to him, clinging to his surrender and his openness, we can and do experience a letting go of our external self with all of its fears and desires and an openness to God's *basileia*, where healing and liberation put us in harmony with the elegance of the universe and its divine source and goal.

Ecological Consciousness in Sacramental Community

Contemplative prayer and the mystical vision it brings are only part of the rich array of practices within the Catholic tradition that offer healing, reactivation, and communion. Another source of transformation and conversion comes in the sacramental community, where ritual opens our eyes to the numinous character of the cosmos and symbolic action connects us with the dynamic of Christ risen. In Catholic liturgy, the divinization of the material universe is celebrated in symbolic transformation, and the numinous depths of the elements (earth, air, fire, and water) are disclosed. The transforming character of divine compassion is celebrated in the remembering and making present of Jesus Christ, who is not only the peasant sage healer and liberator of Galilee, but the cosmic Christ whose risen presence continues the healing and the liberating transformation of humankind and the whole of creation. He is past, present, and future — drawing us into the pursuit of a cosmic goal: God all in all, the intense fullness of radial energy in the reconciliation of all creation. The universe as a whole is the sacrament of God — the visible, physical, bodily presence of God. "The cosmic Christ metaphor," says Sallie McFague, "suggests that Jesus' paradigmatic ministry is not limited to the years 1–30 C.E.... but is available to us throughout nature. It is available everywhere, it is unlimited — with one qualification: it is mediated *through bodies*.... The entire cosmos is the habitat of God, but we know this only through the mediation of the physical world."[19]

In sacramental community, the cosmic Christ is mediated to us through bodies, human and nonhuman, and the paradigmatic ministry of Jesus stretches across the centuries to touch us. But there is something more: in sacramental community we learn a pattern of perception that opens up *all of nature* as the presence of the cosmic Christ. The bodies that mediate the compassionate, healing, liberating reality of Christ to us are not limited to those we encounter in the sacramental community, but what goes on there opens our eyes to that same numinous presence everywhere we go. An encounter with any body can become a sacramental experience — that is the perception we gain through participation in sacramental community. In this sense, a nature mysticism is nurtured by our sacramental perception of divine presence in water and fire, bread and wine. "Traditional sacramentalism is an important perspective, for it is the major way Christianity has preserved and developed an appreciation of nature," according to Sallie McFague.

> It has encouraged Christians to look upon the world as valuable — indeed, as holy — and has served as a counterforce to two other perspectives on nature within Christian history, one that divorces it totally from God through secularizing it and one that dominates and exploits it.... Christian sacramentalism has included nature as a concern of God and way to God rather than limiting divine activity to human history.... From its incarnational base, it claims that in analogy with the body of Jesus the Christ all bodies can serve as ways to God, all can be open to and give news of the divine presence.[20]

Today we need to reconstruct Catholic ritual to more clearly teach its ecological and cosmic mysteries. We need to transform sacramental community to better emphasize the incarnation and the cosmic Christ. We need to make liturgy less heady and more bodily, more feminine and less masculine, including more movement, more touching, more contact with the nonhuman aspects of creation, more closely tied to the rhythms of the natural world. Liturgy in sacramental community must celebrate not only the memory of the historical Jesus and his risen presence, not only our psychological transformation in conversion, but also the elegance and integrity of cosmos and nature and its numinous character. The sun, the stars, the moon, and the movements of these heavenly bodies; the wonder of Mother Earth with all her beautiful life forms; the dynamics of fertility and fecundity; the rich diversity of creation; the interdependence of the intricate web of life; the seasonal cycles and the changes in weather that they bring — all of this needs to be celebrated with humility and gratitude, reactivating our awareness, drawing us into a deep communion with the body of God.

My Father's Funeral

My father died on Easter Sunday in 1992. We buried him a few days later, on Earth Day. The stunning coincidence of his death, Easter, and Earth Day initiated in me a mystical experience of the cosmic Christ. Death and resurrection, the continuity and buoyancy of life, the great mystery of our coming to be and our passing away, the ongoing process of change and transformation, the earthiness of grace and the vessels that bear it — all of this flooded my consciousness in perhaps the most profound spiritual experience of my life. Dad drawing his last breath as spring emerged in the singing birds and budding trees seen from the many windows that surrounded him in his last hours — on the very day when we celebrate the fact that death is not the last word or the final reality. Taking his body back to the bowels of Mother Earth on the day we celebrate her wondrous fecundity and gratefully acknowledge our utter dependence on and love for her. While my inner self was brimming with mystical insight and a deep experience of the unity of all things in God, there was little expression of this in the sacramental community's funeral ritual. Nothing was said of Earth Day. Nobody noted the coincidence. What bothered me the most were the casket and the vault, inhibiting the recycling of my father's remains. Conventional wisdom prevailed. The ecological and cosmic dimensions of the energy map named Charles Ludwig and his relationship to the body of Christ and the Earth body, the body of God and our bodies, his genes, received and given, received by his children and given again to his grandchildren, all of us connected with the nonhuman world that precedes us and endures after we are gone, the deep and profound mystery of all this found little expression in the ritual prayer.

Still, there was enough in the sprinkling of the casket with water and the reminder that he had felt this same water in baptism decades earlier, dying with Christ and rising with him; in the Gospel reading of the risen Jesus eating with the disciples on the shore of Lake Tiberias; in the embrace of family and friends and the eating and drinking with one another and with the risen Christ; in the spring sunlight and verdant greenness of the cemetery, the bright blue skies and multicolored flowers that decorated the burial site — enough to *feel* the incarnation as the deepest reality of our common existence, the cosmic Christ as what Dad's life was all about, a numinous universe as the context for our shared moment in conscious self-awareness for the years of our lives.

Celebrating the Earth and Its Liberation in Christ

The natural cycles of birth and death, the seasons, the patterns of darkness and light, the gifts that nature yields for our sustenance have all been largely eclipsed in our focus on the biblical and the ecclesial. We need to broaden our liturgical horizon, beyond the confines of juridical consciousness, to include more explicitly the material, the physical, the natural world. Some of this can happen simply by calling greater attention to what is already integral to liturgy: the darkness of Advent as we move toward winter solstice, the light that dawns anew in Christmas and Epiphany, the new life that emerges in the natural world at Easter. We can also retrieve from the liturgical past planting and harvesting feasts, recognizing food and fiber as gifts of Earth, the sun, and rainfall. But we need, too, to create new liturgical events, preferably celebrated outside, where our communion with nature can *feel* more authentic. Sean McDonagh suggests that we institute a "Feast of Creation," noting that no such ritual exists in Catholicism:

> We have no ritual celebration for the original moments of the emerging cosmos. We should celebrate that most sacred moment — the initial fireball. Without that mystery of energy and fire, nothing in time or space would ever have existed. The formation of the stars, the birth of our sun and planet Earth present unique opportunity for ritual. A ritual focused on nurturing could celebrate the gradual emergence of the ocean as both the mother and cradle of life....Each new moment in the progressive unfolding of life — the appearance of plants, flowers, animals, birds, and humans — presents its own special possibility for creating rituals based on the story of the Earth and

the theology of creation to emerge from it. This search for appropriate rituals could spark a new period of creativity among Christians in
music, art, dance, and sacred texts.[21]

Such a Feast of Creation could coincide with the broader celebration of Earth Day, providing a cultural as well as a religious focus on
the natural world. Other sacramental rituals come to mind: celebrating together the beauty of autumn's colors and the first snowfall, the
return of the sun's warmth in spring, the harvest of summer's fruits
and vegetables; giving thanks for the animals whose habitat we share,
our pets, the squirrels, the birds, the rabbits; hiking in the mountains
or a morning at the beach and taking time to gratefully notice and
celebrate these gifts of nature. These are liturgical patterns that can
emerge within sacramental communities everywhere, giving expression to our new ecological and cosmic sensibilities. But there is also
a need in our time to make serious liturgical connections between the
liberating and healing mission of Christ and the realities of a devas-
tated natural environment, between the proclamation of good news
to the poor and the poverty we have visited on the Earth.

> The story of Jesus suggests that the shape of God's body includes
> all, especially the needy and outcast. While there are many distinctive
> features of the Christian notion of embodiment, in an ecological age
> when the development of our sensibility concerning the vulnerability
> and destruction of nonhuman creatures and the natural environment
> is critical, we ought to focus on one: the inclusion of the neglected op-
> pressed — the planet itself and its many different creatures, including
> outcast human ones. The distinctive characteristic of Christian em-
> bodiment is its focus on oppressed, vulnerable, suffering *bodies,* those
> who are in pain due to the indifference or greed of the more power-
> ful. In an ecological age, this ought to include oppressed nonhuman
> animals and the earth itself.[22]

Liberation and Eco-Justice

A cosmic and ecological perspective today demands that the radical inclusiveness of divine compassion proclaimed by Jesus in and
through his overturning of conventional hierarchies be extended to
the nonhuman world of nature: to *nature as the new poor.* The
basileia of God proclaimed by Jesus includes the Earth and her creatures, the whole of nature, not merely the human. The central aspects
of Jesus' message and activity — his parables, his healings, his open
commensality — push Christians toward the liberation and healing
of the Earth in what has come to be known as "eco-justice." The

ethical problems stemming from our anti-nature attitudes and behaviors are multidimensional, including at least three levels: (1) the
impact of ecological devastation on poor, mostly Third-World and
indigenous peoples; (2) the responsibility we bear for future generations of human beings; and (3) the immorality of our violating
the integrity of nature and its many life forms in and of itself.
The first two levels are valid ethical concerns even in an anthropocentric approach to reality: we are increasing human poverty and
oppression in our assault on the natural environment in the underdeveloped nations of the world, and we are robbing future human
generations of health and economic well-being, perhaps even of life
itself, by the negative impact we are having on the natural world.
The third level is an expansion of ethical rights beyond the human
community, recognizing an intrinsic value and worth within the nonhuman world: the Earth and her many life forms have their own
dignity and rights that are being violated by our human species.
Biocide and ecocide are immeasurable evils, creating massive suffering for present and future generations of human beings and within
the natural world itself. Biocide and ecocide are species-level suicide for humanity, and, to the extent that we affirm the numinous
and Christic character of the cosmos, we are about a profound assault on the divine purpose of creation. Eco-justice is the redressing
of these profound injustices operative in the human impact on the
natural world.

Increasingly today, in light of the ecological crisis and the broadened understanding of the physical universe we now have, the experience of liberation (as developed in chapter 7) is being extended to
the Earth and the biosphere. Sallie McFague, noting that the vulnerable and needy bodies of Earth today cry out for compassion and
care, poses the question precisely: "In what ways should the Christic
paradigm be applied to the natural world?" Her response demonstrates how Christ as Liberator is brought to bear on ecological
concerns:

> In the same ways as applied to other outcasts: the deconstructive
> phase (liberation from oppressive hierarchies as seen in the parables),
> the reconstructive (physical sustainability as suggested by the heal-
> ing stories), and the prospective (inclusion of all as manifest in the
> eating practices). These primary, active dimensions of the Christic
> paradigm — the shape of the cosmic Christ given to God's body —
> are balanced by a secondary, passive phase, the suffering of God with
> the despairing and defeated.[23]

Overcoming the Human-Nature Hierarchy

Jesus challenged the hierarchies of his world, proclaiming instead a radical egalitarianism. Today, Christians need to challenge the hierarchies of male over female and human over nature. Ecofeminism sees these patterns of domination as connected. Mind over matter, the rational controlling the physical and the emotive, the patriarchal and sexist domination of women by men, the human controlling and dominating the larger natural world. The goal envisioned by Jesus and by the community that seeks to follow him is radically egalitarian. As Rosemary Ruether writes,

> This vision must start with a principle of equity: equity between men and women, between human groups living within regions; equity across human communities globally; equity between the human species and all other members to the biotic community of which we are a part; and finally equity between generations of living things, between the needs of those alive now and those who are to come.[24]

The dualistic hierarchy of people over nature stretches back some five thousand years to the beginnings of the patriarchal era, but today because of the scientific and technological revolutions it has become more lethal, infinitely more dangerous. The deconstructive phase of liberating nature, then, means breaking down this hierarchy in the recognition of an egalitarianism that extends to the nonhuman world — challenging the conventional biases against nature: "our prejudices that it is, at best, only useful for our needs; our rationalizations in regard to activities that profit us but destroy it."[25] The assertion that the land and its creatures have rights and are intrinsically valuable is so contrary to conventional wisdom that it is shocking and perceived by many as absurd. We have lived for so long with, and so thoroughly integrated, the human-over-nature paradigm, that challenging it and asserting rights and intrinsic value for the nonhuman seems bizarre. In a world where so many are weary of "political correctness" and are increasingly uncomfortable with the challenges against racism, sexism, and heterosexism, the challenge of "anthropocentrism" is not readily or happily received. Yet the connection between Jesus' Gospel and how we now understand the nature of nature means that this pattern of domination must be challenged. "We need to think holistically, and not just in terms of the well-being of human beings," writes McFague. "We need to move beyond democracy to biocracy, seeing ourselves as one species among millions of other species on a planet that is our common home.... The preferential option for the poor is uncomfortable wherever it is applied; it will be no less so when applied to the new poor, nature."[26]

Healing a Sick and Damaged Earth

The reconstructive phase of connecting the historical Jesus with today's ecological concerns suggests a focus on healing the Earth. "It is increasingly evident," writes McFague, "that the metaphors of sickness, degeneration, and dysfunction are significant when discussing the state of our planet." Today the healing of human freedom and the healing of our eco-systems go hand-in-hand. We need to recognize that we have a particular responsibility as guardians and caretakers of nature, that, in a twist of irony, now we are responsible for insuring the health and well-being of all the rest upon which we are so profoundly dependent. Realizing and activating this sense of responsibility for, but not domination of, the rest of creation is tied to the healing mission of Christ: being freed from our own addictions and demons, made whole in our allegiance to the rule of God. Then, as healed healers, we can be about the challenge of healing the damage we have done. Rather than an easy spiritualizing of salvation that overlooks or denies the Earth's sickness, we must face it and seek to heal it.

> Most of us, most of the time, refuse to acknowledge the degree of that sickness. It is convenient to do so, since curing the planet's illnesses will force human inhabitants to make sacrifices. Hence, denial sets in, a denial not unlike the denial many practice in relation to serious, perhaps terminal, illness when it strikes their own bodies. But the denial of the planet's profoundly deteriorating condition is neither wise nor Christian: it is not wise because, as we increasingly know, we cannot survive on a sick planet, and it is not Christian because, if we extend the Christic healing ministry to all of creation, then we must work for the health of its many creatures and the planet itself.[27]

Radical Inclusiveness and Sustainability

Finally, the liberating mission of Jesus is connected to the present-day ecological crisis in demanding a sense of radical inclusiveness. Human exclusivity must give way to a sense of cooperation and harmony, an inclusive sense that all of us — the whole web of life and our Mother Earth — must be fed at a common table. Just as Jesus practiced open commensality, eating and drinking with the outcasts (tax collectors and prostitutes, gentiles and Samaritans), Christians today must work for human systems that insure the sustainability of the Earth and her eco-systems. Thinking of sharing food in terms of its *literal meaning* (rather than, again, spiritualizing it) is most appropriate: "sustainability for bodies, especially the many bodies on our planet that Christians as well as others in our society think of as superfluous." This, of course, is again an ironic twist, since "many people assume that creatures not only do not *deserve* food but are themselves *only* food — food for us."[28]

Catholicism Green and Cosmic

Retrieving the Christic paradigm expressed in the patterns of Jesus of Nazareth — proclaiming the *basileia* of God as liberation and healing in and through the radical and universal compassion of God — moves Catholicism toward an ecological consciousness and a sense of the cosmic Christ who seeks to reconcile all of creation. The reconstructed cosmos (the universe in process, still becoming), imaged by Einstein decades ago but only now becoming a popular understanding, looks and feels very different from Newton's mechanical universe. It is the gradual unfolding of space-time in spirited matter, groping, guided by the principles of differentiation, subjectivity, and communion. The human is now seen as integral to all this, growing from all that came before in evolutive development, radically dependent on the whole and its many distinct parts. Yet human being appears as novel and unique and has a special role. We are the reflexive consciousness of the universe, the place in time wherein the cosmos becomes self-aware, seeing itself for the first time. This reflexive awareness calls us to realize, more fully than ever before, the deepest and most profound mystery of the universe: its numinous character. At the center of cosmogenesis and its reflexive awareness is a personal center that radiates the energy of compassion and love. This compassion, which seeks to heal human freedom and reactivate reflexive consciousness for wonder and celebration, emerges in human form in Jesus of Nazareth. Jesus is liberator, one who challenges conventional wisdom and its hierarchies, healer, radically egalitarian and inclusive, the mirror of a universal and divine compassion. He is the new track for evolution's direction and the manifestation of its goal, inaugurating a new phase in evolution's journey, the cosmic Christ. Today, the challenge is to make universal the liberating work of Christ, healing human freedom and reconciling all of creation.

Reconstructing Catholicism today moves us beyond any narrow juridical and ecclesial parameters, moves us into the great mysteries of Earth and cosmos. But it also brings us down to Earth, off our lofty triumphalistic pedestals and into the concrete physical world of bodies. It is an exciting place to be. One can only hope that Teilhard de Chardin's comments, written decades past, apply prophetically to Catholicism as we move toward a new millennium:

> There is now incontrovertible evidence that humankind has just entered upon the greatest period of change the world has ever known. The ills from which we are suffering have had their seat in the very foundations of human thought. But today something is happening to the whole structure of human consciousness. A fresh kind of life is starting.[29]

— Epilogue —

Catholicism for a New Generation

The challenges facing today's young people are daunting. They have been born into and are coming to maturity in a cultural and social context that is falling apart. The institutions and structures meant to serve their development toward realization of their highest potential have, in many ways, failed them. The family, the school, higher education, government, business, religion, the arts, health care — all have failed to provide an environment that fosters healthy growth by introducing them to a world of transcendent meaning and value. Generation X has been abandoned and left alone to figure out the meaning of life. They have inherited massive problems and few resources. Now they are criticized as slackers and deadbeats, people who are filled with anger and oriented toward cynicism and violence, lazy nonconformists preoccupied with themselves, lacking reverence and respect for their elders and the institutions about them, unwilling to participate and contribute. There is an African aphorism that says, "It takes a village to raise a child." The village in this case has been so crippled that it hasn't served the child very well.

But there is a resilience in life, and the human spirit gropes toward meaning and fulfillment, no less so with this generation than with all those that have gone before. Thus, despite the cultural poverty and social chaos, today's young people pursue life with freshness and candor, with generosity and a search for purpose. They are poised for reconstruction, wanting to rebuild, as best they can, the world they are becoming responsible for. That it needs rebuilding, not just more criticism, is a point that requires more consensus, even among the young. Rebuilding is a daunting task, demanding imagination, creativity, hard work, commitment, and sacrifice. Some are more eager and better equipped than others, but there are signs that all of us want to get beyond gridlock, to face our problems squarely, to begin again, to reconstruct.

This is today's context for Catholicism. Its potential for the work of reconstruction is immense, bearing within its traditions and its people centuries of spiritual wisdom springing from Jesus of Nazareth and his proclamation in word and deed of the *basileia* of God. Fidelity to him and to the experience he provoked, to the path he blazed and the faith with which he blazed it, has, over these centuries, sometimes been weak and fledgling, sometimes intense and ardent. Yet his memory endures, his presence is celebrated, his pathway offered. Catholicism is but one bridge to that memory and presence and pathway. These pages have sought to make that bridge accessible so that it might open up a rich and powerful spiritual experience for this generation and for many to come. The mysticism and sacramentality of Catholicism, its emphasis on community and liberating justice, its long tradition of grace and the lifelong path of conversion, its desire to locate spirituality within cosmos and extend itself to the whole of creation — these aspects of a particular approach to living discipleship to Jesus make it attractive and relevant.

Reconstructing Catholicism is about rehabilitating our tradition so that it can provide direction and inspiration for the reconstructing of our civilization. Our world cries out for meaning, for reconciliation and love, for justice and community, for harmony and balance. Human freedom seeks healing and the restoration of its creativity, of its capacity for empathy, compassion, and spontaneity. Catholicism can be a resource for the reconstructing of culture and society, can contribute to the rebuilding of civilization — but not without its own reconstruction. The young inherit a tradition rich with potential, but one that asks of them an imaginative refashioning necessary to reactivate that potential and make it accessible to a spiritually hungry world. They must make this tradition their own by entering into dialogue, bringing their own experience of grief and deconstruction, of hope and resilience, into conversation with Jesus and his interpreters, with the experience of the many others who have come to Catholicism grieving and hoping. Such a dialogue will yield spiritual treasures, the insight and the energy to rebuild civilization.

We stand at the threshold of a new millennium. It offers us pause, time to reflect and consider. Who are we, and what are we about? What kind of future do we want, and how can we shape it? A millennial vision beckons us toward a new and different future, toward reconciliation and mutuality within the natural world, toward the risks of groping for new patterns in cosmogenesis, toward the retrieval and reactivation of reflexive consciousness, toward the rebuilding of society and culture grounded in spirit and the numinous. Such a vision is worth whatever price is exacted for its embrace:

subduing our own cynicism, forgiving ourselves and each other, confronting and resisting conventional powers and conventional wisdom, struggling with conversion and reconversion toward liberation. A millennial vision, if it is to be personally integrated and socially transformative, means forfeiting lesser visions, the petty but virulent desires of acquisitiveness, competition, immediate gratification, of addiction to the controlling expectations of others. Hope for a new and different future asks of us nothing less than death and resurrection. But that is exactly Catholicism's point: a path of death and resurrection so that we can give ourselves to what we hope for.

Today there is a new eagerness for spirituality, particularly among the young, who search for a meaning that seems absent within their immediate world. Ersatz spiritual wisdom is plentiful, offering miracles and supernatural powers to the gullible. A reconstructed Catholicism suggests another path, less dramatic, more down-to-earth. Daniel Berrigan, a Jesuit priest and poet who has spent most of his seventy-five years moving back and forth between resisting and building, spending many months in prison for his pacifist protest, trying to be faithful to Jesus Christ as well as his own experience, offers us insight and inspiration in a Zen poem, a poem for the reconstructing of Catholicism and for the rebuilding of culture:

Zen Poem

How I long for supernatural powers!
said the novice mournfully to the holy one.
I see a dead child
and I long to say, *Arise!*
I see a sick man
I want to say, *Be healed!*
I see a bent old woman
I long to say, *Walk straight!*
Alas, I feel like a dead stick in paradise.
Master can you confer on me
supernatural powers?

The holy one shook his head fretfully;
How long have I been with you
and you know nothing?
How long have you known me
and learned nothing?
Listen; I have walked the earth for 80 years
I have never raised a dead child
I have never healed a sick man
I have never straightened an old woman's spine

Children die
men grow sick
the aged fall
under a stigma of frost

and what is that to you or me
but the turn of the wheel
but the way of the world
but the gateway to paradise?

Supernatural powers!
Then you would play God
would spin the thread of life
and measure the thread
5 years, 50 years, 80 years
and cut the thread?

Supernatural powers!
I have wandered the earth for 80 years
I confess to you
sprout with root
root with flower
I know nothing of supernatural powers
I have yet to perfect my natural powers!

to see and not be seduced
to hear and not be deafened
to taste and not be eaten
to touch and not be huxtered

But you —
would you walk on water
would you master the air
would you swallow fire?

Go talk with the dolphins
they will teach you glibly
how to grow gills

Go listen to eagles
they will hatch you, nest you
eaglet and airman

Go join the circus
those tricksters will train you
in deception for dimes —

Bird man, bag man, poor fish
sprouting fire, moon crawling
at sea forever —
supernatural powers!

Do you seek miracles?
listen — go
draw water, hew wood
break stones —
how miraculous!

Blessed is the one
who walks the earth
5 years, 50 years, 80 years
and deceives no one
and curses no one
and kills no one

On such a one
the angels whisper in wonder;
behold the irresistible power
of natural powers —
of height, of joy, of soul, of non belittling

You dry stick —
in the crude soil of this world
spring, root, leaf, flower!
trace
around and around
and around —
an inch, a mile, the world's green extent,
a liberated zone
of paradise![1]

Notes

Introduction

1. Charlene Spretnak, *States of Grace: The Recovery of Meaning in the Postmodern Age* (San Francisco: HarperSanFrancisco, 1991), 3–4.
2. Charlene Spretnak, "The Regeneration Perspective: Catholic Exploration of a Post-Modern America," Joe Holland and Anne Barsanti, eds., *American and Catholic: The New Debate,* (South Orange, N.J.: Pillar Books), 104.
3. Ibid., 105.
4. Richard Rohr, "Reconstruction: Let Us Be Up and Building," *Radical Grace* 6, no. 5 (November 1993): 1–2.

Part One: A Time for Reconstruction

1. Douglas Coupland, *Life after God* (New York: Pocket Books, 1994), 50–51.
2. See Michael Crosby, *The Dysfunctional Church* (Notre Dame, Ind.: Ave Maria Press, 1991).
3. Patrick Brennan, "Re-Imagining Parishes, Evangelization, Small Communities," notes from a presentation at the 1993 Call to Action Conference, edited from the tape by Bill Thompson, *Call to Action Churchwatch,* May 1994, 6–7.

Chapter 1: A New Generation's Spiritual Hungers

1. Douglas Rushkoff, *The GenX Reader* (New York: Ballantine Books, 1994), 3.
2. Neil Howe and Bill Strauss, *13th Gen* (New York: Vintage Books, 1993), 7.
3. "A Generation of Gripers," *Psychology Today* (May/June, 1992): 11.
4. Howe and Strauss, *13th Gen,* 7, 13.
5. See Douglas Coupland's three recent books, *Generation X, Shampoo Planet,* and *Life after God,* and Kim France's interview with him in *Elle* magazine (September 1993), reprinted in *The GenX Reader,* 11–16.
6. *Elle* interview quoted in *The GenX Reader,* 15.
7. Douglas Coupland, *Life after God* (New York: Pocket Books, 1994), 286–87.
8. Ibid., 273–74.

9. Nancy O'Malley, *Suicide on Campus* (Madison, Wis.: Magna Publications, 1987).

10. Howe and Strauss, *13th Gen,* 60–61.

11. Ibid., 61.

12. Ibid., 62.

13. Dennis P. Hogan, David J. Eggebeen, and Clifford C. Clogg, "The Structure of Intergenerational Exchanges in American Families," *American Journal of Sociology* 98, no. 6 (May 1993): 1429.

14. Ibid., 1430.

15. Sharon Daloz Parks, "Reimagining the Role of the Human in the Earth Community," in Fritz Hull, ed., *Earth and Spirit* (New York: Continuum, 1993), 87.

16. *The Religious Life of Young Americans,* with commentary and analysis by George Gallup, Jr., and Robert Bezilla (Princeton, N.J.: George H. Gallup International Institute, 1992), 11.

17. Ibid., 12–14.

18. Coupland, *Life after God,* 359.

19. Rushkoff, *The GenX Reader,* 6.

20. Ibid., 7.

21. *The Religious Life of Young Americans,* 17.

Chapter 2: Vatican II and the Graying of Catholicism

1. E. E. Y. Hales, *Pope John and His Revolution* (London: Eyre and Spottiswoode, 1965), 122.

2. Ibid., 123.

3. One news report put the vote of the whole commission as 52–4 in favor of changing the teaching on contraception (see William H. Shannon, *The Lively Debate: Response to Humanae Vitae* [New York: Sheed & Ward, 1970]). For a full report on the workings of the commission, see Robert McClory, *Turning Point: The Inside Story of the Papal Birth Control Commission* (New York: Crossroad, 1995).

4. See Joseph J. Koury's essay "The Rediscovery of a Tradition: The 'Ends' of Marriage according to Vatican II," Lucien Richard, O.M.I., Daniel Harrington, S.J., and John W. O'Malley, S.J., eds., *Vatican II: The Unfinished Agenda* (New York: Paulist, 1987), 129–45.

5. T. Howland Sanks, "Education for Ministry Since Vatican II," *Theological Studies* 45, no. 3 (September 1984): 481ff.

6. Hales, *Pope John and His Revolution,* 80.

7. See the English translation of the encyclical, *Peace on Earth* (New York: Paulist Press, 1963).

8. Al Ries and Jack Trout, *Positioning: The Battle for Your Mind* (New York: Warner Books, 1986), 178.

9. Ibid., 178–79.

10. Ibid., 179.

11. John Grindel, *Whither the U.S. Church?* (Maryknoll, N.Y.: Orbis,

1991), 90. The author is quoting Jay Dolan, *The American Catholic Experience* (Garden City, N.Y.: Doubleday, 1985), 111.

12. Ibid., 90, following Dolan's ideas, *The American Catholic Experience,* 310–11.

13. Ibid., 91. The author is quoting James Hennesey, S.J., *American Catholics: A History of the Roman Catholic Community in the United States* (New York: Oxford University Press, 1981), who in turn is quoting William Halsey.

14. Dennis McCann, *New Experiment in Democracy* (Kansas City, Mo.: Sheed & Ward, 1987), 13, as quoted by Grindel, *Whither the U.S. Church?* 91.

15. "America's Catholics: Who They Are," *Christianity Today* (November 7, 1986): 19.

16. Ibid.

17. Andrew Greeley, *American Catholics: A Social Portrait* (New York: Basic Books, 1977), 71.

18. See Grindel, *Whither the U.S. Church?* 93.

19. *The Emerging Parish: The Notre Dame Study of Catholic Life since Vatican II* (San Francisco: Harper & Row, 1987), 37f., as quoted by Grindel, *Whither the U.S. Church?* 93.

20. Greeley, *American Catholics,* 272, quoted by Grindel, *Whither the U.S. Church?* 93.

21. See John A. Coleman, *An American Strategic Theology* (Mahwah, N.J.: Paulist, 1982), 178, and Grindel, *Whither the U.S. Church?* 93.

22. Rosemary Radford Ruether, "The Future Church according to the Gospels: How to Get There from Here," presentation at the Call to Action Conference, Chicago, November 5, 1994.

23. See Eugene C. Bianchi and Rosemary Radford Ruether, eds., *A Democratic Catholic Church* (New York: Crossroad, 1992).

Chapter 3: Retrieving the Experiential Base of Religion

1. James Redfield, *The Celestine Prophecy* (New York: Warner Books, 1993), 26–27.

2. Charlene Spretnak, *States of Grace: The Recovery of Meaning in the Postmodern Age* (San Francisco: HarperSanFrancisco, 1991), 2–3.

3. Peter Berger, *The Heretical Imperative* (Garden City, N.Y.: Anchor/ Doubleday, 1979), 58.

4. Gabriel Moran, *Theology of Revelation* (New York: Herder & Herder, 1966), 46.

5. Mircea Eliade, *Myth and Reality* (New York: Harper & Row, 1963), 6.

6. See especially Mircea Eliade, *The Sacred and the Profane: The Nature of Religion* (Orlando, Fla.: Harcourt Brace and Company, 1959). Chapter 2, "Sacred Time and Myths," and chapter 4, "Human Existence and the Sanctified Life," are particularly helpful.

7. C. G. Jung, *Psychology and Religion* (New Haven, Conn.: Yale University Press, 1938), 4.

8. Among the twenty books Campbell wrote and edited, the best known are *The Hero with a Thousand Faces* (Princeton, N.J.: Princeton University Press, 1949) and *The Masks of God* (London: Martin Secker & Warburg, 1960).

9. Joseph Campbell with Bill Moyers, *The Power of Myth* (New York: Doubleday, 1988), 5–6; emphasis added.

10. Quote from the *Power of Myth* video series, tape 1.

11. Campbell and Moyers, *The Power of Myth*, 14.

12. Ibid., 6.

13. Ibid., 22.

14. Ibid., 10.

15. Quoted by Pythia Peay in "Campbell and Catholicism," *Common Boundary* (March/April 1992): 28, 30; emphasis added.

16. Ibid., 31.

17. *The Power of Myth* video, cassette 6.

18. Quoted by Pythia Peay in "Campbell and Catholicism," 31.

19. Ibid.

20. Campbell's wife, Jean Erdman, as quoted by Pythia Peay, "Campbell and Catholicism," 31.

21. Ibid.

22. Bernard Cooke, *Sacraments and Sacramentality* (Mystic, Conn.: Twenty-Third Publications, 1983), 31.

23. Ibid.

24. Alan W. Watts, *Myth and Ritual in Christianity* (Boston: Beacon Press, 1968), 7.

25. Ibid., 15.

26. Ibid., 23, 235–36.

27. Andrew M. Greeley, *The Catholic Myth* (New York: Charles Scribner's Sons, 1990), 13.

28. Ibid., 272–73.

Chapter 4: The Jesus Experience

1. See Jaroslav Pelikan, *Jesus through the Centuries: His Place in the History of Culture* (New Haven, Conn.: Yale University Press, 1985).

2. Karl Rahner, *The Love of Jesus and the Love of Neighbor* (New York: Crossroad, 1983), 23.

3. See Marcus Borg, *Meeting Jesus Again for the First Time* (HarperSanFrancisco, 1994), 121ff.

4. Ibid., 10. See also Jerome Neyrey's excellent book *Christ in Community: The Christologies of the New Testament* (Wilmington, Del.: Glazier, 1985).

5. For a description of historical method and sources, see John Dominic Crossan, *The Historical Jesus* (New York: HarperCollins, 1991), xxvii–

xxxiv. For an excellent commentary on Crossan's method, see Bernard Brandon Scott, "to impose is not / To Discover," in Jeffrey Carlson and Robert A. Ludwig, eds., *Jesus and Faith: A Conversation on the Work of John Dominic Crossan* (Maryknoll, N.Y.: Orbis, 1994), 22ff.

6. Ibid., xii.

7. Borg, *Meeting Jesus Again for the First Time,* 32.

8. Ibid., 47.

9. John Dominic Crossan, *Jesus: A Revolutionary Biography* (Harper-SanFrancisco, 1994), 25.

10. Borg, *Meeting Jesus Again for the First Time,* 49.

11. Ibid., 30.

12. Crossan, *Jesus: A Revolutionary Biography,* 55.

13. James C. Scott, "Protest and Profanation: Agrarian Revolt and the Little Tradition," *Theory and Society* 30 (1977): 225–26, as quoted by Crossan, *Jesus: A Revolutionary Biography,* 71–72.

14. See Borg's chapter "Jesus, Compassion, and Politics," in *Meeting Jesus Again for the First Time,* 46–68, and Crossan's chapter, "A Kingdom of Nuisances and Nobodies" in *Jesus: A Revolutionary Biography,* 54–74.

15. Borg, *Meeting Jesus Again for the First Time,* 69–70.

16. Ibid., 71.

17. See John Dominic Crossan, *In Parables: The Challenge of the Historical Jesus* (New York: Harper & Row, 1973).

18. Crossan, *The Historical Jesus,* xii.

19. Martin Hengel, *Crucifixion in the Ancient World and the Folly of the Message of the Cross* (Philadelphia: Fortress, 1977), as quoted in Crossan, *Jesus: A Revolutionary Biography,* 123–24.

20. Francis Schüssler Fiorenza, *Foundational Theology* (New York: Cross-road, 1986), 45.

21. Crossan, *The Historical Jesus,* xiii.

22. Michael Cook, *The Jesus of Faith* (New York: Paulist, 1981), 82.

23. Robert Goss, *Jesus Acted Up: A Gay and Lesbian Manifesto* (Harper-SanFrancisco, 1993), 77–78.

24. John Shea, *An Experience Named Spirit* (Chicago: Thomas More Press, 1983), 20; emphasis added.

25. Ibid., 21–22.

26. Borg, *Meeting Jesus Again for the First Time,* 121–33.

27. Ibid., 122.

28. Ibid., 123.

29. Ibid., 124–25.

30. Ibid., 125.

31. Ibid., 126.

Chapter 5: The Experience of Grace

1. See Galatians 1:11–16, Acts 9:1–9, Acts 22:4–16, and Acts 26:9–18 for various accounts of Paul's conversion experience.

2. Robin Scroggs, *Paul for a New Day* (Philadelphia: Fortress, 1982), 25.

3. See Geoffrey Parrinder, ed., *World Religions: From Ancient History to the Present* (New York: Facts on File Publications, 1971, 1983), 272–74.

4. See Karl Rahner, S.J., *Spiritual Exercises* (New York: Herder & Herder, 1965).

5. See David Ray Griffin's "Introduction to SUNY Series in Constructive Postmodern Thought," in *Varieties of Postmodern Theology* (Albany: SUNY Press, 1989), xii.

6. See Karl Rahner, "The Mystery of Human Existence," in *The Content of Faith* (New York: Crossroad, 1992), 73ff.

7. See Karl Rahner, "The Hearer of the Message," in *Foundations of Christian Faith* (New York: Seabury/Crossroad, 1978), 24ff.

8. Ibid., 44ff.

9. Ibid., 46.

10. Ibid., 50–51.

11. Michael Buckley, "Within the Holy Mystery," in *A World of Grace* (New York: Seabury, 1980), 35.

12. See Karl Rahner, "Man as the Event of God's Free and Forgiving Self-Communication," in *Foundations of Christian Faith*, 116ff.

13. Gerald May, M.D., *Addiction and Grace: Love and Spirituality in the Healing of Addictions* (San Francisco: HarperSanFrancisco, 1988).

14. Ibid., 13.

15. Ibid.

16. Ibid., 15.

17. Ibid., 16–17.

Chapter 6: The Experience of Sacramental Community

1. Marcus Borg, *Meeting Jesus Again for the First Time* (HarperSanFrancisco, 1994), 96.

2. See Kenan B. Osborne, O.F.M., "Jesus as Primordial Sacrament," *Sacramental Theology: A General Introduction* (New York: Paulist Press, 1988), 69ff.

3. See Klemens Richter, *The Meaning of Sacramental Symbols* (Collegeville, Minn.: Liturgical Press, 1990).

4. Karl Rahner, *The Church and the Sacraments* (New York: Herder and Herder, 1963), 15–16.

5. John G. Gager, *Kingdom and Community: The Social World of Early Christianity* (Englewood Cliffs, N.J.: Prentice-Hall, 1975), 140.

6. Ibid., 129.

7. Ibid., 130.

8. Tad Guzie, *The Book of Sacramental Basics* (New York: Paulist Press, 1981), 78.

9. See Kenan B. Osborne, O.F.M., "The Church as Basic Sacrament," 86ff., and Bernard Cooke, "Christian Community: Sacrament of Christ,"

Sacraments and Sacramentality (Mystic, Conn.: Twenty-Third Publications, 1983), 68ff.

10. Rahner, *The Church and the Sacraments*, 18.

11. Edward Schillebeeckx, *Christ: The Sacrament of the Encounter with God* (New York: Sheed & Ward, 1963), 47–48.

12. Guzie, *The Book of Sacramental Basics*, 48.

13. "We Come to Tell Our Story," GIA Publications, 1989.

14. Sandra DeGidio, *Sacraments Alive* (Mystic, Conn.: Twenty-Third Publications, 1991), 16.

15. See Tom F. Driver, "Christian Sacraments as the Performance of Freedom," *The Magic of Ritual* (San Francisco: HarperSanFrancisco, 1991), 195ff.

16. See Tad Guzie's study of the Eucharist, *Jesus and the Eucharist* (New York: Paulist, 1974).

17. Marty Haugen, "We Remember," GIA Publications, 1980.

18. Daniel L. Schutte, "Behold the Wood," Daniel L. Schutte and New Dawn Music, 1980.

19. Marty Haugen, "Light of Christ/*Exsultet*," GIA Publications, 1987.

20. See Mary Durkin, *Guidelines for Contemporary Catholics: The Eucharist* (Chicago: Thomas More, 1990).

21. See Richard A. Horsley's excellent study of the infancy narratives in the Gospels, *The Liberation of Christmas: The Infancy Narratives in Social Context* (New York: Crossroad, 1989).

22. Marty Haugen, "Send Down Your Fire," GIA Publications, 1989.

23. See Patrick J. Brennan, *Re-Imagining the Parish* (New York: Crossroad, 1990), particularly his chapters "Ecclesiology — Vision Influencing Praxis" (9–15), "Small Communities and Neighborhood Ministries" (16–23), "Models — North American and Roman Catholic" (63–75).

24. Marcello de C. Azevedo, *Basic Ecclesial Communities in Brazil* (Washington, D.C.: Georgetown University Press, 1987), 245–46, as quoted by Dokecki, Newbrough, and O'Gorman in "Community and Leadership in the Postmodern Church: Leadership for Community," *PACE* (December 1993): 36.

25. Robert T. O'Gorman, Paul R. Dokecki, and J. R. Newbrough, "Communiogenesis: Society at Peril," keynote address for *Communiogenesis: Birthing the Communal*, a symposium held at the Institute of Pastoral Studies, Loyola University Chicago, July 8–10, 1994, 64.

26. Paul R. Dokecki, J. Robert Newbrough, and Robert T. O'Gorman, "Community and Leadership in the Postmodern Church: Lessons from Latin America — the Basic Ecclesial Communities," *PACE* (October 1993): 30.

27. See Patrick Brennan, "The Latin American Experience: Basic Ecclesial Communities," in *Re-Imagining the Parish*, 30–40.

28. See Bernard J. Lee and Michael A. Cowan, *Dangerous Memories* (Kansas City, Mo.: Sheed & Ward, 1986), particularly their chapter on "U.S. Culture & Christian Communities," 61ff.

29. O'Gorman, Dokecki, and Newbrough, "Communiogenesis: Society at Peril," 63.

30. Brennan, *Re-Imagining the Parish*, 14.

31. O'Gorman, Dokecki, and Newbrough, "Communiogenesis," 66.

32. See Dean Hoge, *Future of Catholic Leadership: Responses to the Priest Shortage* (Kansas City, Mo.: Sheed & Ward, 1987); and Jay P. Dolan, R. Scott Appleby, Patricia Byrne, and Debra Campbell, *Transforming Parish Ministry. The Changing Roles of Catholic Clergy, Laity, and Women Religious* (New York: Crossroad, 1989).

33. See Thomas Franklin O'Meara, *Theology of Ministry* (New York: Paulist Press, 1983), particularly his chapters "Beyond Religion: Spirit, Freedom, Charism, and Ministry" (47ff.) and "Primal Ministry" (76ff.).

34. O'Meara, *Theology of Ministry,* 136.

Chapter 7: The Experience of Liberation

1. John Dominic Crossan, *The Essential Jesus* (San Francisco: Harper-SanFrancisco, 1994), 3.

2. Bob Hurd, "Pan de Vida," OCP Publications, 1988.

3. Crossan, *The Essential Jesus,* 12.

4. In addition to Gutiérrez, some of the best-known liberation theologians whose works are available in English are Hugo Assmann, Brazil (*Theology for a Nomad Church*); Leonardo Boff, Brazil (*Jesus Christ Liberator, Liberating Grace, Ecclesiogenesis*); Ignacio Ellacuría, El Salvador (*Freedom Made Flesh*); Paulo Freire, Brazil (*Pedagogy of the Oppressed*); Juan Luis Segundo, Uruguay (*The Liberation of Theology*); and Jon Sobrino, El Salvador (*Christology at the Crossroads, Jesus the Liberator*).

5. Gustavo Gutiérrez, *A Theology of Liberation,* 15th Anniversary Edition (Maryknoll, N.Y.: Orbis, 1988), xx.

6. See Leonard Swidler and Herbert O'Brien, eds., *A Catholic Bill of Rights* (Kansas City, Mo.: Sheed & Ward, 1988).

7. Gregory Baum, *Compassion and Solidarity* (New York: Paulist, 1990), 22–23.

8. Robert McAfee Brown, *Gustavo Gutiérrez: An introduction to Liberation Theology* (Maryknoll, N.Y.: Orbis, 1990), 4.

9. David J. O'Brien and Thomas A. Shannon, *Catholic Social Thought: The Documentary Heritage* (Maryknoll, N.Y.: Orbis, 1972), 41.

10. Ibid., 40.

11. John XXIII, *Pacem in Terris,* no. 51. The quote from Aquinas comes from the *Summa Theologica,* Ia-IIe, q. 93, a. 3 ad 2.

12. *Pacem in Terris,* no. 61.

13. Ibid., no. 44; emphasis added.

14. Ibid., no. 127.

15. See O'Brien and Shannon's introduction to this document in *Catholic Social Thought,* 164–65.

16. *Pastoral Constitution on the Church in the Modern World* (*Gaudium et Spes*), no. 69.

17. Baum, *Compassion and Solidarity,* 24.

18. Ibid., 25.

19. Brown, *Gustavo Gutiérrez,* 13.

20. See *Justice in the World* in O'Brien and Shannon, *Catholic Social Thought,* 288–89; emphasis added.

21. Quoted by Brown, *Gustavo Gutiérrez,* 17; emphasis added.

22. Baum, *Compassion and Solidarity,* 28.

23. Ibid., 28–29.

24. See Rosemary Radford Ruether, *Women-Church* (San Francisco: Harper & Row, 1985) for discussion of feminist theology and practice.

25. See Robert Nugent and Jeannine Gramick, *Building Bridges: Gay and Lesbian Reality and the Catholic Church* (Mystic, Conn.: Twenty-Third Publications, 1992).

26. Gloria Steinem, *Revolution from Within* (Boston: Little, Brown and Company, 1992), 16.

27. See Michael H. Crosby, *Spirituality of the Beatitudes* (Maryknoll, N.Y.: Orbis Books, 1981). His structural analysis of American society in the light of the Gospel according to Matthew is excellent. The book is especially insightful about the hidden authority of consumerism: "Consumerism has become the new authority infecting every element of our individual and group lives. It has become the underlying base, the network that touches each individual, family, and community. As *the central project of this infrastructure,* it is reinforced by an ideology through the persuasion of mass media advertising in such a way that individuals and families are valued only in the light of this central project.... People exist to keep the central project alive" (40–41).

28. Again, Michael Crosby's *Spirituality of the Beatitudes* is helpful. He proposes a model for faith communities: "There is significance in gathering regularly with people having similar problems. The twelve steps of dealing with addictions can become the agenda for communities of conscientization who seek conversion from their cultural addictions. Thus, whenever the community gathers with its gifts, it can operate from a model of reflection and mutual sharing, guided by the twelve steps, to deal with its enslavements" (66).

29. O'Brien and Shannon, *Catholic Social Thought,* 491.

30. Michael Crosby, *The Dysfunctional Church* (Notre Dame, Ind.: Ave Maria Press, 1991).

31. Ibid., 175.

32. Ibid.

33. Ibid., 177.

Part Three: Catholicism in a Reconstructed Universe

1. Brian Swimme, *The Universe Is a Green Dragon* (Santa Fe, N.M.: Bear and Company, 1984), 39–40.

Chapter 8: Reconstructing Cosmos

1. Daniel Sitarz, ed., *Agenda 21: The Earth Summit Strategy to Save Our Planet* (Boulder, Colo.: Earthpress, 1993), 1–2.
2. Ibid., 2.
3. Al Gore, *Earth in the Balance* (Boston: Houghton Mifflin, 1992). According to Gore, "The most dangerous form of deforestation is the destruction of the rain forests, especially the tropical rain forests clustered around the equator. These are the most important sources of biodiversity on earth and the most vulnerable ecosystems now suffering the effects of our determined onslaught.... Most biologists believe that the rapid destruction of the tropical rain forests, and the irretrievable loss of living species dying along with them, represent the single most serious damage to nature now occurring.... The wholesale annihilation of so many living species in such a breathless moment of geological time represents a deadly wound to the integrity of the earth's painstakingly intricate web of life, a wound so nearly permanent that scientists estimate that recuperation would take *100 million years*" (*Earth in the Balance,* 116; emphasis added).
4. Ibid., 53–54.
5. Gerald O. Barney, with Jane Blewett and Kristen R. Barney, *Global 2000 Revisited: What Shall We Do?* (Arlington, Va.: Millennium Institute, 1993), 2.
6. Gore, *Earth in the Balance,* 31.
7. Ibid., 30.
8. Sitarz, *Agenda 21,* 12.
9. Barney, *Global 2000 Revisited,* 4.
10. Gore, *Earth in the Balance,* 12.
11. Lynn White, Jr., "The Historical Roots of Our Ecological Crisis," *Science* 155 (March 10, 1967): 1207; emphasis added.
12. Thomas Berry, *The Dream of the Earth* (San Francisco: Sierra Club Books, 1988), 125.
13. Ibid., 41.
14. White, "The Historical Roots of Our Ecological Crisis," 1205.
15. Charlene Spretnak, *States of Grace: The Recovery of Meaning in the Postmodern Age* (San Francisco: HarperSanFrancisco, 1991), 90.
16. Ibid., 89.
17. Ibid., 90. Spretnak is citing Joseph Epes Brown, *The Spiritual Legacy of the American Indian* (New York: Crossroad, 1982), 39.
18. Fritjof Capra, *The Turning Point: Science, Society, and the Rising Culture* (New York: Simon & Schuster, 1982), 25.
19. Ibid., 25–26; emphasis added.
20. Ibid., 31.

21. Ibid., 56.

22. Ibid., 57.

23. Descartes's words, quoted by Daniel Garber, "Science and Certainty in Descartes," in Michael Hooker, ed., *Descartes* (Baltimore: Johns Hopkins University Press, 1978).

24. Capra, *The Turning Point,* 59.

25. Ibid., 60.

26. Ibid., 60–61.

27. Ibid., 65.

28. Ibid., 66.

29. Ibid., 78.

30. J. McKim Malville, *The Fermenting Universe* (Menlo Park, Calif.: Cummings Publishing, 1975), 22.

31. I want to acknowledge the influence of public lectures given by Kevin O'Shea at the University of Notre Dame in my development of this description of Einstein's insights about the universe.

32. George Gamow, *My World Line* (New York: Viking, 1970).

33. Adam Ford, *Universe* (Mystic, Conn.: Twenty-Third Publications, 1987), 52.

34. See ibid., 51–53. Much of this information was obtained in lectures given by Kevin O'Shea.

35. For an interesting description of the Big Bang and the earliest moments of the universe, see *The Cosmos: Voyage through the Universe* (Alexandria, Va.: Time-Life, 1988).

36. Berry, *The Dream of the Earth,* 123.

37. James Conlon, *Earth Story, Sacred Story* (Mystic, Conn.: Twenty-Third Publications, 1994), 10.

38. Berry, "Introduction," in *Earth Story, Sacred Story,* 3.

39. Thomas Berry, *The Dream of the Earth,* 132.

40. Brian Swimme and Thomas Berry, *The Universe Story* (San Francisco: HarperSanFrancisco, 1992), 1.

41. Ibid., 2–3.

42. Sallie McFague, "A Square in the Quilt," in Steven C. Rockefeller and John C. Elder, eds., *Spirit and Nature* (Boston: Beacon Press, 1992), 54.

43. Ibid.

44. James E. Lovelock, *GAIA: A New Look at Life on Earth* (New York: Oxford University Press, 1979), viii.

45. See chapters 4 and 5 in ibid., 48–83.

46. See Michael J. Cohen, *How Nature Works* (Portland, Ore.: Stillpoint Press, 1988), 84–86.

47. Elizabeth Roberts, "Gaian Buddhism," in Allan Hunt Badiner, ed., *Dharma Gaia* (Berkeley, Calif.: Parallax Press, 1990), 147.

48. Rachel Rosenthal, *Gaia mon amor: A Performance by Rachel Rosenthal* (Buffalo, N.Y.: Hallwalls, 1983), 5–6.

49. Richard Morris, *The Edges of Science* (New York: Prentice-Hall, 1990).

50. Pierre Teilhard de Chardin, *The Phenomenon of Man* (New York: Harper & Row, 1959), 45.

51. See ibid., 39–74.

52. Ibid., 31.

Chapter 9: Reconstructing the Human

1. John Seed and Joanna Macy, "Gaia Meditations," in *Thinking Like a Mountain* (Philadelphia: New Society Publishers, 1988), 41–43.

2. Brian Swimme and Thomas Berry, *The Universe Story* (San Francisco: HarperSanFrancisco, 1992), 145–46.

3. Ibid., 147–48.

4. Ibid., 149.

5. Ibid., 152–53.

6. Ibid., 153.

7. Ibid., 157–58.

8. Ibid., 158.

9. Ibid., 159.

10. Thomas Berry, *The Dream of the Earth* (San Francisco: Sierra Club Books, 1988) 202, 207–8.

11. Ibid., 37.

12. Ibid., 208.

13. Ibid., 6–7.

14. Edward O. Wilson, *The Diversity of Life* (New York: W. W. Norton & Company, 1992), 344.

15. Swimme and Berry, *The Universe Story*, 72–73.

16. Ibid., 74.

17. Ibid., 75.

18. James Conlon, *Earth Story, Sacred Story* (Mystic, Conn.: Twenty-Third Publications, 1994), 35, 42.

19. Swimme and Berry, *The Universe Story*, 77.

20. Ibid., 78.

21. Joanna Macy, "The Greening of the Self," in Allan Hunt Badiner, ed., *Dharma Gaia* (Berkeley, Calif.: Parallax Press, 1990), 56–57.

22. Ibid., 58–59.

Chapter 10: Catholicism Green and Cosmic

1. Charlene Spretnak, *States of Grace: The Recovery of Meaning in the Postmodern Age* (San Francisco: HarperSanFrancisco, 1991), 9.

2. Sallie McFague, *The Body of God* (Minneapolis: Fortress Press, 1993), 102.

3. Ibid., 179.

4. Ibid., 181.

5. Ibid., 102.

6. This translation appears in Paulos Mar Gregorios, "New Testament Foundations for Understanding the Creation," in Charles Birch, William Eakin, and Jay B. McDaniel, eds., *Liberating Life: Contemporary Approaches to Ecological Theology* (Maryknoll, N.Y.: Orbis, 1990), 41.

7. James Redfield, *The Celestine Prophecy* (New York: Warner Books, 1993), 42.

8. Robert Faricy, S.J., *The Spirituality of Teilhard de Chardin* (London: Collins Publishers, 1981), 24.

9. Pierre Teilhard de Chardin, *Human Energy* (New York: Harcourt Brace Jovanovich, 1969), 156–57.

10. Ewert Cousins, *Christ of the 21st Century* (Rockport, Mass.: Element, 1992), 173.

11. See his discussion of Francis of Assisi: Matthew Fox, *The Coming of the Cosmic Christ* (San Francisco: Harper & Row, 1988), 112–14.

12. Sean McDonagh, *To Care for the Earth* (Santa Fe, N.M.: Bear and Company, 1986), 205.

13. Sean McDonagh, *The Greening of the Church* (Maryknoll, N.Y.: Orbis Books, 1990), 171–72.

14. Cousins, *Christ of the 21st Century*, 135.

15. Ibid., 148.

16. St. Francis of Assisi, *The Canticle of Brother Sun,* in M. A. Habig, ed., *St. Francis of Assisi: Omnibus of Sources* (Chicago: Franciscan Herald Press, 1983), 130–31.

17. Cousins, *Christ of the 21st Century*, 135.

18. Thomas Merton, *New Seeds of Contemplation,* in Thomas P. McDonnell, ed., *A Thomas Merton Reader,* rev. ed. (Garden City, N.Y.: New York: Doubleday Image, 1974), 427–28.

19. McFague, *The Body of God,* 182–83.

20. Ibid., 184.

21. McDonagh, *To Care for the Earth* (Santa Fe, N.M.: Bear and Company, 1986), 158–59.

22. McFague, *The Body of God,* 164.

23. Ibid., 186.

24. Rosemary Radford Ruether, *Gaia and God* (San Francisco: HarperSanFrancisco, 1992), 258.

25. Ibid., 187.

26. Ibid., 109, 188.

27. Ibid., 188–89.

28. Ibid., 189.

29. Pierre Teilhard de Chardin, *Building the Earth* (New York: Dimension Books, 1965), 49.

Epilogue: Catholicism for a New Generation

1. Daniel Berrigan, "Zen Poem," in *Tulips in the Prison Yard* (Dublin, Ireland: Dedalus Press, 1992), 56–58.

Index